A GUIDE FOR SOCIAL SCIENCE METHODS

REASONING AND RESEARCH

THELMA F. BATTEN

REASONING AND RESEARCH

REASONING AND RESEARCH
a guide for social science methods

Thelma F. Batten, *California State College at Hayward*

 LITTLE, BROWN AND COMPANY   BOSTON

LIBRARY OF CONGRESS CATALOG CARD NO. 79-145568

FIRST PRINTING

Printed simultaneously in Canada by
Little, Brown & Company (Canada) Limited

PRINTED IN THE UNITED STATES OF AMERICA

To my husband and our children, because . . .

Acknowledgments

No book, especially one devoted to some aspects of that cooperative enterprise called science, is the product of one person. My debt to others is great, not only to those whose ideas I have learned about through personal conversations but also and primarily to those far more numerous individuals whose ideas have come to me solely in written form, sometimes written a good many years ago.

Citing certain books under the heading "Suggestions for Beginning Further Reading" only in very small part indicates my debt to prior writers. But at least I can more obviously indicate my debt to some of the many who have guided my ideas through personal contact.

In chronological order of influence, I would first like to thank Amos H. Hawley, sociologist and human ecologist. Fortunately for me, I needed a job while going through the University of Michigan and was privileged enough to have one for several years as a research assistant to him. I learned much from him, both through observation and questioning, during this apprenticeship and through more limited association in later years.

While a sociology graduate student at Michigan, I participated in the first of the "Detroit Area Study" year-long training programs, conducted in cooperation with the Survey Research Center. The experience I gained during this period turned out to be very helpful. I would particularly like to thank Ronald Freedman of the Sociology Department and Leslie Kish of the Survey Research Center for their patient guidance and their willingness to put up with my many questions.

My first full-time job as a Ph.D. was with the huge California Health Survey conducted by the State of California Department of Public Health during the mid-1950's, which served as one of the pilot studies for the National Health Survey. My chief co-worker was a statistician, Mary Elizabeth Laughlin, whose advice I have been happy to seek out on many occasions since. In addition to her other talents, she has a remarkable grasp of the kinds of practical problems likely to be encountered in both large- and small-scale research and the ability to suggest ways to overcome them.

After some years devoted largely to child bearing and rearing, I began teaching at California State College at Hayward. Among my colleagues in the Sociology Department, I would particularly like to thank Peter Geiser and Judith Cohen. As department chairman, Peter Geiser provided initial and continuing support for my efforts to develop material appropriate for the beginning student. Judith Cohen and I have been the staff members most directly involved in class-testing the material, and her suggestions have been invaluable. Both Professors Geiser and Cohen were kind enough to read carefully my several preliminary drafts and friend enough to suggest many places where changes were needed. I cannot thank them enough.

Finally, many of the more than two thousand students on whom the material has been class-tested made helpful comments and suggestions. A few of them worked with the material both as students trying to master it and later as graduate assistants helping others master it during the activity sessions devoted to carrying out the exercises. Three deserve special thanks: Eileen Eastman, Elizabeth Hoag, and James Gray.

While I hope I have treated fairly the many ideas I have tried to synthesize and present here on an elementary level, the responsibility for any defects in the synthesis and presentation is of course mine.

Contents

PART III

Second Portion of the Research Process
from collecting observations through writing report   201

Exercise Set III   232

Introduction

PURPOSES

What kinds of decisions typically have to be made during the various stages of trying to specify and solve a scientific problem? What are the major merits and demerits of the usual options available for each kind of decision? What are the implications of picking one set of alternatives along the way rather than another for the kinds and quality of the conclusions that may be drawn later?

This book is an outgrowth of several years of attempting to provide beginning students in sociology and related social science disciplines with some existing answers to these questions and with some practice in applying the principles involved. Most of these answers have long been in the public domain, though in rather scattered form. I have tried to pull some basic information together under one cover, primarily for the novice.

People who have been engaged in research for some time are not likely to find here any guiding principles that they are not already using in some form. People who will find this book useful are those who are considering a career in science (especially social science) and would like some overview of what can be anticipated on the job and those who have no thought of becoming professional scientists but, particularly in a science-dominated society such as ours, are willing to make some effort to try to understand how a scientist's mind works. This book, then, is concerned with science in its broad outlines, in order to achieve two equally important purposes.

On the one hand, an awareness of the kinds of decisions to be made and their implications for the kind and quality of knowledge subsequently attained should provide a methodological foundation on which to build, should an individual later decide to engage in the production of scientific knowledge. Of course, only a foundation is provided because he will soon need to add specialized information. He will need detailed knowledge of *tools* and *techniques* (centrifuges, computers, matrix algebra, questionnaire design, and the like) useful for his specific branch of science.

Tools and techniques in vogue can change fairly rapidly, at least in details, and the serious researcher will soon find he needs to keep abreast of professional journals and monographs in his field. The general principles — the underlying rationale — remain. If the beginner masters them first, he should find the process of learning required details a more understandable one, and less like having to "follow a cookbook."

In this book tools and techniques are covered primarily in passing. Necessarily, they are used as illustrations when discussing or doing, in the form of practice exercises to be completed, one or another stage of the entire decision-making process.

On the other hand, whether engaged in the actual production of scientific information or not, all citizens will be consumers of knowledge at least purporting to be scientific. They are especially likely to be consumers of knowledge gained by the social sciences. "Knowledge explosion" is a term in the vernacular by now. It would seem that every educated citizen needs some standards of judgment, some principles for evaluating the research reports he reads. This is true whether he reads them directly in the various professional journals or as filtered by the more mass-oriented communications media.

It can be said that one of the purposes of securing an education — especially, although hardly exclusively, a college education — is to learn how to change one's mind efficiently. A major premise motivating this book is that to the extent a person possesses some criteria for evaluating evidence and some skill in using those criteria, the more efficient his mind-changing will be. In science as perhaps elsewhere, it turns out that what a person "knows" and in particular the probability and hence the degree of confidence he can have that what he knows is likely to be "true" depends very heavily indeed on *how* (or the conditions under which) that knowledge was obtained.

If a citizen has an awareness of what is involved in specifying the "conditions under which" acceptable scientific knowledge is obtained, he will be aided in developing his criteria for evaluation. An awareness is needed of the kinds of decisions likely to be made when a scientist formulates his problem in this way rather than in that, when he chooses some specific set of observations as a sample from all the relevant observations he could have used, when he determines the kind and extent of controls to be employed on his observations, when he develops some description based on his observations, and when he provides an explanation for his description.

Some of a scientist's decisions are more directly related to the process by which he obtains observations ("research"), and some are more directly related to why he selects those specific observations and what he does with them once they are obtained ("reasoning"). As its title implies, this book is concerned with both kinds of decisions, although in actuality they are so closely intertwined that they are separable only analytically. To use a familiar and appropriate analogy, reasoning and research — or theory and method — are like a team of horses. If they do not pull together, progress in science will be halting and fitful at best.

This book, then, has two major goals: providing some guides for the consumer of scientific knowledge; and providing a methodological foundation for the eventual producer of scientific knowledge. I believe the same content can meet both goals. In practice, the difference between a consumer and a producer rests on whether an individual will use the principles described and the experience gained in trying to apply them in the exercises solely to evaluate later the work of others *or* whether he will use them to evaluate the work both of others and of himself. A producer of scientific knowledge needs to evaluate the work of others in his specific branch of science, and for that purpose he must also be a consumer. Further, he will need to evaluate and to improve his own work while it is in progress. Both producers and consumers must learn and apply the same principles.

PLAN

A combination of discussing *and* doing is used in this book. The same general ideas are covered in two ways: text and exercises.

The text is divided into three main parts. Associated with each of these is a set of practice exercises, each containing the same three types of practice. The first is akin to a drill or self-training type of practice in what I have labeled for shorthand purposes "some desirable skills." The second type is practice of an "apprentice-type" nature, designed to guide the application to a specific project of the principles discussed in the just preceding text portion. The third I have called "on-your-own" practice, intended to give freedom and flexibility both in choosing a topic to investigate and in applying what has been learned from the text and prior exercises.

Since this book is aimed at the novice in the social sciences, I have not assumed any initial mathematical ability beyond that required to compute and interpret a percentage distribution. Nor have I assumed any social science knowledge beyond what the average seventeen- or eighteen-year-old might have picked up in his day-to-day reading. I have tried to prepare the exercises so that the questions to be investigated in them might have spontaneously occurred to someone with the minimal background assumed. And, although the discussion and instructions in the exercises are couched as though a classroom situation were present, I have tried to prepare the material so that it would be possible for someone working alone to complete most of the exercises. Throughout, I have tried to select homely examples, to use what might be referred to as standard English, and to limit the use of footnotes, which so often seem to result in a formidable appearance to the beginner. Preliminary student response has indicated that this approach is successful in eliminating much of the aura of magic that many beginning students seem to feel surrounds the process by which scientists reach their conclusions.

The first part of the text is devoted to an overview of the game called science. The general scientific enterprise can be viewed as a game of strategy played by the human mind in order to gain understanding of Nature, or the observable world. Particular sciences, of course, are devoted to trying to understand particular aspects of the observable world, but there are some "rules of the game" and some general processes involved in playing that are applicable to all the sciences, and Part I of the text is concerned with these.

Carrying out a research project from start to finish can be considered playing a specific instance of the basic game. For convenience in exposition I have divided the overall research process into two portions. The first takes the researcher from the point where he is trying to get an idea to investigate to the point where he is ready to gather his observations. The second takes him from collecting observations through writing a final report on his project.

In practice, the decisions involved for the entire process are highly interdependent, but Part II of the text attempts to cover those most obviously related to the first portion of the process while Part III tries to cover those for the second portion. Following a description of the type of decision needed is a discussion of the major options available and some guides for evaluating each, always in light of the implications of each option for the strength and soundness of any later conclusions to be drawn from the project. Throughout Parts II and III of the text the orientation is toward major social science options, although the same *kinds* of decisions need to be made for a project in any of the sciences.

The principles contained in the text portion are elaborated in the discussions and comments for the exercise portion. Even if they are not actually carried out, then, the exercises should at least be read.

In Exercise Set I, following Part I of the text, the first kind of exercise provides some self-training in table preparation and reading. For reasons elaborated in Exercise I-1, I feel these are desirable skills to have, no matter what type or level of project is of interest. The second kind of exercise, Exercise I-2, is a guided carrying out of a highly simplified project from the initial stage of getting an idea to the final stage of writing a report. The problem investigated has to do with an aspect of the internal functioning of groups, and the data used take the form of direct observations made by the students in a field type of situation. In the third, or on-your-own kind of exercise, Exercise I-3, the student begins thinking about and trying to select a topic for study, and begins to try to narrow it so that his investigation will be completed by the end of the course.

Following Part II of the text, emphasizing the first portion of the research process, the same three kinds of exercises are contained in Exercise Set II. This time, the desirable skills stressed are those of locating and evaluating already available information. For the second kind of exercise two separate projects are carried through from the idea stage through a small pretest, or pilot study, of the student's plan for obtaining information, with the pretest designed to enable him to judge the workability of his plan.

The problem selected for the first project has to do with certain factors related to changes in the relation of a group to its social environment (or to the other groups and individuals with which the group interacts), and the student develops a questionnaire to gather the information needed. The second project's problem has to do with changes in a group's functioning as related to changes in the resources available to it to carry out a specific task, and this time the data consist of observations in an experimental, or laboratory, setting.

For Exercise II-3, the student carries his own project through developing a detailed research proposal. To gain maximum benefit from this exercise, each student should submit his proposal to at least one other classmate playing the role of consultant. I have found that over and above whatever advice his instructor may give him, the experience in critical thinking gained by having to serve as a consultant to a classmate typically improves each student's *own* project as well.

Part III of the text stresses the second portion of the research process, from collecting data through report preparation. In the associated Exercise Set III, some brief practice is provided for the following skills: analysis of simple sets of data and preparation of common types of graphic devices; engaging in the interplay of evidence, interpretation, and speculation needed to solve rather more complicated problems; and trying to translate some typically obscure prose material into clear and readable English. The second kind of exercise, Exercise III-2, involves the guided completion of a project from sample selection and data collection stages through report preparation. This project's problem has to do with describing certain characteristics of a group. The data used come from available records that consist partly of observations and partly of answers to questions. For the third kind of exercise, the student finishes his own project and turns in his report.

Thus, by the time the student has completed the first kind of exercise in each Exercise Set, he will have received some self-training in certain skills desirable no matter what type of project he later engages in or reads about. When he has completed all of the exercises of the second kind, or apprentice-type, he will have had some — admittedly superficial — practice in the use of data in the form of direct field observations, answers to questions, laboratory-type observations, and available records. His completion of parts of his own project is intended to parallel the sequence followed in the text discussion and applied in the first two kinds of exercises in each Exercise Set.

One of the hazards encountered by a teacher who tries to use exercises as part of student training is that too often the exercises are so structured that they tend to become obsolete, in the sense that after the first year earlier students can simply provide later students with "the answer." In that case, it is difficult to sort out how much of a student's performance is attributable to his own learning and how much to the width of his circle of friends.

The difficulty is likely to be most pronounced for the second kind, or apprentice-type, of exercise. Whether or not the student has truly mastered the first, or self-training, kind of exercise can be determined through the choice of appropriate and easily altered examination questions. And, if there is time to carry out the third, or on-your-own, kind of exercise, this can be used to check the student's understanding. In my choices for the apprentice-type exercises, I have most consciously tried to minimize the hazard of obsolescence. While the steps involved will be essentially the same each time, the data that result will not be. I think I have managed to overcome the problem even in Exercise III-2, where the students are to use a certain kind of record which is already available and easily accessible to them. The basic data in the kind of record suggested change enough from one year to the next to alter the results the students will obtain. Further, although the data would come from an identical set of records each time during a *given* year that the exercise is conducted, it is a relatively easy matter to find at least four (assuming a quarter-system) slight alterations in the way the problem is specifically examined.

SUGGESTIONS FOR USE

As far as levels of mastery of the material are concerned, the highest level would involve completion of all the exercises, something that can be accomplished if a semester-long course is available. The next highest level would involve completing just the first and second kinds from each Exercise Set, which can be done in a quarter-long course. The third level of mastery would involve completing the first kind as outside assignments and just reading the other two kinds of exercises. This third level could be achieved by using the text and the material in the first kind of exercise during the time spent on the "_____ as a science" portion of the customary introductory text in each of the social sciences. I think this substitution might be especially beneficial where a single introductory course is intended to serve as both initial and terminal exposure to a given social science, as is frequently the case in our junior colleges, or even high schools.

To take sociology as an illustrative social science, I think a good "single exposure" course could be developed as follows. Use some material like that contained in this book along with something like the recent survey of the field contained in the small and inexpensive pocketbook, *Sociology* (Prentice-Hall, 1969), edited by Neil J. Smelser and James A. Davis and based on the efforts of a panel of practicing sociologists. For each of the principal areas within the discipline, *Sociology* gives an overview of what is known, the kinds of methods used to find out, and some major questions still to be answered. If it were read first, the student should have lots of ideas to help him in selecting his own project. Then the material in this book could be covered, relating it to the material in *Sociology* and perhaps supplementing it by having the student read some of the original articles for the studies mentioned there. It seems to me that a student completing only an introductory course like this would have a much better ability to read and critically evaluate any sociologically-oriented literature he might later encounter than is typical in students exposed to just one course.

Finally, the material in this book might be either used as a beginning for an upper-division or graduate level methods course or interspersed with reading one of the better methods texts, such as Kerlinger, 1964, Phillips, 1966, or Selltiz et al., 1959 (see "Suggestions for Beginning Further Reading," p. 253). In the usual upper-division methods course one can assume a more extensive background on the student's part than I have assumed here, both as far as knowledge of the content of a particular discipline and as far as general background in statistics and other techniques. In that case, it should be possible either to expect a more advanced level of performance on the exercises described in this book or else be relatively easy to provide more sophisticated versions of some or all of them.

REASONING AND RESEARCH

PART I

Overview of the Game Called Science

Not truth, nor certainty. These I foreswore
In my novitiate, as young men called
To holy orders must abjure the world.
"If . . . ," then . . . ," this only I assert;
And my successes are but pretty chains
Linking twin doubts, for it is vain to ask
If what I postulate be justified,
Or what I prove possess the stamp of fact.

Yet bridges stand, and men no longer crawl
In two dimensions. And such triumphs stem
In no small measure from the power this game,
Played with the thrice-attenuated shades
Of things, has over their originals.
How frail the wand, but how profound the spell!

CLARENCE R. WYLIE, JR.,
poet and mathematician

"Paradox" reprinted from *Scientific Monthly* LXVII
(July–December, 1948), p. 63, by permission of *Science*.

1. Science as a Game

Scientific activity can be thought of as game-playing activity. As in any game, there are one or more reasons for playing the game, goals to be achieved, criteria for deciding how well the goals have been met, and rules for admissible pieces and their manipulations. And, as in most games, some pieces and moves are better than others, in the sense that their use yields a higher probability of successful game-playing.

There are other similarities. Participants tend to take about as much pleasure in the process of playing as in the results, while spectators frequently seem interested just in the results. But even for spectators, observing the game and appreciating its outcome can be enhanced in enjoyment by an understanding of the basic rules and an awareness of possible strategies and their implications. Further, while anyone who wants to play can learn the rules and be aware of better and worse strategies, still some players will be more skillful than others.

The game is played to understand the world, or at least some aspect of it. In particular, science can be viewed as a kind of guessing or puzzle-solving game. The basic puzzle is given by the occurrence of, and changes in, events in the observable world. Any single scientific discipline takes some aspect of that world as its specific version of the puzzle to be solved. Trying to solve the puzzle involves guessing at an explanation of why events occur and change as they do, checking it to see that it proves to be scientifically acceptable, and presenting it in a form such that anyone with the competence and desire to do so may examine and check it for himself.

To achieve a satisfactory explanation as to why events occur and change as they do, the scientist needs some descriptions. He needs to know what occurrences and changes there *are*. To achieve this, he needs some observations. As the game continues, scientists try to fit particular explanatory propositions into the broadest, most confirmed, most consistent, and logically simplest set possible at any given time. Thus the pieces to be manipulated at one point or another while playing the game called science are of three kinds: observations, descriptions, and explanations.

Usually when you decide to solve a puzzle, such as a jigsaw puzzle, you have certain expectations. You expect (*a*) to be given a picture on the outside of the box that can be used as a guide to play and is the only appropriate one for the pieces inside; (*b*) the pieces located to stay rigid in their outlines, no matter what maneuvers you make to try to fit them together; and (*c*) enough of the needed pieces to be available that fitting them together will give an essentially complete picture. When these expectations are met, with enough patience and perseverance even the slowest and least imaginative puzzle-solver can produce the picture eventually.

The situation is somewhat different when you try to solve scientific puzzles. You do always have some picture or possible solution to the puzzle as a guide: the explanation or theory currently available. But the guiding picture may be incomplete or fuzzy in detail, and you cannot be sure it is the only appropriate one for the pieces of the puzzle you or others manage to locate. The solution is guessed at, not given, and there may be several guesses that could be solutions. Further, any guess is always to some degree tentative and subject to revision as the game continues.

At any given time during the puzzle-solving process, one guess may be more appropriate than others as a guide to some regions of the picture, especially as more pieces are located and acceptably fitted together. Unfortunately, what is an acceptable fit for a given region may not remain so. In trying to fit the pieces together, you cannot count on their outlines remaining rigid. The outlines depend on descriptions that are interpretations of any observations made. These interpretations may change, either because the tentative guiding picture is revised or because additional observations are made that are relevant to a particular piece and merit alteration of its outline.

Nor can you be sure all the pieces will be located, or at least enough to be satisfied you know what the solution is. However, some ideas about where and how to look are always available and as the game progresses some areas and techniques of search may be exploited as especially productive and other areas and techniques discarded as apparently unproductive of useful pieces. Also, as the game continues some of the tentative guesses (your own or those of others) may be reliably eliminated, raising the probability that a correspondence to the picture is among those remaining.

Patience and perseverance can help, but they are hardly enough for solving the puzzles of science. A prepared, imaginative, and flexible mind is essential. You need to be prepared enough that you can recognize relevant pieces when you come across them, imaginative in finding pieces, deciding on their outlines, and fitting them together, and flexible enough to alter your decisions or your procedures when such change can be justified as aiding progress.

The game is complex and challenging, which accounts for much of its fascination for the players. The interest of the spectators typically rests on the fact that solutions to particular portions of the basic puzzle — Why do events in the observable world occur and change as they do? — often have immediate practical applications. But examples are not hard to find of science being pursued to satisfy the "idle" curiosity of the participants, with the applicability of the results only later, and sometimes much later, being discovered. Familiar instances are those of X-rays and radio. Consequently, the interests of both spectators and participants are usually best served when the game is allowed to continue and perhaps even be actively supported, whether or not practical applications are currently obvious and whether or not progress seems slow.

For the game to be played well requires and therefore fosters certain kinds of behavior. What might be termed a skeptical receptivity is very important. While a scientist needs to be receptive to new and unusual ideas he needs to be skeptical enough to reserve judgment about those ideas unless and until he receives an answer to a fundamental question in science: What is the extent and quality of the evidence?

In addition, scientific behavior should be cooperative, absolutely honest, and democratic. Each player's progress is dependent on the activities of the others. What is left to be explained is contingent on what is already known and so each player's findings need to be freely shared with others. And, if scientific activity is to yield cumulative and self-correcting knowledge, which is merely another way of saying if progress is to be made in the game, then the results of play must be honestly presented. Findings, no matter how seemingly unlikely, have to be accepted as just that, things to be added to the stock of items that needs to be accounted for somehow. They may prove to be illusory, but the illusion should come from theory or technique that need revision, not from dishonest play. Also, progress should be judged solely by how well the game is played, with skin color, nationality, shape of the eyes or of the genitals, or any other such personal characteristics of the participants irrelevant, including whether the player is a professional or not. Until this century the major contributions to scientific knowledge were made by amateurs, or non-paid players, and there is still ample room for the interested and talented amateur.

The equipment needed to work on problems in some branches of science may be beyond the resources of some amateurs, and I would not deny the importance of good tools. The fact that certain additions to knowledge would have been impossible without the telescope and microscope is familiar to every schoolchild. Yet while it is a truism that the most skilled surgeon is hampered if he must work with a dull or defective knife, it is equally a truism that the sharpest and most finely balanced knife is useless in surgery performed by someone without the prepared intelligence to use it.

The most desirable "tool" any scientist can have is a well-prepared, imaginative, and flexible mind. And, for certain parts of what we will discuss later as the cycle of scientific activity, no additional tools are needed in any of the sciences.

The knowledge explosion, with the spread of literacy and the increased number of libraries, makes it feasible for virtually anyone to have a mind that is at least prepared. We live in an age of expressed concern about an increasing amount of leisure and its potential uses. We also live in an age of many unsolved and urgent problems. It would seem unlikely that these problems will be satisfactorily resolved by some version of table-pounding, or "decision by din." The probability would appear to be much higher that these puzzles will be more amenable to solution by reason and research than by rhetoric. Because of all this, as well as because of the habits of thought and behavior fostered by scientific activity, it is my admittedly biased opinion that it would be hard to find a way of filling leisure more worthwhile — or more diverting and absorbing — than to follow the dictate: everyone at least an amateur in some phase of the game called science.

2. AIMS OF THE GAME

The fundamental aim of the game is to achieve understanding of the observable world. To understand events, or phenomena, thoroughly you need to know what they are like as of particular points in time and how they change — a good description, and you also need to know why they are as they are and change as they do — a good explanation.

In science, events are said to be explained when they can be shown both (a) to be members of the general classes of events present in a proposed explanation and (b) to occur and change *as if* the relationships given in the explanation were correct. In order to meet the fundamental aim, then, a more immediate goal is to provide a simulation (an "as if model") that can be shown to correspond to some aspect of the observable world. The kinds of models needed are those called for in trying to answer some version of the basic question posed by all scientists: Just what is going on, and why?

Abstractions based on observations of specific events are used to form classes of events. Relationships between these classes are guessed at and then checked to try to determine the nature of the relationships: sufficient, necessary, both, or neither. That is, the attempt is to provide an explanation that states the conditions under which — if those conditions could be manipulated at will — events could be made to, or prevented from, or both made to *and* prevented from, occurring and changing. (If the relationship is shown to be neither sufficient nor necessary, then what happens to one class of events is irrelevant or accidental as far as occurrence and change in another.)

Therefore, the type of explanation aimed at as a scientifically acceptable answer to a "why" question is not given in terms of ultimate purposes. It turns out to be a "how" answer, statable in terms of the *conditions under which* events do or do not occur and change.

Degree of game-playing success is judged according to the usefulness of the *as if* models developed. Given some time and

ingenuity, especially where little is firmly known about a topic, you could undoubtedly guess at several explanations or models that seem promising. Because of this, two criteria are used for judging models. Each criterion has to do with utility, one related to usefulness for what is already known and the other to usefulness for future work on a topic.

First, does one model aid you more than others in pulling together various propositions about the empirical world into the most broadly coherent set possible? (The term "empirical" refers to the observable behavior of physical things: heat, water, lightbulbs, families, cities, and so on.) What is possible at a given time is of course bounded by existing knowledge on a topic and by the tools and techniques for studying it. Within these bounds, you attempt to explain as much as you can as simply as you can; have as high a degree of confidence as you can that the model does in fact correspond to some aspect of the world; and have as little inconsistency as possible. That guessed-at model which turns out to be the broadest, simplest, most confirmed, and most consistent at any given time is the most useful in systematizing and accounting for already available findings.

To say that you aim at providing the simplest model possible is not necessarily equivalent to saying that you aim at the most easily understandable model. Rather, logical simplicity is meant. For instance, Einstein's famous equation $E = MC^2$ is a mathematically or logically simple one, yet hardly understandable in all its implications without some training in physics.

One model is logically simpler than another when it can use a smaller number of independent concepts than another in order to account adequately for the same phenomena. Further, one is simpler than another when it requires fewer "special rules" or exceptions to the overall explanation in order to account for certain kinds of phenomena within the same general class (such as certain kinds of delinquent behavior among juveniles within the general class of "juvenile delinquency").

To say that you aim at providing a consistent explanation is to say that you want an explanation that is both internally and externally consistent. To begin with the latter, you want any proposed explanation to be consistent with, or not to contradict, any existing and already well-confirmed propositions about whatever it is you are interested in. But it is not rare in the history of science for various proposed explanations to seem inconsistent for a time, only to have further reasoning and research make it clear that a broader explanation is acceptable, from which the earlier and supposedly inconsistent partial explanations can each be derived. Distinguishing *in practice* between those contradictions that are real and those that are only apparent is not always as easy as we might wish.

Internal consistency is the same as logical plausibility. Any explanation should be translatable into the form of an argument: a set of propositions in which one or more represent the conclusion and the remainder are called premises, used to justify the conclusion. An argument is logically plausible when it is the case that *if* the premises in the argument are true then the conclusion is highly unlikely to be false. Whether or not the premises *are* true is a separate question from the plausibility of the argument, and is checked by testing the implications of the argument against empirical observations, or in other words trying to confirm it.

Since you not only want to explain, or account for, as much as you can but also be as sure as you can that you are probably correct in thinking you have achieved the best accounting currently possible for what

is going on and why, all four bases for judging *current* utility are needed: breadth, simplicity, existing degree of confirmation, and extent of consistency.

The second criterion for utility is related to usefulness for future work. As far as the second criterion is concerned, in general you ask yourself whether one model can aid you more than others in drawing inferences, or conclusions about the world, that can then be tested. In particular, if one model can aid you more than another in drawing testable inferences about important regions of the puzzle that as yet have been little explored or confirmed, then that model is more useful for guiding future efforts at understanding some topic.

Whichever model, or explanation, best satisfies *both* criteria — bringing order into what is already known and guiding future efforts — is the most useful one. It is the guide to puzzle solution to be accepted, at least until you can find an even better one.

Frequently, spectators of the game are concerned solely with how well existing explanations can satisfy the first criterion. That is, they are most concerned with science in its "existing body of knowledge" aspect. Players of the game are at least equally concerned with the second criterion, or science as a growing, changing guide to improving our understanding of the world. To a scientist, any explanation is always tentative to some degree. It is always subject to revision or even outright discard whenever a better one can be developed on the basis of an evaluation of additional evidence or a more satisfactory re-evaluation of old evidence.

In practice, when it comes to initially developing explanations the basic rule is to use anything that works — analogy, hunches, logic, going fishing or doing the ironing, even toe-counting and navel-contemplating if these help you to get ideas. In science, far more important than how you manage to begin to develop your explanations is what can be done with them. Do they help bring order into what is already known, by providing an account that can be shown to be scientifically acceptable? Can testable inferences legitimately be derived from them to guide future work, and do those inferences turn out to be corroborated or not?

Designing and carrying out any particular research project can be thought of as playing an instance of the basic game. While the fundamental aim is to understand the observable world and the more immediate aim is to provide an increasingly acceptable correspondence, or as if model, for that world, an even more immediate aim is to play each instance of the game as well as possible.

As in any game, using inadmissible pieces or making inadmissible moves is considered fouling. And, as in any game, those who commit fouls may be penalized. The penalty for anyone committing fouls in the game of science tends to take one or more of the following forms. His published work may be discounted or even ridiculed by his fellow scientists. His work may not be accepted for publication, or if it is, it may not be published in leading journals in his field. If he becomes widely known as a committer of fouls, any future work he manages to get published somewhere may remain unread. Penalization by ridicule and some form of shunning is remarkably effective, in science as elsewhere.

On a more positive note, those who play the game particularly well are rewarded. Citations, medals, and substantial grants of money to support ongoing work are among the "trophies" available for excellence in play. Further, as in other games there are some highly valued less tangible rewards. Among these are the appreciation and respect shown by your fellow players for a well-played game. In science, there is also the satisfaction that comes from seeing your explanation accepted and used by others, and from having it survive the acid test of checking it against empirical observations. Finally, the pleasure gained from occasionally stretching your mental muscles beyond what you thought they were capable of should not be minimized. Frequently, the possibility of this kind of reward is enough to guarantee continuing efforts to play the game.

As will be discussed later, for the kinds of pieces (observations, descriptions, and explanations) as well as the kinds of moves made with the pieces, some will not meet certain criteria adequately and should be avoided. Some will be considerably better than others. The immediate aim while trying to play any instance of the basic game is, of course, to work with the best pieces and make the best, or most efficient, moves that you can.

2.1 A NOTE ON TERMINOLOGY. Drawing checkable inferences from a proposed explanation can be thought of as making predictions. Throughout this book I use the term "prediction" in a general sense, to refer to assertions about situations not yet examined, whether those situations are in the future or in the past.

Where an explanation has a great deal of evidence in support of it, some writers refer to it as a law or principle. Where there is little or no supporting evidence, the terms "hypothesis" or "working hypothesis" may be used. And, where an explanation covers few relationships among few classes of events some writers may use the term "hypothesis," reserving the term "theory" for explanations that consist of a set of interrelated hypotheses covering many relationships or many classes of events, or both.

However, terminology is not consistently

used. What is theory or law to some writers may be hypothesis to others. I think it best for the beginner to grasp the basic idea that all he will ever have to work with as an aid to understanding the observable world is a guess. It may have more or less supporting evidence; it may be more or less complex; it may be more or less useful to him. It is still a guess and still somewhat tentative.

Throughout this book, I use the terms "hypothesis," "theory," "explanation," and "as if model" (or just "model") interchange-ably. I use the latter two rather more often because I feel the term "explanation" helps remind us of the purpose behind scientific activity and the term "model" helps remind us that science no longer even pretends to be interested in discovering absolute truth but only in providing increasingly useful simulations of, or correspondences to, reality. A good deal of the fascination, as well as some of the frustration, for players of the game of science comes from just this aspect of it: it is a never-ending game.

3. Manner in Which Played: The Cycle of Science

A scientist proceeds to try to solve his puzzle by observing, describing what he observes, and developing an explanation that can be used in both of two ways: to account for what has already been observed and described; to draw inferences about additional situations to be observed, described, and explained.

Descriptions and explanations are two of the three main kinds of pieces used in playing the game of science; observations make up the third. Because of the continual interplay of observation, description, and explanation, as a set the pieces are manipulated in cyclical fashion. The cycle is a never-ending one, as illustrated in the accompanying schematic diagram, Fig. I.1.

What is observed is always in some part determined by an idea (*expl* on the diagram), no matter how vague and tentative, about what is worth noting in the ongoing flow of reality. Even the so-called accidental observations that sometimes lead to scientific advances are not truly such, since they are made only when the mind of the observer is both prepared and imaginative. As a familiar case in point, the events that led to the discovery of penicillin occurred in the presence of others before Sir Alexander Fleming, but were ignored.

One sometimes hears (or even worse, reads in published form) a researcher state he is simply going to observe "everything" about, say, families and see what he finds out, without using an explanation or theory to guide him. He may go on to state that he is just going to "let the facts speak for themselves." When examined, the statements become rather absurd.

His guiding theory or explanation may be extremely vague and tentative, but it is nonetheless there, helping him decide what units to observe and what kinds of observations to make. What he really means is that the theory he is actually using is implicit, he has not yet made the effort to bring it to the surface of his mind.

If he truly has no guiding theory, how did he decide on his units? That is, how did he decide what constitutes a "family"? (Were second cousins twice removed included, no matter how far away they lived or how often kept in touch with? Or did he decide to include all living in the same household, no matter how close or remote the blood tie? Or just what *was* the guiding

Fig. I. 1. THE CYCLE OF SCIENCE

Explanation constructing and revising to . . .
   (observation to   *Explanation developing and testing to . . .*
   description to   (explanation to   *Explanation constructing and . . .*
   explanation)   description to
                     observation)

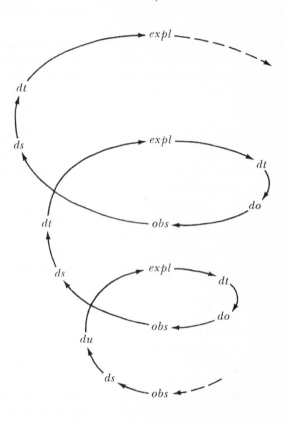

where:

    obs: observations or evidence

      ds: description of pattern in
         sample of observations
         obtained

      du: description of pattern in
         parent class (or universe)
         to which sample belongs

    expl: explanation or theory to
         account for described
         observations and guide
         further investigation

      dt: descriptive inference
         derived from theory

      do: empirical interpretation
         (in operationalized or
         procedural terms) of
         theoretical inference to
         be investigated

basis on which his choice was made?) If he is really going to observe everything, why would he ignore, as he undoubtedly would, the length of the toenails or eyelashes of each family member? These observations would not be made because his implicit explanation or theory dictated they were not relevant for his topic of investigation.

Further, facts never speak for themselves. They are quite passive and never volunteer information. Sometimes they answer questions, but only if you ask and even so they require an interpreter. Deciding what to ask and how to interpret the answers depends on what the researcher's guiding explanation tells him to ask and what it tells him about how the answers might be interpreted.

Once a set of observations (*obs* in the diagram) has been made, two kinds of descriptions are developed, the *ds* and then the *du* descriptions shown on the left side of the diagramed cycle. Every set of concrete observations actually obtained is always just a portion of some parent class of observations of the same type. In the terminology often used in research reports, every set of observations is a "sample" from some broader set, called a "population" or "universe" and containing the sample as a subset. Both the pattern seen in the sample and the pattern thought likely to be present in the parent class from which it comes need to be described, with the description of the sample (*ds* on the cycle) followed by the *du*, or universe description.

The *du* descriptions constitute what is to be accounted for, or explained. Once an explanation is developed, it is checked for plausibility, that is, checked to see that *if* the explanation were correct the *du* descriptions available should logically follow.

But, especially when few described observations are available, a number of plaus-

ible accounts can be more or less easily constructed. The task then becomes one of further elaborating and testing proposed and plausible explanations. To do this the scientific process moves on to the right side of the cycle.

Two kinds of descriptions are again developed, and again in sequence. Additional plausible inferences are developed from a proposed explanation. These inferences are in general, or theoretical, form both as to variables and relationships and are noted on the cycle as *dt* descriptions. Before their truth or falsity can be tested, using empirical observations, a choice must be made as to which empirical interpretation will be given them. An empirical interpretation of a description stated in general terms is shown as a *do* on the cycle. A *do* description is stated in terms of the operations, or procedures, which will be used: those used to determine when concrete events can be considered to be members of particular categories of variables (or classes of events); those used to determine when specific relationships can be considered to be empirical counterparts of relationships in the original *dt* description.

Observations are then selected to serve as a direct test of the description and an indirect test of the explanation from which it was derived. Depending on the results of the test, the explanation is re-examined and the cycle continues.

The explanation will be judged as either more confirmed or less confirmed than before the test. If more confirmed, the probability will have been raised that it does correspond to some aspect of the observable world, and the cycle proceeds by developing further inferences and checking them. If less confirmed, it is in need of revision to try to ensure that the correspondence will become closer than it is now. In that case, the cycle continues by first revising the explanation and then checking it in its revised form.

On either the left or right sides of the cycle, then, two kinds of descriptions are developed. One kind is more empirically oriented, or in specific terms. The other is more theoretically oriented, or in general terms. The *order* of development is reversed, however, depending on whether the left (explanation constructing and revising) side or the right (explanation developing and testing) side is involved. The left side moves from observations to specific and then more general descriptions and on to explanations. The right side moves from explanations to general and then more specific descriptions and on to observations.

In addition to mentally splitting a turn of the cycle vertically, a split may be made horizontally. This split results in upper and lower, or theory and methodology, halves.

Skill in constructing and developing explanations or theories (roughly the upper half of a turn of the cycle, from *du* through *expl* to *dt*) and skill in methodology (roughly the lower half of a turn of the cycle, from *do* through *obs* to *ds*) are both needed if any particular project is to be as useful as possible for scientific progress on a topic. And, both skill in the upper half and skill in the lower half require the ability to discover as well as prove.

In the theory half, you are involved in discovery when you try to invent or guess at an explanation to account for whatever *du* descriptions are available and you are involved in proof when you try to show that your explanation does adequately so account. Further, you are engaged in discovery when you hunt about for additional consequences, or *dt* descriptions, that can be derived from your explanation and in proof when you try to show they do legitimately follow. In temporal rather than log-

ical order, explanations and consequences frequently are guessed at first, with the logical underpinning later developed to show that *if* the explanation or theory is assumed to be true then it *can* adequately account for what is already known and other consequences *can* legitimately be derived.

Both discovery and proof are also involved in the methodology half. You try to discover some empirical counterparts (*do* descriptions) to your theoretical problem. Then you try to show that these empirical counterparts *are* satisfactory. Also, you try to discover whatever patterns (*ds* descriptions) do exist in your observations and are likely to exist more generally and then try to show that your descriptions, and not some alternative ones, *are* justified by the evidence available.

To repeat, skill in the theory half and skill in the method half of the basic cycle are needed equally for the game of science to be played well. And in either half, both skill in discovery and skill in proof are required.

Some individuals may feel their explanatory, or theory, skills are better than their method skills, while others may feel the reverse is true about themselves. Nonetheless, at least to some minimum extent, every scientist needs to possess each kind. It is both artificial and misleading to consider it acceptable to separate these skills physically, with a given researcher embodying solely one kind. If science is to progress, both skills are necessary — in the same skull — and it is a wise beginner who tries to acquire some facility in both as early as he can.

Sometimes a complete turn of the basic cycle seems to resemble a circle, in the sense that we are no further ahead at the end of the manipulations of the pieces than at the beginning, as far as the knowledge obtained about a topic. But what is hoped for, is more typical, and is the way I have prepared the diagram, is that repeated turns of the cycle resemble an ever-widening spiral. Hopefully, the cycle (which is a self-corrective one by the nature of the procedures) represents cumulative knowledge, becoming more and more precise and filling in more and more gaps in the puzzle to be solved.

4. SELECTION OF PIECES AND MOVES

Science attempts to account for events by showing that they are members of certain classes of events and by showing that relationships among them are such as would be expected if the relationships given in a proposed explanation were correct. The basis for any claim to belief in scientific knowledge rests on that knowledge being shareable, or public, in the sense that *any* member of the public with the competence and desire to check it should be able to do so. Because of this, several things follow.

The events referred to should be repeatable, at least in type although not necessarily in all details. Otherwise, scientific knowledge would be highly specific, referring only to particular events at particular times and in particular places. If this were so, it would be difficult for someone else to check any claims made. After all, if it is claimed that water boils at 212 degrees Fahrenheit, you would like to feel that this event is repeatable: it will do so again, no matter who does the observing or the heating, or when and in what type of container.

Further, any assertions about classes of events should be checkable, or testable, so that independent observers can agree. To do this, they need some shared rules for assigning labels to events and relationships. This means that communication should be objective, not subjective. Objectivity and subjectivity are not inherent in the subject matter, but have to do with how knowledge about that subject matter is communicated.

For instance, if I state Sally is a beautiful girl, I might find that you agree with me. But without some shared rules for assigning labels, we could be agreeing on the basis of private, subjective definitions. I might decide she is beautiful because of her long brown hair even though I wish she weren't quite so skinny, while you might find her beautiful because of her slenderness although you wish she wouldn't wear her hair in such a mop.

Mere agreement among many observers is not enough; you need to know the basis for their agreement. It is not so long ago in human history when everyone agreed that the earth was flat, or that witches existed, or that parents who saw more than half their children survive to adulthood were blessed with extraordinary good luck. This was so despite the fact that anyone might have, to take the first illustration, observed that the top of a ship sailing beyond the horizon disappeared last. Agreement among independent observers is essential to have confidence in an assertion, but it is not enough in science unless you also know the basis for testing the assertion — what kinds of observations might be used to show it false — as well as the results of the available tests: do they tend to confirm or deny the assertion?

In addition to repeatable observations and objectively stated, potentially testable assertions or propositions, you want to know the interrelations between propositions: why do events occur and change as they do? To have this kind of understanding, you want explanations that can be couched in terms of relationships that are necessary or sufficient, or both. Otherwise, we might find ourselves merely stumbling around in the dark.

Finally, you would like to know that the reasoning involved when manipulating the pieces is adequate. You don't want fallacious reasoning to be used, or in other words drawing conclusions not merited by the premises used.

Therefore, there are certain pieces among the basic kinds used (observations, descriptions, and explanations) that you will want to avoid, as well as certain moves, or manipulations of the pieces, that you will want to avoid. Beyond this, you would like to use the best pieces and make the best, or most efficient, moves that you can. The next two subsections elaborate the kinds of pieces and moves to be avoided, while the following subsections try to provide some guides for picking better pieces and moves.

4.1 PIECES TO BE AVOIDED. You aim at making descriptions and providing explanations that hold beyond the here and now. These descriptions and explanations, then, should be about classes of events.

It is the repeatability of patterns that is the repeatability the scientist asks of nature. It is these patterns he seeks to describe and explain. It is quite true that nature never quite repeats specific events. To borrow an example dating at least from the Greeks, one cannot step into the same stream twice. The time is not identical, the molecules in the stream are not identical, the individual himself is not identical. While the specific event is not repeatable in every detail, the abstracted and generalized pattern of placing a dry foot into a stream with the resulting condition of having a wet foot *is* repeatable many, many times.

Observations should be of events that are repeatable in type, although not necessarily in specifics. Unique events are not of interest to scientists, unless and until they can be shown to be members of a repeatable set, or class of events. Observations that do not meet this criterion are not likely to be useful in developing scientific knowledge, and should be avoided.

Potentially testable assertions, the only propositions admissible in the game of science, may be termed contingent. All other kinds, namely contradictory and empty propositions, should be excluded.

Contradictory propositions are always false. The assertion that something is both X *and* not-X simultaneously must always be false, no matter what is observed.

An empty proposition is also one that is "not potentially falsifiable." This statement means that it is not possible even to conceive of evidence, in the form of possible observations, that could show the assertion is false. However, the statement is not equivalent to saying that an empty proposition must always be true, regardless of what is observed. While this may happen, another possibility is that, based on observations, the truth or falsity of the proposition cannot be *determined*.

To give an obvious example of one kind of empty proposition, suppose you assert that sometime tomorrow your house either will be rained on *or else* it will not be rained on. No matter what the weather observed tomorrow in your neighborhood, your assertion will be true. Such all-inclusive statements are empty and should be avoided.

In addition to all-inclusive assertions, statements that are ambiguous in one way or another are almost always empty. Consider the following statement which might have come from an ancient oracle about a forthcoming battle: The Roman Army, the Greek Army will overcome. No matter who wins, the statement will be true. It would be false only if there were a tie, and so is an almost completely empty statement. Even though it is clear which armies are referred to and what is meant by one army overcoming another, the statement as a whole still represents one kind of ambiguity.

Sometimes in an ambiguous statement it is *not* clear what is referred to. Fortune-tellers and astrologers earn their livings by using statements that are almost always empty in this way. "Something interesting will happen to you soon" is a statement whose truth or falsity is not easily determined. Something interesting could be interpreted (especially after the fact) as anything from trying a new breakfast cereal to inheriting a fortune, and what is meant by "soon" is not exactly clear.

Empty assertions do not always take such obvious forms. To use a final example, in medieval times some writers argued that fossils discovered in the earth had been deliberately placed there by God (or by the Devil, depending on which medieval writer you read) to test man's faith. What conceivable evidence could be used to demonstrate that this proposition is true or false? What possible set of observations would show that fossils had or had not been deliberately placed in the earth by God or the Devil? The proposition is empty and therefore should be avoided as far as the scientist is concerned, and whether or not such a proposition might be "really" true is beside the point.

Propositions may be combined to form descriptions, or they may be combined to form that particular kind of argument called an explanation. Descriptive propositions are directly testable, using observations. Explanatory propositions are indirectly testable. Inferences are derived and take the form of descriptive propositions. These descriptive propositions are then di-

rectly testable, with the test constituting an indirect test of the explanation.

To summarize so far, you should avoid observations that are not repeatable, at least in type although not necessarily in all details. You should also avoid propositions that are not potentially testable, either directly in the case of descriptive propositions or indirectly in the case of explanatory propositions.

Explanations should also meet another criterion in addition to that of potential testability. Explanations should be translatable into a particular kind of argument. (In any argument, one or more of the interrelated propositions contain the conclusion. The others are called premises. The function of the premises is to provide justification for the conclusion.)

The propositions in the argument should refer to *classes* of events, or phenomena — abstracted properties of concrete events in the observable world — and to certain kinds of relationships among these phenomena. The goal is to account for some phenomena by describing their relation to other phenomena.

A phenomenon may be used as *dependent* variable (something to be accounted for) or as *independent* variable (used to account for something else). Typically, we are interested in knowing both kinds of information: What accounts for a phenomenon? What can a phenomenon account for?

But "being accounted for" or "accounting for" requires specifying the *nature* of the relationship between a phenomenon and something else: necessary, sufficient, or both necessary and sufficient. In form, then, an explanation should be capable of being translated into an argument that specifies relationships among abstracted properties of classes of events, where those relationships can be described as necessary, sufficient, or both.

Some property, we can call it A, is said to be in a necessary relationship to (or be a necessary condition for) some other property which we can call B if whenever B occurs A must also be present. Necessary conditions, then, are those whose presence is essential to, but need not guarantee, the presence or occurrence of something else.

Some property A is said to be a sufficient condition for some other property B if whenever A is present B must be present too. Sufficient conditions, then, are those whose presence will guarantee, but may not be essential for, the presence or occurrence of something else.

Some property A is both necessary and sufficient for some other property B if A's presence is both essential to *and* can guarantee the occurrence of B.

These various relationships need not be one way, since it is possible to have interdependence present. If this is the case, then depending on the type of interdependence present each property is necessary for, or sufficient for, or both necessary and sufficient for, the other. Five illustrations follow:

1. Having lungs is a necessary condition for the development of lung cancer, although it is not also sufficient. It will not guarantee the occurrence of the disease.

2. In the United States as in some other countries, being born to a legally married woman is sufficient for, or will guarantee, a child's legitimacy by the time he enters school. But this is not essential, or a necessary condition, for legitimacy by that time, since another way to guarantee a child's legitimacy is to adopt him.

3. It used to be that cessation of the heart's beating was considered both necessary and sufficient for death to be said to have occurred. Because of some recent developments in medicated survival, it is now proposed that a necessary and sufficient condition for death is that the electrical tracing of the brain's activity form a straight line.

4. The current interdependence of poverty and inadequate formal education in this society is well known, even though as yet the particular kind of interdependence present — necessary, sufficient, or both — has not been firmly established. And, as may well be the case for this illustration, the interdependence may be such that the occurrence of a factor is necessary or sufficient for the occurrence of a second factor, which then in turn is necessary or sufficient for the continuance of the first factor, and so on.

5. My last illustration is a version of an ancient joke, probably told in virtually every course in introductory logic. You can use it to further clarify for yourself the ideas of necessity and sufficiency. As pointed out in the remarks following it, you can also use it to anticipate some things to be elaborated later.

> On the first Saturday evening in May, a blithe young bachelor went out with a redhead and during the evening consumed a large quantity of Scotch and soda. The following Sunday morning he had a terrible hangover. On the second Saturday in May he again went out for the evening but this time dated a brunette and drank a large quantity of bourbon and soda. The next morning he again had a terrible hangover. Undaunted, the following Saturday he again went out, but with a blond and drank a large quantity of gin and soda. When he awoke the next morning with a terrible hangover he vowed, priding himself on being a logical young man, "That does it! From now on I'm giving up soda."

When I first heard this joke in an introductory logic class some time ago, the subject of the story was referred to as a gay young bachelor. As we all know, everyday language can change in its connotations and in order not to distract you from the main point of the joke I thought it wisest now to refer to the gentleman as a *blithe* young bachelor. This "slipperiness" of everyday language is only one of the reasons for the scientist's insistence on precise specifications for the terms he uses in any given empirical interpretation of a theoretical statement.

The implied conclusion our hypothetical bachelor came to was that drinking soda was responsible for his hangovers. As premise for this conclusion he might be using either a claim that drinking soda was necessary for, or was sufficient for, or possibly both necessary and sufficient for, hangovers. But suppose that he has a skeptical friend, who claims that the association observed by the bachelor is an irrelevant one. By this the friend would mean that the association is accidental only. More precisely, this is the same as saying that the relation between drinking soda and having a hangover is *neither* necessary *nor* sufficient. What situations would our blithe bachelor have to be willing to subject himself to if he were to try to check his friend's claim? (*Hint:* The situations needed to show drinking soda is not necessary for a hangover to occur may not be the same as the situations needed to show drinking soda is not sufficient.)

What are considered reasonable contenders for necessary or sufficient conditions, or both, depends to a large extent on what is already known or presumed to be true. For instance, regardless of hair color, the bachelor's dates were all female. Further, all the observed situations occurred in May. Yet neither of these common properties of the specific observed events figures in the bachelor's explanation. He must have discounted them as insignificant, presumably on the basis of prior knowledge of some

kind. Whatever tentative explanation about hangovers guided him in making his observations — and some initial explanation will always be present as a guide to selecting what to observe, no matter how vague and tentative it may be — led him to regard these properties as irrelevant.

But what is considered irrelevant or relevant always depends largely on the information we already have and how we interpret it. To us the joke is funny because we are aware that the bachelor has overlooked what to us is the most reasonable contender of all, the alcohol content in all the other substances drunk besides soda: Scotch, bourbon, and gin. That is, we know an *alternative* or competing explanation about hangovers, and based on other knowledge that we have we find this alternative explanation preferable. To a proverbial man from Mars, however, or for a scientist working on the exploratory fringe of his discipline, where little is known in any reliable form, determining just which properties of events represent "reasonable contenders" may be far from easy.

To return to the main discussion, both participants and spectators of the game of science are interested in information about relationships that are necessary, sufficient, or possibly both. For the producer of scientific knowledge such information can aid him in developing and checking his tentative explanations. For the consumer or user of scientific knowledge such information may aid him in preventing, or producing, or at least adjusting to, events of concern to him. For each, the prime interest lies in the application of any understanding gained about these kinds of relationships.

As one application, if A is necessary for B then if you can prevent A from occurring you will thereby also prevent B from occurring. What has been described involves one interpretation of the somewhat loose term "cause." You search for the cause of something in order to prevent that something from taking place.

In another use of the term "cause," you search for the cause of something in order to ensure, or guarantee, that that something will happen. This use corresponds to an application of knowledge of sufficient conditions.

Sometimes the term "cause" is used to mean that by knowing the cause of something you can either prevent or ensure its occurrence, at will. Doing this amounts to applying knowledge of conditions that are both necessary *and* sufficient.

Of course, knowledge of these various kinds of relationships can be useful even when you do not actually have the power to manipulate them, as was implied in the preceding paragraphs. Whether or not you are able to manipulate the observable world, such knowledge can be a great aid in enabling adjustment to what can and cannot happen in that world. Adjustment to predictions of the weather, even though manipulation of it was not possible, used to be given as a prime example, although even manipulation of the weather is now an increasingly real possibility. If only because some of the capriciousness of life seems to have been eliminated by gaining understanding of necessary and sufficient conditions, this kind of understanding seems to make life a little more comfortable and secure even when no manipulation is possible and when no obvious adjustments are called for.

I referred earlier to the term "cause" being used somewhat loosely. In addition to sometimes using it to refer to relationships that we want to prevent, or guarantee, or both, we also sometimes use the term "cause" in everyday language to refer to signs or symptoms.

For example, when we say the cause of a high fever is a certain disease, what we mean is that the fever is a symptom of the disease's presence. Here the particular disease is a sufficient condition. It may not be necessary, though, since there may be several diseases accompanied by a high fever. As an illustration of the term "cause" to mean sign, suppose we were to light a match in a small closed container and it immediately went out. We might say that the cause of the flame's being extinguished was a lack of oxygen. What we seem to mean here by the term "cause" is that we have a sign of the lack of oxygen. In this case, the presence of oxygen is interpreted as a necessary condition for the flame to continue to burn.

Since there are these assorted meanings of the word "cause" as used in everyday life, scientific communication could be improved in clarity by using the term as little as possible and instead specifying whether we are actually talking about necessary conditions, sufficient ones, or both. However, the term "cause" is so much a part of our communication about events that you will often see it used. Whenever it is, in scientific as well as in other kinds of reports, it is helpful to be sure you understand what is specifically meant, by trying to determine just which usage of cause is intended. It will turn out, in the case of signs and symptoms as well as the other uses, that what is being discussed is a certain relationship that is implied to be necessary, or sufficient, or both, and your job will be to determine which.

Explanations, after all, are potential solutions to the basic puzzle of science: Why do events occur and change as they do? Because we not only want to be able to account plausibly for described observations but we also want to be able to show that a proposed and plausible explanation is probably correct, both criteria are essential: an explanation should actually *explain,* or account for what is going on, which means it should take a certain form as described above; an explanation should be potentially verifiable, or testable.

Both criteria are necessary because, difficult though it may be to accept the idea at first, it turns out that for any set of observations whatsoever you can always find *some* regularity, some pattern of relationships, in what has so far been observed to license whatever prediction you might feel like making. Frequently, the beginner is so delighted to be able to come up with any regularity to support a prediction that he may be easily lulled into thinking that therefore this must be the only regularity possible and so must be the correct one, and need not be checked.

However, finding some kind of pattern that you can extend to justify a prediction may take a little time and ingenuity, but it can always be done. Usually, the less known about a subject — especially as long as there are no restrictions on the relationships allowable, such as restriction to necessary, sufficient, or both relationships — the easier it is to find several different possibilities from which you can then move on to make the same prediction.

Some time ago the mathematicians showed that for any set of numbers arranged in any sequence it is always possible, though not always obvious and easy, to find some generating function that can be used both to give a pattern to the numbers already available and to predict any number whatever as the next in the sequence. (A generating function is simply a formula. This formula has an unknown in it, k, such that if the number 1 is substituted and the operations or procedures called for in the formula are carried out, such as multiplication or taking square root or whatever

operations the formula tells you to do, you get the first member of the series; if 2 is substituted for k you get the second member of the sequence, and so on.)

Since any objects or events could always be assigned numbers to label them, it follows that finding some regularity to support any prediction about any set of objects or symbols for objects can always be done. This can be done even when there seems to be a patently nonsense association present, as long as there is no restriction on the type of regularity allowed. To use a kind of nonsense association often given to illustrate the point in logic classes, the set might consist of a pink umbrella, a yellow feather, and a flower whose color you would like to predict, perhaps as red or blue or whatever color pleases you. And, if it were impossible to go on to observe the flower, to check your prediction, you would have no way of knowing which of your various possible (based on extending some pattern or other) predictions was correct. Hence, for explanations in science both criteria are needed: plausibility and testability.

To summarize, the pieces used in the game of science are observations, explanations, and descriptions. Pieces that do not meet certain criteria should be avoided. Observations should be of a repeatable type, although not necessarily repeatable in all details. Explanations and descriptions should be potentially checkable, or testable. Therefore, contradictory and empty propositions should be excluded. Descriptions are directly testable, using observations. Explanations are indirectly testable, by drawing inferences in the form of descriptive propositions that are then directly tested. Explanations should meet an additional criterion besides testability: they should actually explain, or account for what is going on. Thus an explanation should be translatable into a particular form. It should be capable of being put in the form of arguments that state certain relationships between classes of events, namely relationships that are necessary, or sufficient, or both.

4.2 MOVES TO BE AVOIDED. The scientific process involves a continuous interplay between explanation, description, and observation. At *every* stage in the game reasoning is more or less explicitly used. Reasoning consists of making inferences or drawing conclusions on the basis of premises, which are either known or assumed to be true. Taken as a set, a conclusion and the premises used to justify it constitute an argument.

You are engaged more or less consciously and explicitly in making arguments and drawing conclusions (or reasoning) when you claim: particular descriptive statements can be legitimately derived from an explanation; a particular empirical interpretation of a derived inference is an appropriate one to use; evidence has been collected in a fashion that adequately conforms to the intentions of your research design; examination of the evidence or observations yields particular descriptions of them and of the parent class from which they come; descriptions of the results of a test of inferences support the conclusion that the original explanation has been verified and so raise the probability that the explanation is correct, *or* support the conclusion that the original explanation needs revision; some particular explanation can account for the described observations available; and your report on your project is prepared in the best way to interest, inform, and convince the reader.

For any of the moves you make to enable you to justify these claims, using inadequate or fallacious reasoning is a foul in the game. A fallacy is committed whenever a conclusion is not legitimately drawn.

Fallacies can take many specific forms. The ones discussed below are those I feel you should most be on guard for, stating them in as stark a form as I can. Unfortunately, fallacious arguments will seldom take such clear-cut forms or they would not be so troublesome. However, if you are alerted to the basic forms and deliberately remind yourself to check for them in your own work as well as that of others, you should be able to spot similar fallacies even in their more subtle guises.

I will briefly discuss four general kinds of fallacies to be avoided: incompleteness, circularity, ambiguity, and logical invalidity. The last kind will be discussed somewhat more fully than the first three.

A. Incompleteness. There are three versions of this kind of fallacy that I will discuss here. They have in common that the set of premises used to justify the conclusion is inadequate to do so because it is incomplete.

In one version of this fallacy, the premises are incomplete because they are rather obviously irrelevant — typically personal preferences. This kind of argument tends to take one of the following two patterns. Either:

Mr. X is a ——ist
I don't like ——ists
Therefore, what Mr. X says must be false

or:

Mr. X is a ——ist
I like ——ists
Therefore, what Mr. X says must be true

The conclusion that what Mr. X says is true (or false) may be factually correct, but it is not a legitimately drawn inference from the premises given. The set of premises is incomplete. It does not contain premises justifying moving from your personal preferences to the truth or falsity of Mr. X's statements.

A second version of the fallacy of incomplete premises occurs in two related forms: the fallacy of composition and the fallacy of division.

In the fallacy of composition you state that because certain things are true of the units making up a whole they must also be true of the whole. In the fallacy of division you state that because certain things are true of the whole they must also be true of the units making up the whole.

Let me give two examples. Suppose you state that since hydrogen and oxygen separately have certain properties, then water (which is made up of hydrogen and oxygen) must have those same properties. Or, suppose you state that since individuals have certain properties when alone (rational, law-abiding, or whatever) then a mob made up of those individuals, such as a lynch mob, must have the same properties. In each case, you are committing a fallacy of composition. You would need to complete your set of premises by adding one or more that *justify* moving from the properties of the parts to the properties of the whole.

Conversely, if you stated that since water is made up of hydrogen and oxygen then the properties of water must also hold true for hydrogen and oxygen when considered separately, or that since a mob is made up of individuals then the properties of the mob must hold for the individuals when alone, you would be committing a fallacy of division. Again, your premises are incomplete. You need to add premises to justify moving from the properties of the whole to the properties of the parts.

A third version of the fallacy of incomplete premises is usually known as a *post hoc* fallacy. The longer Latin phrase is *post hoc, ergo propter hoc,* or "after this, there-fore because of this." The *post hoc* fallacy is one kind of a broader fallacy: concluding that because two things occur together, one must cause the other. In statistical terminology, this broader fallacy is warned against in the caution that correlation (or association) does not necessarily prove causation.

I will give just one extreme example, often given in introductory statistics courses. At a time when Holland was more rural than it is now there was a strong correlation between the stork population and the number of babies born. Past kindergarten age, or perhaps even earlier nowadays, no one is likely to construe this empirical association as evidence for the conclusion that an increase or decrease in births is caused by an increase or decrease in storks. Of course, the reason we easily spot this conclusion as a fallacy is that we have learned an alternative argument and so find it hard to see any reasonable connection between the presence or absence of storks and the presence or absence of babies.

Typically, it is those premises stating a reasonable link between two or more phenomena that are customarily missing in a *post hoc* argument. The premises are not complete enough to justify the conclusion that one phenomenon is responsible for another.

B. Circularity. In this kind of fallacy the conclusion has been somehow concealed as one of the premises. Thus what you are trying to conclude as true has already been assumed as true. You have not gone anywhere in your reasoning except around in a circle. In its simplest pattern, the argument is:

> A is true
> B is true
> Therefore, A is true

As an illustration, suppose we let A stand for: happy marriages are intact; B stand for: intact marriages are not broken by divorce; and the conclusion would be: happy marriages are not broken by divorce. If we substitute in the schematic form above, we see that the second premise is a definition of a term, "intact," contained in the first premise. After the substitution the first premise becomes: happy marriages are not broken by divorce; and the conclusion to the argument remains as before: happy marriages are not broken by divorce.

Because of the circularity of the argument, the conclusion is true if the premises are true, but the conclusion is only trivially true since in essence it was *assumed* to be true as one of the premises.

C. Ambiguity. Many kinds of ambiguity are possible, but I want to stress those fallacies that have in common that the argument seems to be a correct one but is not, because a verbal illusion is present. The argument *seems* to follow a correct pattern:

> All A's are B's
> All B's are C's
> Therefore, all A's are C's

You probably learned this correct form in early mathematics, as "when A is contained in B and B is contained in C, then A must be contained in C." While the fallacious version seems to be of this form, it really isn't. Instead, the pattern is:

> All A's are B's
> All C's are D's
> Therefore, all A's are D's

The difficulty comes because, when replaced by verbal terms, the B's and C's sound as though they referred to the same things. But in fact, two different meanings of the same or similar verbal terms are employed. Because this kind of fallacy can take extremely subtle forms, scientists frequently find it necessary to use what are seemingly almost fastidiously precise definitions of terms, especially if those terms are used in everyday language as well. Also, avoidance of this kind of fallacy justifies the occasional use of neologisms, even though these invented terms can at times hinder communication between scientist and citizen.

D. Logical invalidity. Using logic or reasoning consists of combining statements, doing this over and over again, and drawing conclusions about these combined statements. The reasoning is logically invalid, or a fallacy is committed, when the conclusion about the truth or falsity of the combination is not warranted.

There are many ways of combining statements or propositions but these various ways are the result of using one or another of four fundamental ways: conjunction, disjunction, negation, and implication. For each of these ways I will describe the kind of combination meant and when the combination is considered to be true or false.

When you form that compound proposition called a *conjunction,* you place an "and" between propositions. The conjunction "A and B" is true only when *both* components are true, and is false otherwise. Thus if either or both components are false the combined proposition is false.

When you form a *disjunction* you place an "or" between propositions. The disjunction "A or B" is false only when both components are false. If one or the other or both are true, then the disjunction is true. Hence, in disjunctions "or" is used in what is called an *inclusive* sense, which is not always the way it is used in everyday language. In everyday language we sometimes use "or" in an inclusive sense and sometimes in an exclusive sense: to mean either one or the other but *not* both. In logic, when you intend the exclusive sense you can make your meaning clear by using combinations of the four basic ways, and so in forming disjunctions the agreed-on meaning of "or" is always the inclusive one.

If A is any proposition, the *negation* of A is formed by placing "not" or else "it is false that" in front of A. The negation of a proposition always has the opposite truth value of the proposition: if the proposition is true, its negation is false, while if the proposition is false, its negation is true.

You form an *implication* between two propositions, A and B, by placing "if" before one of them and "then" before the other. The implication "if A then B" is false *only when* the "if . . ." part (called the antecedent) is true and the "then . . ." part (called the consequent or conclusion) is false. Thus two major types of fallacies are possible and extremely important to avoid. One is called the fallacy of affirming the consequent and the other is called the fallacy of denying the antecedent.

In the fallacy of affirming the consequent, you unwarrantedly conclude that because the consequent is true, therefore the antecedent *must* also be true. This is a fallacy because the consequent *may* be true either when the antecedent is true or when it is false. Let me give two examples. Example 1: *If* all turkeys are birds, *and if* all birds have wings, *then* all turkeys have wings. Example 2: *If* all turkeys are green fish, *and if* all green fish have wings, *then* all turkeys have wings.

In each of the examples the *implication* is correct, since it is impossible for the conclusion to be false if the antecedent is true (the examples are both of a type encountered earlier: if the set of A's is contained in the set of B's and the set of B's is contained in the set of C's, then the set of A's must be contained in the set of C's).

But in the first case the conclusion is true and so also is the antecedent, while in the second case the conclusion is true but the antecedent is false.

Whether or not the antecedents are *factually* correct is a separate issue from whether the implication (if A then B) is a *logically* correct, or valid, one. Thus it is a fallacy to conclude solely from the truth of a conclusion either that the antecedent must be true or that it must be false, and this fallacy is known as "affirming the consequent."

In the fallacy of denying the antecedent, you incorrectly reason that because the antecedent is false, then the conclusion *must* be false also. It may be false, but it may be true. Suppose you formed the implication "if X is a mother, then X must also be female." Whereas it is quite correct to conclude that if X is not female (the consequent is false) then X cannot be a mother (the antecedent is false), it is *not* correct to conclude that if X is not a mother (the antecedent is false) then X cannot be female (the consequent is false). It might be factually correct that X is not a mother, but from this information alone, it might be that X *is* female, while it also might be that X is anything from a male to a mangrove tree.

In general, then, it is fallacious to conclude anything definite about the antecedent solely from the truth of the consequent, and it is a fallacy to conclude anything definite about the consequent solely from the falsity of the antecedent. Taken as a whole, the implication "if A then B" is false only when this complex proposition is true: the antecedent is true *and* the consequent is false.

Given these basic ways of combining propositions, "and," "or," "not," and "if . . . then . . . ," many complex propositions can be built up using them. By knowing when these basic ways of combining result in a logically true or false combination, we have a tool for judging the logical correctness of combinations built up by using one or more of the basic ways, or in other words a tool for drawing legitimate inferences about these combinations. As just one example, a complex proposition might be made by combining a negation and a conjunction, or claiming "it is not the case that A and B." By applying our knowledge of when the basic ways of combining are true or false, we can legitimately conclude that either A or B and possibly both *must* be false. In an idle moment or two you might try to see all the legitimate conclusions that could be drawn from the following implication: *if* (p or q) and not (r or s), *then* z. After doing so, you might take any explanation that seems reasonable to you about various alternative conditions that must be present along with various alternative conditions that should not be present in order to account for something of interest to you, say poverty, or delinquency, or the growth of cities, or riots, then substitute them for p, q, r, s, and z, and see to what conclusions you must logically be led when the "if" part is assumed to be true.

Let me now relate the earlier discussion of necessary and sufficient conditions to the question of logical invalidity. To say that A is sufficient for B is the same as saying the implication "if A then B" is true, while saying A is necessary for B is the same as saying that the implication "if B then A" is true, and to say that A is both sufficient and necessary for B is the same as saying that the complex proposition "if A then B *and* if B then A" is true. In other words, to claim that A is sufficient and necessary for B is the same thing as making two separate claims simultaneously. Sometimes this is referred to by saying that a relationship that

is both sufficient and necessary is an "if and only if" relationship. A small diagram may be useful:

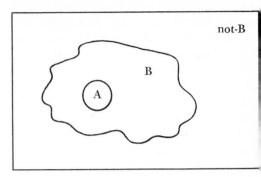

In the diagram, the small circle labeled *A* corresponds to all cases where A is true (or exists), the roundish blob labeled *B* corresponds to all cases where B is true (or exists), while the remainder is labeled *not-B* and corresponds to all cases where B is false (or does not exist). To claim that A is sufficient for B is the same as claiming that whenever A exists B must also exist, or to claim "if A then B." From the diagram, the fallacy of affirming the consequent or of concluding that if B is true, or exists, then A must also be true, becomes evident. When B exists A may exist too, but it may not. The diagram also illustrates the fallacy of denying the antecedent, or concluding that if A does not exist then B must also not exist. It may not, but it also may.

Note that the diagram also contains the claim that B is necessary for A, or "A only if B." A cannot occur unless B also occurs. But the diagram does *not* contain an "if and only if" claim, or one of both sufficiency and necessity.

In a diagram containing an "if and only if" claim, the space occupied by A and B would be identical. And, if we *could* legitimately form that complex proposition, I trust you can see that it would no longer be a fallacy to conclude from the truth of

B that A must be true or to conclude from the falsity of A the falsity of B. Since these conclusions would no longer be fallacious, an argument claiming a relationship is both sufficient and necessary is much more desirable than one claiming just sufficiency or necessity.

It is because of the greater desirability of an "if and only if" argument in light of what can be legitimately and not fallaciously concluded, that scientists would prefer to have arguments (or explanations) of that type. So would the citizen.

The aim of the game of science is to understand the world. Knowing the necessary *and* sufficient conditions that account for what is going on would amount to understanding very well indeed. But as citizens (and of course scientists occupy a citizen role as well as a scientist one), our interests are mainly in applying the knowledge gained by science, to predict and perhaps control. Even if we cannot control what happens, being able to predict would help us in adjusting, but if possible we would like to control as well.

If you know the necessary conditions and can manipulate them you can prevent things from happening even though you may not have the ability to guarantee that they will happen. If you know the sufficient conditions and can manipulate them you can guarantee something will happen even though this may not mean you can prevent it from happening. Hence, if you knew and were able to manipulate both, you could produce *and* prevent events, at will. Obviously, then, whether you aim at control, prediction, or understanding alone, knowing necessary and sufficient conditions is the preferred situation to be in.

In actuality, this preference is not typically met. Most scientists (and perhaps most citizens) would be delighted if they could succeed in separating, on the basis of confirmed generalizations, the myriad associations presented by reality into those that are just necessary or those that are just sufficient, even though not both.

Recall that we confirm a theory, or explanation, by deriving consequences from it and then testing those consequences against empirical observations. Logic, or reasoning, can aid us in stating our explanations clearly, so that possible alternative explanations become evident as well. When we have alternative explanations, logic can aid us in legitimately developing their consequences. Then when we do check these consequences against observations we have a way of deciding which explanations can be eliminated and which are still in conformity with observations and so should be retained for further checking.

We have a way of deciding because any proposed explanation can be considered to be in an "if . . . then . . ." relationship to its consequences. Any "if . . . then . . ." combination is false only when the premises or antecedents are true and the consequent or conclusion is false. Thus if a consequence is false, we can legitimately conclude (if we have set up a logically correct implication, or have legitimately drawn inferences from the explanation) that the explanation *must* be false. It would be a fallacy, as we have seen, to conclude that because the consequences are true the explanation must be true, but it would not be a fallacy to conclude that if the reasoning involved in deriving inferences is adequate and those inferences turn out to be false, the explanation must therefore contain a falsity somewhere.

I stress again that if the consequences are false we can make a definite statement that the explanation must be false too, but if the consequences are true we cannot make a definite statement that the explanation must be true — only that the explanation is still consistent with what has been observed. In other words, the test did not enable us to eliminate the explanation.

Because of this, it is sometimes said that scientific results cannot be used to prove that things *are* so, but can only be used in a process of elimination, to prove that some other things are *not* so. As we shall see, deciding when enough other "reasonable contenders" have been eliminated to make us feel confident that what remains is a useful correspondence to what is going on and why is not a matter for conclusive proof, but is a matter of judgment: What is the weight of the evidence? This judgment depends very largely indeed on *how* science learns what it learns, or on how well the game of science is played. That is, were good pieces used and good moves made with those pieces? The next sections provide some guides for selecting better pieces and better moves.

4.3 SOME GUIDES FOR BETTER OBSERVATIONS. Observations are evidence and you would like to use the best evidence you can in trying to solve two related descriptive problems. The first problem is to describe what is going on in the set of observations obtained, in such a way that you are fairly sure that you are right. This means you would like as few as possible alternative descriptions to yours to be legitimate ones of the same observations. The second problem is to describe what is likely going on in the parent class from which the portion of observations you were able to obtain comes, in such a way that you are fairly sure that you are right — in the same sense as before, there are as few as possible legitimate alternative descriptions to yours. Along the cycle of science diagramed earlier, the first problem is that involved in making accurate *ds* descriptions and the second

is that involved in making accurate *du* descriptions.

One set of observations is better than another to the extent that it enables solving the two problems. Solving the first hinges largely on the adequacy of the *controls* on the set of observations. That is, it hinges on what kinds of information were obtained in what kinds of situations. You want to be able to eliminate the alternative interpretation that the pattern you say you see in your sample is an illusion. In particular, you don't want to be in the position where someone else can come along and say that those factors you describe as being responsible for the pattern are not, because your controls were so inadequate that you were really observing the effect of some other factors.

Solving the second problem hinges largely on the adequacy of the *sampling* procedures used to obtain the set of observations from its parent class. Again, you want to be able to eliminate some alternative interpretations. You want to be able to eliminate the possible interpretation that the pattern you see in your sample cannot be generalized more broadly because it was just a chance result, or that your sampling procedures were so inadequate that your set of observations might well be biased and so the pattern in them cannot legitimately be generalized.

The two solutions are interdependent. They proceed in tandem and each is in part determined by what you consider theoretically relevant for the topic at hand and in part by what is feasible for you to do in light of the resources you have available for examination of the topic.

As far as the first descriptive problem, what items should be controlled when making observations depends on what the tentative explanation guiding your selection of observations indicates is relevant. Once this is determined, there are more or less specialized techniques for achieving appropriate controls, some used before selecting observations and some used in manipulating data on observations once they have been made.

You are aiming at making descriptions of the type where you say that when something occurs or changes (call it X) then something else occurs or changes (call that Y). To make such statements, you would like to be able to discount the other factors besides X (call them A and B and so on) that might be relevant for Y. You might try to discount A, B, etc. by "talking them away," but the surest way of discounting them, and the only legitimate or valid way, is to control these other factors when examining the relation between X and Y. Of the various items that might be considered relevant, then, you control those other than the ones you are especially interested in investigating at any given time.

To put a very modest amount of flesh on the symbolic bones, suppose you were interested in why children become delinquents. You might have reason to think that the amount of parental abuse inflicted on the children may have something to do with this, and so you would like to describe the effect of parental abuse on the probability of children becoming delinquents.

Suppose further that you have reason to believe that the socioeconomic status of the family has some effect on the chances of a child's future delinquency. In addition to obtaining an adequate sample of the range of parental abuse and the range of socioeconomic status, you want to discount the effect of socioeconomic status when observing the effect of parental abuse.

You could hold socioeconomic status constant, or control on that factor, by looking at the relationship between parental abuse and delinquency *within* each category you used to group families with similar socioeconomic status levels. That way, you should be able to determine the effect of parental abuse over and above the effect of socioeconomic status. Without such control, there is the possibility of the alternative interpretation that perhaps abuse is more prevalent in certain socioeconomic levels than others and so rather than seeing the effect of parental abuse alone, you might merely be seeing the effect of socioeconomic status.

Discounting alternative *du* descriptions to the one you would like to make (the second problem) depends heavily on the adequacy of the sample of observations you were able to obtain. If only because man is mortal, you are likely to be able to examine only a subset of observations — a sample — from the entire set of observations of the same kind — the parent class, or population, or universe. But it is the entire set you want to describe, or to which you want to generalize.

In order to have confidence in your generalizations you would like to feel that what you are able to observe is a fair or adequate sample from the appropriate universe. Typically, you would like to pick your sample in such a way that it is adequate both in the sense that whatever properties are relevant in its parent class also appear in the sample *and* in the sense that those properties appear in the sample according to the same pattern, or in the same relative proportions or distribution, as they do in its universe. That is, you want your sample to be a fair reflection of its universe, so that you can be relatively sure you are right in your description of that universe.

For example, if you wanted to describe the particular income distribution of some population (such as households in the United States in 19——) from a sample of that population, you want both the range of household income and the correct proportions for each income level to be reflected in the sample. If you picked a sample that contained the range from poverty to millionaire status but 50 percent of those in your sample were in the millionaire category, you would likely feel some qualms about the adequacy of your sample as a fair reflection of its universe. Available theory and knowledge about income distribution in industrialized countries would make you suspicious of such a sample.

And in general, available theory can serve as at least a partial guide to sampling. It ought to be able to provide help as to which properties might be relevant and perhaps even some help as to their likely distribution in the appropriate universe. In addition, there are specialized and often rather simple to use techniques of sampling which, if feasible to use for a particular project, can help in raising the probability that the distribution of selected properties is adequately reflected in the sample. However, these sampling techniques cannot aid in determining which situations (or sample units) are appropriate for your problem, nor in determining which properties of those situations are likely to be relevant. This determination is part of the reasoning portion of your job as researcher, using whatever theories or explanations you have to help you.

It is always good strategy, then, to make your assumptions, your guiding explanation, as explicit as you can (at least to yourself!), specifying what properties you consider important and how you propose to handle them. The better job you do of this, the better job you are likely to do of both picking an adequate sample and placing adequate controls on the observations you select. And, the better job you do on sampling and controlling, the more useful your observations will be for solving the two problems of describing your sample of observations and of describing the parent class from which they come, with as few as possible alternative descriptions being legitimate.

4.4 SOME GUIDES FOR BETTER DESCRIPTIONS. Descriptions have two uses in the scientific cycle. On the right side they are used in explanation developing and testing, while on the left side they are used in explanation constructing and revising. On the right side of the cycle, inferences are derived from an explanation or theory and take the form of descriptions. Checking these descriptions empirically, using observations, tests the theory. On the left side, descriptions are developed, based on a set of observations. These descriptions summarize the set and state the likely pattern in the set's parent class. Descriptions developed in this way comprise what is to be explained and so affect the construction or revision of a theory to explain, or account for, them.

In connection with the use of descriptions in theory constructing, there is a chain leading from observations through descriptions to explanations. For use in theory testing, the chain leads from explanations through descriptions to observations. In a sense, descriptions resemble the ancient god Janus, who faced in opposite directions. Criteria for choosing better descriptions differ somewhat, depending on which direction is under consideration.

Descriptions to be used in theory testing are inferences derived from an existing explanation. As such, they are in general, or *dt,* form and are not directly testable. Before a test can occur, they need to be made more specific or put in *do* form. An empirical interpretation must be given the descriptions, in order that they may be checked by observations, which after all are always specific and concrete events.

Giving an empirical interpretation means that the classes of events and relationships between them which are in theoretical form must be translated into empirical form. Decisions need to be made as to what specific variables, according to what specific categories of those variables, will be used, and as to what procedures will be used to determine when a particular observation belongs in one category rather than another. Decisions also need to be made on how a theoretical relationship will be empirically examined and what procedures are necessary to determine whether and to what degree the observed relationships embody the theoretical ones.

These two kinds of essential decisions are sometimes summarized by saying that the researcher needs to decide how he will operationalize. This is simply a shorthand way of saying that he has to decide how to specify the procedures, or operations, involved in providing an empirical interpretation for the theoretical statements he wants to examine.

Developing a *do* description, or placing descriptive propositions in operationalized form, requires the scientist to specify the steps or operations to be performed in making actual observations. He is required, in other words, to use propositions which refer to things that *are* observable, and so concern himself with questions that are "settleable" or resolvable. Think how quickly the ancient argument about how many angels could stand on the head of a pin could have been resolved if agreed on operational definitions of terms had been used: agreed on steps or procedures to follow to determine whether an angel was present or absent and how much standing space would be required for each one.

Or, to take a more recent example,

within the past few years several scientists at Stanford University made newspaper headlines. The headlines somewhat simplified and sensationalized the matter and referred to the scientists as having created life in the laboratory. If you followed the more detailed accounts of the reporters' questions and the scientists' replies, they tended to take this format:

> Reporter: Is it true that you have created life in the laboratory?
> Scientist: If you would care to give me a definition of "life," I might be able to answer your question.

The scientist is, of course, requesting an *operational* definition, so that he may address himself to an answerable question and avoid misunderstanding.

Using operational definitions for terms in propositions ensures that the questions a scientist asks in theoretical form are answerable empirically. These definitions provide links between the theoretical model and the observable world. Their use does not mean there will be no honest disagreement among scientists. Their use helps ensure minimal disagreement on what the evidence *is*. Disagreement, if any, is likely to come in the assessment of the utility of the evidence provided, because the "links" can typically be specified in more than one way. Since more than one operational definition of the same concepts could be used, there might well be some disagreement on which links are better, in the sense of more theoretically appropriate, than others.

Suppose you were investigating a problem in which the relatively simple concept "income" is used. In beginning to specify this concept, you might well ask yourself such questions as the following. Should I pick money income only or also include income in kind, such as the value of the vegetables a farmer grows for his family's own use rather than purchasing them? Should I use money income of all family members lumped together or just that of the head of the family? Money income during the most recent calendar year or an average for several years? Should any allowance be made for inflation or not? And so on and on.

The answer can only be an equivocal, "It depends." Choice rests on two bases. Which of the various operational definitions possible are more theoretically relevant for a particular problem than the others? Which of these "more theoretically relevant" ones are feasible to use in light of the resources in time, money, and personnel available for a particular project?

To stick with the general concept of income, once you do pick a particular empirical definition for it, you will probably need to divide the income into several categories, or levels. You might decide to use just three: high, medium, and low. You might decide to specifically use "$3,000 and above," "between $2,000 and $2,999," and "less than $2,000." However, some question could be raised about the theoretical appropriateness of your particular choices for high, medium, and low income levels. At least if you intended to investigate the relationship between income level and something else in a modern industrialized country, it is questionable whether your choices would be very relevant. They may be, but you should be aware that the burden of proof would be on you, as the deciding researcher, to justify them.

On the one hand you want to test the explanation as adequately as you can and so one criterion guiding your choice is theoretical relevance. On the other hand you must get around to actually collecting evidence and evidence comes in the form of concrete observations, some of which may be considerably easier to obtain than

others. Thus the other guiding criterion is feasibility. You would like to maximize both. Final operationalizing is guided according to what seems to yield the best balance between theoretical relevance and feasibility for the specific project involved.

The other main use for descriptions is on the other side of the basic cycle, explanation constructing and revising. Descriptions are most useful here when they are stated in general form, referring to properties of classes of events, rather than describing the highly specific properties of a particular sample of observations. In the diagramed cycle, this means a move from a *ds* to a *du* description.

While the *du* descriptions comprise what is to be accounted for, theory construction never starts *de novo*. Some tentative explanation guided the selection of observations to begin with. Even in those cases where observations seem to be accidentally stumbled on, they would tend to be ignored except that some tentative theory alerts the researcher to take notice of them. Most typically, then, descriptions used in theory construction affect possible amplifications and revisions of an existing explanation of what is going on and why. Thus, the *ds* descriptions and the *du* descriptions based on them are not about just any properties of events. Which specific properties in the set of observations merit generalization depends largely on what is judged most important as far as aiding confirmation or revision of the explanation used in the immediately preceding right side of the basic cycle.

Further, you need to decide which of several possible parent classes you will try to generalize to. For instance, a sample of households in your state of residence as of 19—— belongs to the parent class of all households in that state as of that date. It also belongs to the parent class of all households in your nation, and to the even broader parent class of households in all nations at comparable levels of industrial development, and of households in all nations.

Possible parent classes can be conceived as broader and broader laterally, or through space, and broader and broader vertically, or through time. Which, then, should you pick? It is certainly true that the broader *du* description you can justifiably provide the better. A theory able to account satisfactorily for some aspects of households in the broadest parent class, both laterally and vertically, could *a fortiori* account for those aspects of households in a particular area at a particular time as well. (An *a fortiori* argument is one "from the stronger or more extreme cases to those less so." In this case, stronger means more general.)

Some sort of balance needs to be achieved between a *du* description, or what is to be accounted for, being too general and not as general as it usefully could be. A concern with being "fairly sure that you are right" aids in achieving balance. To what extent can you *justifiably* feel that you can eliminate the alternative interpretation that your sample of households would not give a fair representation of the pattern present in each of the possible parent classes?

It may be that you feel your method of picking your sample ensured it was representative of all households in your state of residence yet not representative of households in the nation. For that, you might feel you would need a different sample. Or, you might feel that your sample *is* representative of this broader class and a different sample would not be needed.

While there are some techniques and procedures that can be used to aid you in making this decision (some of which will be briefly described later), they are just that: aids. Ultimately, this decision too is a matter of judgment, based on the weight of the evidence available to you, and as before the burden of proof is on you, as the deciding researcher, to justify your choice so that others may judge for themselves whether or not they agree.

To summarize, descriptions are used for two purposes in the cycle of science: explanation constructing and revising; explanation developing and testing. Within certain limits, the descriptions employed for theory construction and revision should be as general as possible, both with respect to the properties and the classes of events described. For use in theory elaboration and testing, descriptions need to be specific, or given an empirical interpretation. The actual interpretation, or operationalization, chosen is guided by the attempt to achieve the best balance possible between theoretical relevance and feasibility, in light of the particular topic to be investigated.

4.5 SOME GUIDES FOR BETTER EXPLANATIONS. Explanations (or theories or as if models) are produced because they are a means to understanding the observable world — the underlying aim of the game of science. Whatever aspect of the observable world is of interest, explanations have two functions in the basic cycle of science. One is to bring order and coherence to as much as possible of what has already been described, and the other is to guide the process of obtaining further understanding.

When attempting to decide whether any proposed explanation is useful enough to be worth retaining, developing, and testing, the scientist evaluates the answers he gets to questions that are in a sense very similar to those a voter might ask a congressman up for re-election: What have you done for me up to now that was worthwhile? What can you do for me in the future? Just as a voter might do, a scientist evaluates past and probable future power in making his decision.

The power of any argument, not solely those in the form called scientifically admissible explanations, is judged according to strength and soundness. Strength has to do with the likelihood that the conclusion to an argument is true *if* the premises are true and soundness has to do with the likelihood that the premises *are* in fact true.

In theory construction and revision, or bringing order into what is now known, the task is to guess at or otherwise locate premises that can be shown to have a link to the conclusion (what has been observed and described) such that if the premises were true the conclusion would follow. In theory developing, other consequences are derived in addition to what has already been plausibly accounted for. The task is to set up additional arguments such that if the premises were true these other consequences would follow.

These two tasks involve the strength of the argument. Adequate strength would appear to be the minimum to ask of any explanations we are considering keeping. This plausibility is not enough because, as discussed some time earlier, typically the same conclusion could plausibly be drawn from several different sets of premises. It is essential that an explanation also be adequately sound, and the purpose of theory testing is to make it as likely as possible that the premises are true.

Arguments range in strength from none, or fallacious, through increasing degrees of inductive strength to deductive validity. In a deductively valid argument the link between the premises and conclusion is such that it is *impossible* for the conclusion to be false if the premises are true. In arguments of intermediate strength the link between premises and conclusion is such that it is more or less *improbable* for the con-

clusion to be false if the premises are true.

You may sometimes read that deductive arguments go from the general to the specific while inductive arguments go from the specific to the general. But either kind may go from the general to the general, the general to the specific, the specific to the specific, or the specific to the general. Brief examples of such deductively valid arguments are given on p. 33, along with arguments with some degree of inductive strength. As the examples illustrate, the difference between deduction and induction rests on whether the link is one of impossibility or only improbability that the conclusion could be false *if* the premises were true. In each of the illustrative arguments, the link between the premises and the conclusion is such that it is either impossible, in the case of the deductively valid ones, or else it is more or less improbable, as in the case of the inductively strong ones, for the conclusion to be false if the premises are true. The degree to which the premises are indeed empirically true is the degree to which the argument is sound.

It is not difficult to think of strong arguments that are not sound, even though they may have true conclusions. If you think back to the argument used as one of the illustrations in the section on fallacies, or moves to be avoided, you will recall that the conclusion, "All turkeys have wings," could be derived through a deductively valid argument (so it certainly had adequate strength) even though at least one of the premises was obviously false: All turkeys are green fish.

Someone once wrote that scientists carry on an "incessant internal dialogue" with themselves. They must. Trying to develop arguments that prove to be useful is seldom a straightforward process. Usually the conclusions aimed at are noted first and the logical underpinnings then guessed at,

Deductively valid	*Inductively strong*

A. General to general

All men are primates All primates are mammals Therefore, all men are mammals	All persons reading this book are highly intelligent All persons reading this book are motivated to do well on its exercises Therefore, all persons reading this book will do well on its exercises

B. General to specific

All chimpanzees are primates Chi-Chi is a chimpanzee Therefore, Chi-Chi is a primate	All men located so far have died before their 300th birthday Sam Jones is a man Therefore, Sam Jones will die before his 300th birthday

C. Specific to specific

Mickey Mouse is a fictional character Mickey Mouse has ears Therefore, Mickey Mouse's ears are the ears of a fictional character	Countries A and B had a rapid drop in their death rate, followed by a rapid increase in population Country C recently had a rapid drop in its death rate and its population is now increasing rapidly Country A's population was stabilized by having large numbers of people migrate out each generation Country B's population was stabilized by lowering its birth rate Country C's people are not permitted to migrate out of the country Therefore, if country C's population is to become stabilized, its birth rate will have to be lowered

D. Specific to general

May is a good month to eat oysters June is a good month to eat oysters July and August are good months to eat oysters Therefore, all months of the year without an *r* in the name of the month are good months to eat oysters	In groups A, B, C, and D the economically dominant roles are occupied by females In groups A, B, C, and D the family form is matriarchal Groups A, B, C, and D are an adequate sample of all groups where the economically dominant roles are occupied by females Therefore, in all groups where the economically dominant roles are occupied by females and family form will be matriarchal

groped for, stumbled over, or even missed completely during a number of attempts. Once developed, though, then the overall argument needs to be checked for strength and finally for soundness. The logical structure finally produced for public gaze may be neat, quite elegant, and even briefly statable. But the order in which assumption builds on assumption to the conclusion, the order in which the logical structure is publicly presented, and the temporal order involved in discovery can be rather different sequences.

Whatever the process gone through in its development, for an argument to be very powerful it must have both adequate strength and adequate soundness. This means it must either have deductive validity or a high degree of inductive strength, so that there is little likelihood that the conclusion could be false if the premises are true, *and* there must be a high probability that the premises are true.

Both criteria for choosing better explanations are essential: degree of strength, or plausibility; degree of soundness. It would seem that adequate strength is a minimum requirement. After all, if we are going to go to the trouble to test an explanation, the least we ought to be able to ask is that it is plausible, in the sense that it has adequate strength. If it doesn't meet this minimum requirement, we would likely be further ahead if we ignored it and spent our effort in hunting around and trying to find one that does.

Providing what purport to be theories when these theories seem to have been guided in their development without much, if any, concern with utility in accounting for what is already known empirically would seem to be a singularly unproductive form of professional specialization. It is. Granted that given enough time and ingenuity, particularly where little is firmly established, several plausible explanations might be developed in scientifically acceptable form to account for the same phenomena, surely plausibility in the face of what is already known is the least we should ask any theory worth remembering to provide. This is not enough, but it's a start, and is indispensable to the other phases of the scientific cycle: elaborating, testing, and possibly revising what must always be a somewhat tentative explanation of the observable world.

Since we would like our explanations to be strong, you might wonder why I did not state that an argument should always be deductively valid, rather than merely stating it should have adequate strength, which includes high inductive strength as well as deductive validity. The reason is because of the kind of link between premises and conclusion in the two types of arguments.

For it to be logically impossible for a conclusion to be false if the premises are true, the conclusion cannot go beyond what is logically implicit in the set of premises taken as a whole. Thus, for instance, the argument could not go on to make situations not yet examined (see inductive illustration under "D. Specific to general"). Nor could an argument be deductively valid and be based on an analogy (see inductive illustration under "C. Specific to specific") and arguments using analogy are often very useful in science.

To say that deductively valid arguments are limited to elaborating and making explicit what is already implicit in the set of premises is hardly to say that deductive arguments are simple, obvious, or unimportant, as the history of the development and application of mathematics amply shows. But in science we do often want to argue beyond what is already logically implicit in the set of premises. For those arguments we want the degree of inductive strength to be as high as possible, even though an inductively strong argument cannot ever, by definition, be a deductively valid one. In an inductive argument, no matter how strong, there is always some possibility that the conclusion might be false even if the premises are true.

Even the strongest of arguments needs to be confirmed, or shown that it is likely to be empirically true. Confirming (or verifying) an explanation can never prove it to be true, although as the degree of confirmation increases it can be rendered increasingly likely to be acceptable.

An explanation can be confirmed, or rendered more probable, either by trying to verify its premises (what "accounts for" the conclusion — in an illustration given earlier this would amount to checking the extent to which it seems to be true that turkeys *are* green fish) or by trying to verify some additional consequences derived from it (what the existing argument can account for). What happens to the probability that an argument is sound if its consequences are shown to be true? What happens if they are shown to be false?

Recalling the previous discussion of fallacies classified under logical invalidity aids in giving answers to the questions. There we discussed that combination of propositions called an implication, or if A then B, and stated and illustrated that from the falsity of B it was legitimate to infer the falsity of A, while from the truth of B it was not legitimate to infer anything definite about the truth or falsity of A. As an aside, if the argument is deductively valid the falsity of B legitimates the inference that A must be false; if the argument has high inductive strength, the falsity of B legitimates the inference that it is highly *probable* that A is false. Whether deductively valid or highly inductively strong arguments are used, however, it is still falla-

cious to conclude from the truth of B either that A must be true or that it is very probably true.

Why, then, do we work so hard and consider it so important to show that B (the consequent) is true? We certainly seem to behave as if by so doing we raise the probability of the truth of A (the explanation from which consequences were derived), and in fact we do. We raise its probability because if B is true we have eliminated all those possible arguments of adequate strength (A′ and A″ and so on) which claim that B is false. By eliminating some arguments about B, we thereby raise the probability for the truth of the remaining ones. Raising the probability for an argument means the same as increasing its degree of confirmation, or as making it more highly verified, or as increasing the chances that it is sound.

Thus it is always good strategy to try to think of reasonable *competing* explanations in addition to the one in which you are primarily interested, and to try to design your research project to eliminate as many of them as you can at any given time. The more competing hypotheses you can eliminate "in one fell swoop" the more rapidly you raise the probability for, or confirm, the explanations that remain.

Regardless of the details for any particular research design, one or both of two basic principles of elimination are used, one for the elimination of potentially necessary conditions and the other for the elimination of potentially sufficient conditions:

1. A necessary condition for something cannot be absent when that something is present.
2. A sufficient condition for something cannot be present when that something is absent.

If we let C stand for "condition" and

E for "something" else, and a diagonal through a symbol stand for "is absent" (or "is false"), then the two principles can be stated in a more suggestive form as follows: Principle one: if $\not{C}E$ exists, C cannot be necessary for E. Principle two: if $C\not{E}$ exists, C cannot be sufficient for E.

Devising reasonable alternatives and devising efficient ways of eliminating them is something easier said than done, however. It requires an awareness *in depth* of relevant theory and techniques for study of a given topic. It also requires the far from common creative ability fully to utilize this awareness, and is one of the reasons why some play the game of science better than others.

An additional difficulty is often encountered and is not at all limited to beginners, although perhaps more common among them. There is a tendency to become as fond of a product of your intellectual self, the theory or explanation you brought forth and developed, as you would become of a child of yours and in either the intellectual or biological case to be equally blind to the merits of competitors.

Fully aware of this tendency, Darwin said that whenever he became especially certain he was on the right track he consciously redoubled his efforts to try to think of possible alternative explanations of the data. Well aware of another familiar human tendency, he also said he kept a special notebook to record evidence *against* whatever was his favorite hypothesis, so that he would be sure not to overlook or forget it — a much more remote possibility for evidence in favor.

Much of any discussion about research design boils down to the questions of how to pick situations to observe (or to "sample") and how to pick what will be observed in those situations (or to "control") so that as many as possible reasonable competing contenders, either for necessary or sufficient conditions, can be eliminated in a given project. It is always good strategy to do this, preferably by using both principles of elimination and not just one, because by so doing you waste a minimum of effort while trying to confirm, or raise the probability for, the contenders remaining.

Raising the probability for an argument's soundness, or theory testing, is an important part of the cycle of science. Therefore, a highly simplified illustration follows. I have selected a murder mystery of the old-fashioned "whodunit" type.

Suppose Mr. Gotrocks was found murdered on the sandy beach beside his island mansion on a Sunday morning. Mr. and Mrs. Gotrocks have a live-in butler and maid (I said the illustration was old-fashioned!) and had three other couples as overnight guests. Whodunit?

With no other information than this, nine explanations (or hypotheses) are possible, one for each person present. Each is equally likely and to be specific, each has a probability of one-ninth.

If we want to feel justified in choosing one of the explanations, we need to show that it is likely to be true. We can proceed in either or both of two ways. We can try to establish possible premises (a motive, for instance) for an argument in which an explanation as to who is the murderer would be the conclusion, or by trying to derive consequences from the various explanations and then check those consequences. If we took the former course, we might try to find out whether any of those present had a violent quarrel with Mr. Gotrocks, or needs money, or was the beneficiary in Mr. Gotrocks' will, and so on. If we took the latter course, we might reason in the following way.

Since we are being old-fashioned anyway, let us be very traditional and focus on the possibility that the butler did it. Now we need to draw some consequences. We might argue from the properties of sand and the weight of human adults that there might be footprints around the spot on the sandy beach where the body was found. If we are very lucky, there will be only two sets of footprints leading up to the body and only one set leading away. If this were true we could argue that it is highly *improbable* that the footprints leading away from the body would belong to anyone other than the murderer.

Then, assuming this conclusion to be true, and since the butler is male, and if our guess that he is the murderer is correct, then we can argue that it is *impossible* that the single set leading away from the body will be other than male footprints. So, we dash off to the beach to take a look.

Suppose we are lucky and the footprints were indeed made by male shoes. Our explanation that the butler did it is by no means proven true, but it certainly is now much more likely. Its probability (which was one-ninth before we looked at the footprints) is now one-fourth, because some competing explanations have been eliminated: all those from which it could be concluded that the murderer was *not* male. All those hypotheses which stated the murderer was a female, and there were five of them, now have a probability of near zero. (Not completely zero, because it *is* possible that one of the women is really the murderer and donned male shoes to perform her "dastardly deed," but let us discard this as unlikely.)

We then would try to draw further consequences to check, in order to try to eliminate the remaining competing hypotheses involving the other males besides the butler. Of course, if we can establish an adequate motive, so much the better. But it may be possible to raise the probability that the butler did it to near certainty *solely* by testing consequences and eliminating competing explanations.

At a given time, a scientist may be faced with several explanations that are equally simple and yet (if true) capable of accounting for the known facts. This would be comparable to our situation in the murder mystery before checking the footprints. When a scientist finds himself in such a situation he can always try to proceed as we did there — not draw just any inferences but try to draw inferences that are not compatible with all the explanations. Trying to verify the inferences may enable some of the explanations to be eliminated (such as those explanations claiming a female was the murderer in the murder mystery). But incompatible inferences cannot always be found and checked, at least at a given state of knowledge and technique for finding out. What then? That is, how does a scientist proceed to use these "equally useful" models in his future research work?

In this not too rare situation in the history of science, a scientist tries not to choose between the models. He tries to do that difficult thing, suspend judgment as to which is "really" correct. He continues to work with both as equally useful, hoping that one of two things will happen. Either some incompatible inference *will* eventually be made and checked, so that discarding of some of the models will occur. Or eventually additional evidence will be obtained and interpreted such that the currently competing models can be shown to be merely *sub*portions of some broader explanation.

Two simplified cases appear below. While there are many instances of at least partly competing models where resolution of the competition has not yet occurred, I have deliberately selected cases where it has, in order to illustrate the two possibilities for eventual resolution. I have found that a number of students, especially in the social sciences and the humanities, tend to feel it is only in the "less developed" sciences that anything as unsettling as competing explanations would even occur, let alone be tolerated as one of the hazards of the continual interplay of evidence, description, and explanation, in the development of scientifically acceptable yet always somewhat tentative knowledge. Partly because of this, I have selected cases from what is commonly conceded to be the most developed science we have, physics. Further, the second case was not resolved until a very few years ago.

1. Before the eighteenth century a model of heat was available that could account for the then known facts about heat. According to the model, heat was a kind of fluid, called caloric fluid. This fluid was present in the pores of substances and flowed out when an object became cooler and flowed in when the object became warmer. Then an alternative theory was developed. This one too accounted for the then known facts, but stated that there was no caloric fluid. Instead, heat was stated to be a form of motion. Eventually an incompatible inference was drawn and in the beginning of the nineteenth century Sir Humphrey Davy was credited with providing the evidence testing that inference and making the motion theory more verified than the caloric fluid one. The motion theory eventually displaced the caloric fluid theory entirely and is the one now learned in introductory physics classes.

2. For a time during this century wave and quantum theory were competitors. Wave theory said light behaved as if transmitted in continuous form (waves), whereas quantum theory said light behaved as if transmitted in discrete packages (quanta).

One explanation said the phenomenon dealt with was continuous, the other said it was not. On the surface, the inconsistency was obvious and both could not be true. Yet the customary process of drawing inferences and testing them did not provide a definitive choice. For some problems wave theory was more useful and for some problems quantum theory was better. There was a period not many years ago when physicists publicly, although perhaps somewhat ruefully, joked to the effect that they worked with wave theory on Monday, Wednesday, and Friday, and with quantum theory on Tuesday, Thursday, and Saturday. In recent years the two apparently contradictory theories have been reconciled by showing them to be merely subportions of a broader as if model, which might be called a "wavicle" theory.

To summarize, picking explanations proceeds on two bases, both related to usefulness. The scientist would like to be able to account for as much as he can of the described observations currently available and he would also like to be able to use the explanation to guide him in his future efforts by enabling him to draw inferences that he can then test. In either case he would like to be as sure as he can that he is probably correct, and so for either use he would like to pick the best explanation he can. One explanation is better than another if it is more *powerful,* or both stronger and sounder. Strength refers to the probability that the conclusion is true if the premises are true and soundness refers to the probability that the premises are in fact true.

An argument is adequately strong either when it is deductively valid or when it has high inductive strength. If deductively valid, the link between premises and conclusion is such that it is impossible for the conclusion to be false if the premises are true, while if an argument has high inductive strength the link is such that it is highly improbable for the conclusion to be false if the premises are true. An argument is sound to the extent that the probability is high that the argument is true, or in other words to the extent the argument has been confirmed. Confirmation proceeds by eliminating some of the reasonable competing explanations and thereby increasing the likelihood that the remaining ones are correct.

When faced with two or more models to explain the same phenomena the scientist chooses between them, if he can, according to the same criteria used to judge a single model: degree of power relative to the existing state of knowledge; degree of power relative to future work. If several models are judged equally useful, he tries to draw inferences that cannot be compatible with all, in order that he may check them and possibly discard some of the models as less confirmed than those remaining. Where at any given time this is not possible he tries to suspend judgment and work with the competing models as equally useful, hoping that eventually either incompatible inferences will be drawn and tested or the various models will be shown to be just subportions of some broader model developed as the result of later efforts.

4.6 SOME GUIDES FOR BETTER MOVES. The basic strategy attempted, of course, is to use the best pieces you can and move them as efficiently, or with as little wasted effort, as you can in light of the particular topic investigated. Pieces are better to the extent they meet certain criteria. These criteria are related to how the pieces are used, and so describing how to achieve better pieces has also generally described better moves. Because of this and because the remaining two parts of this book are devoted to a

closer examination of "how to" make moves that are desirable, depending on the options available in the phases of the research process being discussed, my remarks here will be brief.

Moves involving reasoning, or drawing conclusions, are used throughout the course of the game. Whenever a move involves reasoning, the better the reasoning the better the move. Therefore you try to use arguments throughout that are as sound and as strong as possible.

In addition to reasoning, there is a research, or evidence collection, aspect to the game. When collecting evidence you try to select your sample of observations and select controls on those observations so that you eliminate as many as you can of possible competing, or alternative, interpretations that might legitimately be made of the same evidence. Whenever making a move particularly related to the research aspect, you will move more efficiently to the extent you are able to think of reasonable competing explanations to the one you favor and are able to design your study to eliminate as many as you can. Two basic principles of elimination are used, one relating to potentially necessary conditions and one relating to potentially sufficient conditions. To the extent you can design your study to employ both principles of elimination and not just one, your research moves will be more efficient, or better.

Moves in the game of science are generally better or more efficient, then, to the extent they result in collecting better evidence, making better descriptions of that evidence, and developing explanations that are better both in accounting for what is already known and in guiding additions to the stock of verified knowledge. In particular, moves are more efficient when any research is designed so that both basic principles of elimination may be used, and when any reasoning involves arguments that have a high degree of power, or strength and soundness.

Several scientists have likened the strategy employed by successful players of the old parlor game, Twenty Questions, to the underlying strategy used in successful scientific work. As an eminent chemist, Dr. Wilder D. Bancroft, put it: That simple little game exemplifies the principles of scientific research and it would be a good thing if our graduate students would play it regularly as part of their research training.

While I tend to agree, I think it a pity to wait until graduate training. And, the strategy evolved by successful players can be used on many everyday problems, not just scientific ones.

In Twenty Questions, the players are told only whether the object sought is animal, vegetable, or mineral. To win the game, it is the job of the players to use no more than twenty questions to identify the object, and they are limited to questions that can be answered with just "yes" or "no." Successful players seem to use the following guides, or strategy: (a) They don't waste questions by asking ones that are just "wild stabs"; (b) they try to ask each question so that it fairly evenly divides the remaining possibilities in half — that way a yes or no answer can eliminate roughly half the remaining possibilities each time; (c) they tend to vary the approach used, so that, for example, they don't just ask questions that would locate the object geographically.

In scientific work, I think these guides might translate as follows. First, try to have your objectives and procedures clearly in mind. In a sense, you are asking questions of Nature, although you have to get the answers for yourself, they will not simply be given to you, and it may take you fewer or many more than twenty questions (or

research projects) before you feel you have a satisfactory solution. Your play is likely to proceed more efficiently if you do not make wild stabs but instead think carefully about what it is you want to know and how you plan to find out: that is, what specific question to ask and how best to phrase it so the answer will be as clear-cut as possible.

Second, the object you are looking for in science is an explanation for what is going on. In trying to decide between possible explanations, you will move more efficiently by selecting from among the logically simplest ones that can account for the known facts and then asking each question (or doing each project) to eliminate as many of these as you can. The hope is that by successive partitioning of the area within which you search you will eventually wind up with just one explanation that seems to be a satisfactory correspondence for what is going on.

Several types of approaches to solving problems are commonly used. You should be aware of the major ones and from time to time re-examine what you are doing to see whether using a different approach for a while might be more productive.

Sometimes a trial and error approach — examining all possibilities in sequence, one after the other — may work. For example, one of the "problems" any large ongoing group must continually try to solve can be called the staffing problem: obtaining a supply of personnel for the available roles or positions in the group; allocating personnel to roles; socializing the personnel as to what is expected of the occupants of particular roles; ensuring at least minimal performance of the activities connected with the roles. If we take just one part of this, allocation of personnel or matching personnel to roles, what happens when there is a temporary discrepancy between the set of personnel and the system of available roles?

There would seem to be four basic possibilities you could check, one after the other: alter the personnel, alter the roles, alter both, alter neither. Can the personnel be altered so that there is again a balance, perhaps by bringing in new personnel or eliminating some of those already present, or else by retraining of some sort? Or will this not work and so will it be necessary to alter the system instead, perhaps by increasing or decreasing the number of roles, or else by altering the requirements for existing roles? Or will this not work, and both the set of personnel and the system of roles have to be somehow altered? Or if nothing is changed to redress the discrepancy, will the group just disintegrate and disappear or will it continue to operate, although perhaps at a lower level of effectiveness?

Rather quickly these four basic possibilities that you might examine subdivide into many more possibilities to be looked at. "Alteration" can vary from a little to a lot, and each degree of alteration could be applied to the personnel, the system, or both. Thus, it often happens that the possibilities to be examined become so large that a complete trial and error approach is not feasible. If so, you can try a partial approach. For each of the major possibilities, set up a decision rule of some sort to guide you as to how long you will work with it before moving on to try another possibility.

Another approach to try to turn a difficult problem into a manageable one might be termed "divide and conquer." Divide the basic problem into smaller pieces and, keeping in mind the relation of the pieces to one another, try to solve each of the smaller pieces. As you proceed, compare what has been solved so far with what is left to be solved. Eventually, you may be able to put these partial solutions together and so solve the original puzzle. For instance, instead of trying to examine the effect of socioeconomic status on "style of life" in general, divide your problem into the effect on housing, or use of leisure time, or family organization, or whatever. Study the pieces separately and then try to put them together.

A third approach is to try to work on a related but more accessible problem that may bring you a bit closer to the main one. Take the problem apart and try to put it back together a different way, which may be more amenable to solution.

A fourth approach is to work on an analogous problem. You may be able to apply the experience gained from solving that problem to find a solution to a number of problems that are superficially different but have analogous relationships among the parts of the problem. Not only may the *method* of solution be analogous, but you may be able to use the *content* of the solution to develop an analogous theory or explanation. For example, there was a time when the activities of the heart were thought to be a forever unknowable mystery. An analogy with the principles involved in a hydraulic system, thinking of the heart as a kind of pump, took science very far indeed toward deciphering this "unknowable" puzzle.

Combinations of these four approaches are also possible, of course. If no single type of approach aids you, perhaps a combination of approaches will.

You should be able to improve your chances of making better moves while playing the game of science if you: (*a*) use the available theories to guide your project, and so don't waste time with unplanned efforts or questions that are just wild stabs; (*b*) deliberately try to consider alternate approaches to solving a problem; (*c*) have your problem, or the question you want to ask, as clearly in mind as you can and try to phrase your question (or specify your method of investigation) in such a way that you are likely to get unambiguous answers that will enable you to narrow the field within which useful explanations might be found; and (*d*) try to be sure that your reasoning throughout is as strong and sound as you can manage.

5. CONCLUDING REMARKS

In this section I will recapitulate by way of an illustration of the basic cycle, along with some comments on the illustration. Then, as a lead into Parts II and III, I will make a few remarks about the major steps to be taken in any specific research project, which after all will be a particular instance of playing the basic game overviewed in Part I.

The musical comedy *You're a Good Man, Charlie Brown* is based on Charles Schulz's popular comic strip *Peanuts*. In the song "Little Known Facts" Lucy attempts to enlighten her little brother Linus about some aspects of the world around him. Among other little known facts, Lucy informs Linus as follows:

> Lucy: And way down there, those tiny little black things, those are bugs. They make the grass grow.
> Linus: Is that so?
> Lucy: That's right. They run around all day long, tugging and tugging at each tiny seedling until it grows into a great tall blade of grass.
> Linus: Boy, that's amazing!
> Charlie Brown: Oh, good grief! [1]

You may well have shared Charlie Brown's, rather than Linus's reaction to Lucy's "enlightenment." Undoubtedly, hers is not the explanation of why grass grows with which you are familiar. But let us temporarily accept Lucy's explanation as a promising as if model and see how we might proceed to try to show her theory wrong.

Beginning with her explanation, we need to derive some consequences from it (*dt* descriptions, on the cycle). Then we need to find a way to check the consequences (*do* descriptions empirically corresponding to the *dt* ones) and actually collect some observations. Once we have the observations, we need to describe what we have learned from them (*ds* descriptions) and decide how far the results can be generalized (*du* descriptions). Then, depending on the results, we will reconsider her original explanation and decide whether it now seems even more likely to be correct than was so before the test was made or whether it seems in need of revision or replacement.

First, we have to decide what Lucy could be claiming the nature of the relationship is. Lucy might be arguing that the grass will not grow *unless* the bugs tug at it, although this alone might not guarantee that the grass will grow. (Here Lucy's claim translates into one about a necessary relationship.) Or, she might be arguing that *one* way, although perhaps not the only way, to get the grass to grow is to have the little bugs tug at it. (Her claim here would be one about a sufficient relationship.) Or, she might be arguing that having the bugs tug at the grass is the *one and only one* way to get it to grow, that is, that the relationship is both sufficient and necessary. Depending on which interpretation of her statement is picked, procedures for trying to show her wrong can vary.

Suppose we could question Lucy further

and she said she meant that the one and only way to get the grass to grow is by having little bugs tug at it. This is a claim about a necessary and sufficient relationship, which you will recall translates into making two subclaims simultaneously. If we can eliminate either one of the two subclaims we can also eliminate her claim. Let us begin by trying to eliminate the subclaim that the tugging of the bugs is a necessary condition.

To shorten the discussion, we will symbolize the tugging of the bugs as C, for condition, and the growth of the grass as E, for effect. If the claim is true then it should also be true, as a consequence, that it is impossible to find situations where E occurs in the absence of C. We will symbolize these situations as $\cancel{C}E$. Thus, if we can set up a situation where the grass grows (E) without the bugs tugging at it ($\cancel{C}$) then we can legitimately conclude that C can *not* be a necessary condition. The task becomes one of setting up a *do* correspondence to this inference.

To do this we would likely turn to an *a fortiori* argument (from the stronger or more extreme cases to the less strong or less extreme cases). If we can get rid of the bugs entirely, then *a fortiori* we have a case where the bugs could not be tugging. We need to try to set up an empirical situation, or one concerned with the observable behavior of some physical things, that would correspond to having the grass grow in the absence of bugs.

We need procedures to ensure that we *are* dealing with "grass" and with "bugs" and so we need some operational definitions to enable us to tell when grass and bugs are present and absent. We need a definition of "growth" and a way to measure it, and to decide on the time period we will use as a reasonable one during which growth could be expected to occur. We

need to assure ourselves we have a fair sample of grass seedlings. And, the hardest part will probably be to find a way to get rid of all the bugs — perhaps through some kind of sterilization procedure — which does not inadvertently damage the grass and so prevent it from growing.

In other words, we want to be as sure as we can that the overall details of the particular method used do not give us misleading results. We don't want to be in the position later where someone else can come along and offer legitimate alternative interpretations of our evidence: that the pattern we see as present is really a chance one because our sample was not adequate; that the pattern we see is not really there because our controls were inadequate and so rather than examining the effect of the absence of C (the tugging of the bugs) we were actually examining the effects of some other conditions.

However, let us assume that we are successful in finding a situation that satisfactorily corresponds empirically to $\cancel{C}E$. Then we could legitimately conclude that the tugging of the bugs was not necessary for the growth of the grass and so C cannot be the one and only way to get E.

What might be Lucy's rejoinder? Well, if Lucy were to behave as a practicing scientist might, she probably would not discard her theory outright, but try to alter it somehow. She would be particularly likely to do this if she could not think of an alternative theory. In practice, a theory is never overthrown by some disquieting observations but only by a better theory. So, Lucy might revise her guess and state that while the tugging of the bugs is not the one and only way to ensure grass growth, nonetheless it *is* sufficient: it is at least one way to get the grass to grow.

If we want to do a thorough job of discounting Lucy's theory and so be able to conclude that what she noted empirically was an accidental association only, then we must try to eliminate this revised explanation as well. Again, we try to draw some consequences and check them.

If it is true that C is sufficient for E, then it should also be true that it is impossible to find situations where C is present and E is absent, symbolized as C$\not$E. If we can find such cases we can legitimately conclude that C is not sufficient for E. If we can do this, then since we already have shown that C is not necessary for E either, it must be that the association between C and E is strictly accidental. While this will not leave us with an explanation that *can* plausibly account for the growth of grass, we will have at least narrowed the area within which plausible explanations might be found: at least we will know that Lucy's theory *cannot* account for grass growth.

As before, we need a *do* interpretation but this time achieving one may be a bit harder. We can't use an *a fortiori* argument and simply get rid of the bugs entirely. This time we need an empirical situation in which the bugs are not only present but are actually *tugging*. Showing this in the form of concrete observations, even using a microscope or some such technical aid to our observational skill and even using our most advanced techniques of bug persuasion in order to get them to tug, may be none too easy.

So, we might try to substitute a more accessible problem for our original one. Instead of trying to observe tiny bugs tugging away at the grass, we could have human beings tug at the seedlings. What we have done is to take another look at our problem and then abstracted "tugging behavior" as the crucial element, and decided that who or what does the tugging is irrelevant.

We still have the task of trying to set up situations in which the grass does not grow even though it is tugged at. By now it has probably occurred to you that it will be easier to prove Lucy wrong if we have some alternative or competing theory to guide us. After all, if we permit the tugging to take place while the conditions of soil, moisture, and sunlight remain the same, the grass may well continue to grow. Then what? We would have to say that Lucy's theory cannot be discounted on the basis of the available evidence. Her theory is still consistent with the observed association — when tugging occurs, grass grows. Using the alternative theory you learned in high school biology, if not earlier, you would probably want to have the tugging take place in the absence of adequate sunlight, moisture, and so on — the factors your alternative theory indicates can guarantee growth.

Suppose we can do this and can show that when the grass is tugged by human beings under certain conditions the grass does not continue to grow. Can we say we have found a case where C$\not$E exists and so C must not be sufficient for E?

This is much more a matter of judgment of the weight of the evidence than in the preceding case where we could *a fortiori* show C was not necessary for E. What might Lucy say? She might counter that we did not have a *do* correspondence that was of adequate theoretical relevance. That is, she would not be disputing what the evidence *is*, but how much *weight* should be given our evidence.

She could claim that no human beings can tug as gently as small bugs can and instead of abstracting "tugging behavior" what should actually be abstracted from reality is "gentleness of tugging." Given this revised explanation, or guess, we have two choices, depending on our judgment. We might decide that some explanation involving tugging was worth pursuing and so we should try to check this revised explanation and so the cycle might continue in this manner. Or, we might decide the evidence has enough weight that we can safely ignore explanations involving tugging and had better look for something else to account for the growth of grass — perhaps while we are looking, also muttering to ourselves about how stubborn and difficult to get along with some people are.

Now let us summarize a little. First, in science a theory is not the last word on a subject but is something to try to disprove. No matter how fond you or your colleagues may be of some pet theory, if the game is to be played successfully (which means if science is to progress in a reliable and cumulative manner), you have an obligation to try to show that your explanation is a powerful one and so should be accepted. To do this requires making the effort to disprove it. Second, the required effort may be considerable. At a minimum, then, any theory worth pursuing should be at least plausible, which means it should be among the simplest ones available that still have enough strength to account satisfactorily for the current facts. But this is not enough to guarantee that it is powerful enough to merit acceptance. It needs to be shown to have adequate soundness: it should be able to withstand empirical tests of its consequences. Third, any particular research project will at least touch all the major points in the basic cycle of science.

Beginning with some *expl*, even though it may be no better than the vague guide that factors X and Y seem to be important somehow, you try to develop some inferences, or consequences in the form of *dt*

descriptions. These must then be given an empirical interpretation, or *do* description, used to guide the collection of concrete observations, or *obs*. Once collected, these observations need to be summarized somehow, in the form of *ds* descriptions. Then you need to decide the extent to which whatever pattern you describe as present in your particular sample of observations can be generalized, or in other words to develop *du* descriptions. Finally, based on the *du* descriptions you return to your original *expl*, and need to decide that it is now more confirmed than before or else needs revision or replacement, and the cycle begins again in a new project on the topic.

Any particular *topic* of investigation will go through a number of turns of the basic cycle. A specific research project, however, may emphasize either the right or left side more heavily as its underlying purpose. The underlying purpose might primarily be to try to some existing explanations. Or the primary intent might be to locate some pieces or better refine some available pieces, to be used on the left or theory construction side. In either case all the points in a complete turn of the cycle will be at least briefly touched, and so a common set of general and highly interdependent decisions must be made.

The set of decisions involved for a particular research project, as an instance of playing the basic game, may be put in a diagrammatic form resembling a flow chart (see Fig. I.2).

The flow chart illustrates the major steps for any specific research project. (Despite

FIG. I. 2. FLOW CHART FOR A RESEARCH PROJECT

| Select problem | Select method of investigation | Collect observations | Analyze and interpret results | Write report |

(First portion of process) (Second portion of process)

the unidirectional effect given by the arrowheads, I would stress again that the decisions needed are highly interdependent.) Selecting a problem involves going from *expl* to *dt;* selecting a method of investigation involves going from *dt* to *do;* collecting observations involves going from *do* to *obs;* analyzing and interpreting involves going from *obs* to *ds,* then to *du* and *expl.* Report writing is the one part of the research process for a particular project that did not appear somewhere on the basic cycle of science.

In practice, reports may be written at almost any convenient point along the never-ending cycle. Some reports pull together known results from other studies and try to develop a coherent and plausible account of them, whether or not the writer of the report goes on to develop further consequences of his account. Some reports are devoted entirely to taking existing explanations and trying to show points of convergence or divergence among them, or else to develop further the consequences of some one or more available explanations. Some reports are devoted to a discussion of techniques for finding out, perhaps pointing out the merits of one way versus another, or perhaps discussing possible (especially so far untried) uses of one or another technique. Sometimes a project may be complex enough that periodic interim reports are prepared. And so on.

These possible kinds of reports are in addition to, and always rest at least in part on the foundation provided by, the general type of report that should be prepared about any completed research project: highlights of the justifications for, and the results of, the decisions made in both the first and second portion of the research process for that project.

Guides for making the decisions in the first and second portions are akin to "how to" suggestions for making efficient progress. Your progress is most likely to be efficient when you have an awareness and understanding of (*a*) the nature of the major decisions needed at each step in the process; (*b*) the principal options available for each decision and the main merits and demerits of each; and (*c*) the implications of deciding one way rather than another at any step in the process, in light of the rest of the highly interdependent steps in the overall process and the kind and quality of the conclusions you can draw when the project is complete.

Part II of this book is an attempt to provide beginning guides for the first portion of the research process. Part III is a similar attempt for the second portion.

Exercise Set I

I-1. SOME DESIRABLE SKILLS: INTRODUCTION TO TABLE PREPARING AND READING

This exercise is in semiprogramed form. Each item that follows is numbered, and each numbered item is called a frame. This system facilitates referral between items. In any programed exposition, the reader is called on to make written responses from time to time. Typically, his written responses are then immediately checked against answers provided. In a fully programed version, virtually every frame asks for a response. In this exercise, however, you are asked to write responses on a separate sheet only on occasion and so I have used the term semiprogramed. Fold a sheet of paper to serve as a slider, sliding it down as you read. Whenever you are asked to make some written response, such as filling in a blank, please do so on a separate sheet of paper before uncovering the suggested answer.

1. Any project requires decisions about variables, categories, and relationships. Decisions must be made about which variables will be related, what categories (at least rough ones) will be used for those variables, how the variables will be related, and how the relationship will be looked at empirically. If these decisions are systematically set down, one or more "tables" are present. Therefore, you need to acquire early some minimum skill in both preparing and reading tables. This should be of aid to you in doing a project, reading a report of a project done by others, or both.

2. Whether explicitly or only implicitly prepared, tables will nonetheless be present. Any t_____ is a way of showing what v_____s are being related, according to what c_____s, and how the relationship is examined empirically.

   (table); (variables); (categories)

3. The most detailed and complex tables you will ever prepare or read are called *appendix*-type, or sometimes master, tables. An a_____-type table is used in analysis. Such tables are set up in order to aid you in seeing the detailed implications of the data. The name comes from the fact that in a final report on the project they, or somewhat condensed versions of them, would appear in the back, or appendix.

   (appendix)

47

4. Based on an analysis of the appendix tables, selected information may be placed into a small table to appear in the body of the report, or text. These small tables are called *text* tables.

5. T_____ tables serve similar functions to those of any graphic device, such as pie charts or bar graphs: to present a <u>selected</u> portion of the basic data, those items you feel merit calling to the reader's attention in some prominent fashion; to avoid the monotony of an unbroken verbal presentation.

(text)

6. All graphic devices, including text tables, present a s_____ portion of information. It is selected according to the investigator's judgment, based on his detailed examination of his evidence, of what he thinks is particularly noteworthy. If the reader wishes to examine the data more fully, and perhaps even do some manipulation of it for himself, he will have to work with whatever analytical, or a_____ tables are present in the back, or appendix, of the report.

(selected); (appendix)

7. Appendix and text tables are prepared for different purposes. Appendix tables are prepared to aid in detailed analysis of the data; text tables are prepared to highlight selected portions of the information. On occasion, you may prepare some auxiliary, or *work*, tables. When needed, they are used to help you get from your initial data to data prepared in a form more suitable for analysis. For instance, a <u>work</u> table might be similar to an appendix table except that it contains raw numbers while the appendix table contains percents.

8. Regardless of the type of table, all tables have certain common features, or parts, and there are some standard labels for those parts. The simple table shown in the next frame can serve as illustration.

9. TABLE NO. _____. AGE, SEX, AND MARITAL STATUS OF COLLEGE SENIORS, UNITED STATES, 19___ (IN PERCENTAGES)

Age and sex	Currently married	Marital Status Never been married	Previously but not currently married[a]	Total
Under 25				
Male				
Female				
25 and over				
Male				
Female				
Total				

[a] Includes annulled.
Source: Appendix table no. _____.

10. The table title is a description of what is contained in the table. If the table is an appendix-type table, the description is usually quite explicit and detailed. Text table titles may be briefly stated since the original table referred to in the source contains the full qualifications.

11. The table t_____ states which variables are related to which others. If the relationship is described in a particular way, such as through the use of percentages, this information should be contained in the title.

> (title)

12. If it is necessary to clarify something in any part of the table, a symbol (small letter, number, or asterisk, usually) is used beside the item to be clarified. The symbol is repeated just below the main portion of the table and the explanation given beside it. Such symbols and their explanations are called *footnotes,* because they appear at the bottom, or foot, of the table. In frame 9 a footnote appears for the third column. The explanation is given because some people might otherwise think that persons who had an annulment would be placed in the never been married column.

13. The source for the information should also appear in a note at the bottom of the table, and this information is called a *source note.* Its purpose is to tell the reader where he can find the detailed table from which the data were selected or else the ultimate source for the information, such as United States College Survey, 19_____.

14. To clarify something in the table a f_____ is used. A table may or may not contain footnotes, but it should always contain a note on the s_____ of the information in the table.

> (footnote); (source)

15. The lengthwise portions of the tables are called *columns.* Each column has a label. If a set of columns represents the categories for a variable then the name given that variable appears over the set. In frame 9, the label "marital status" has a line under it that extends over the first three columns only.

16. The crosswise portions of the table are called *rows.* Each row has a label. The entire set of row labels is referred to as the *stub* of the table.

17. The label given to all the columns as a set is called the column heading, or just *heading;* the label given to the set of rows is called the stub heading, or just *stub.*

18. The h_____ refers to the columns, and the s_____ refers to the rows.

> (heading); (stub)

19. In frame 9 the stub heading refers to two variables and they are

_____ and _____; the column heading refers to just one variable and it is _____.

(age); (sex); (marital status)

20. The intersection of a row and column is called a cell. It tells you the relationship between just one part of the stub and one part of the heading. Because the rows and columns (or stub and heading variables) intersect, the variables are said to be *cross-classified*. In frame 9, age and sex are cross-classified with marital status.

21. The term "body" of the table refers to the entire set of intersections, or c_____s.

(cells)

22. The two sets of cells that give information about the total sample (or set of units examined), according to the variables used, are called *marginals*. They are called marginal cells because they tend to be located at the outer edges, or margins, of the body of the table. In frame 9, the last row and farthest to the right column contain marginal cells.

23. The m_____ cells tell you what the total sample is like with respect to the variables used. The *row marginal* describes the entire sample according to the variables used in the rows, or stub. In frame 9, the row marginal describes the distribution of the total sample according to age and sex categories. In frame 9, this set of cells, called the *row* marginal, is found in the farthest right *column*.

(marginal)

24. If you want to know what your entire set of units is like with respect to the variables in the stub, you look at that column which contains the r_____ m_____ cells. If you want to know what your entire set of units is like with respect to the variables in the heading, or columns, you look at the *column marginal* cells. In frame 9, these cells are contained in the bottom *row*.

(row); (marginal)

25. The row marginal cells will be found in one of the columns at the outer edges of the body of the table. They tell you what your entire sample is like with respect to the variables in the rows, or stub. The c_____ m_____ cells will be found in one of the rows at the outer edges of the body of the table. They tell you what the entire sample is like with respect to the variables in the columns, or heading.

(column); (marginal)

26. In frame 9, age and sex are c_____-classified with marital status. In the stub, the age and sex categories used are merged in such a way that you can look at the relationship of age and sex simultaneously,

or jointly, with marital status. This merged way of setting up categories is called a _joint_ classification, and could be done in the stub, or the heading, or both.

(cross)

27. Suppose age and sex had not been jointly classified but had been shown in the stub this way:

Age and sex

Under 25
25 and over

Male
Female

28. If age and sex had been shown as in frame 27 you would be able to look at the relationship of marital status with just age or just sex, but not simultaneously, or "jointly." But with age and sex classified as in frame 9, you can look at both separate _and_ joint effects.

29. In a joint classification, categories for the first variable used are called the _major breaks._ In frame 9, the major breaks are categories for age. The categories for the second (or more) variable used are called the _minor breaks._ In frame 9, the minor breaks are categories for the variable _____.

(sex)

30. A joint classification enables you to see both simultaneous and separate effects, while a classification as in frame 27 allows you to see separate effects only. In order to see separate effects when a joint classification is used, you may have to do some combining. In frame 9, you would add the second and fifth rows to get a total row for males. You would have to add the raw numbers together and then compute percentages in order to have a total row for males in percentages. Analogously, you would add the third and sixth rows to get a total row for females.

31. Even though a little labor may be involved, a joint classification has the advantage that you are able to examine both simultaneous effects _and_ s_____ ones.

(separate)

32. The table shown in frame 9 is called a _dummy table,_ which means that it is complete except for having the cells filled in with actual data.

33. A dummy appendix-type table can be thought of as a kind of analysis plan. It shows the variables you intend to cross-classify (stub intersected with heading), the categories used for each variable, which if any of the variables will be jointly as well as cross-classified, and

it specifies the manner in which you will be examining relationships between variables, such as by using percentage distributions.

34. In general, the categories used in a table (especially an appendix table) should be both *mutually exclusive* and *exhaustive*. This means there should be no ambiguity about where any unit should be placed, and any unit should be able to be placed somewhere, even if only in a catch-all category like "all other." That is, an observation should be capable of being placed in *one* (the exhaustive criterion) *and only one* (the mutually exclusive criterion) category for a variable.

35. Suppose the third column in frame 9 had appeared this way: Not currently married. If this had been done the categories for the variable marital status would no longer meet the criteria described in frame 34 because they would not be _____ (pick one: mutually exclusive/exhaustive). Why did you pick the one you did?

> (mutually exclusive); (There would be an ambiguity present: someone who has never been married could logically be placed under either the second *or* the third column heading.)

36. Try to set up a possible *stub* for the variables "age" and "educational level" that would enable you to see the joint as well as separate effects. Put your sketch on a separate sheet of paper.

37. Are your categories mutually exclusive and exhaustive for each variable?

38. Joint classifications may be used in headings as well as stubs. Try to set up a possible heading for the variables in frame 36 that would be a joint classification. Put your sketch on a separate sheet of paper.

39. Are your categories mutually exclusive and exhaustive?

40. In order to prepare the sketches for frames 36 and 38, you had to make some decisions on categories. Suppose you had used the following for age: under 25; 25 and over. And suppose you had decided to use years of school completed to measure educational level and used these categories: 8 or less; 9 through 12; more than 12. I will let you decide what the stub would look like in frame 36 if these choices had been made, but here is what the heading might have looked like for frame 38:

Age and educational level[a]								
Under 25			25 and over			Total		
8 or less	9–12	More than 12	8 or less	9–12	More than 12	8 or less	9–12	More than 12

[a] (The footnote would make it clear that educational level is defined according to years of formal schooling completed. Did you need a footnote for your heading?)

41. Major breaks in this heading are for age, while the minor breaks are for educational level. If you had made educational level the major

breaks instead, what would the heading have looked like? (Put your sketch on a separate sheet of paper and compare it with what is shown below.)

	Educational level[a] and age						
8 or less		9 through 12		More than 12		Total	
Under 25	25 and over	Under 25	25 and over	Under 25	25 and over	Under 25	25 and over

[a] (Same footnote clarification as in frame 40.)

42. Note that the overall label in frame 40 says age and educational level, while the overall label in frame 41 says educational level and age. Conventionally, the variable used for the major breaks should be named first.

43. When you go about preparing a table of your own you should do so in light of the purpose of setting up analysis plans in general: to try to devise the best ways for you to see the kind of variation that results in one or more variables (called your "dependent variables") when some other variable or variables (called your "independent variables") are manipulated in some way. How you prepare your table and especially how you make your computations will be influenced by which variables you will at least temporarily consider independent and which dependent.

44. For instance, in the table in frame 9, although the table title tells you that the information to be entered will be percentages, there is no row or column of 100 percents given, so that it is not completely evident which way (along the rows or along the columns) the percentage distributions will be made.

45. Computing in different ways allows you to answer slightly different questions. If the *rows* in frame 9 totaled 100 percent each, you would be able to answer this kind of question: For a given age and sex category, what is the resulting distribution in the marital status categories? On the other hand, if the *columns* each totaled 100 percent, you could answer this kind of question: For a given marital status category, what is the resulting distribution according to age and sex?

46. In the questions for frame 45, the "for a given . . . category" part refers to those variables considered as independent ones, while the "resulting distribution" refers to those considered as dependent ones.

47. Some people prefer to put the independent variables in the stub when they are preparing tables; others prefer to put them in the heading. This is partly a matter of taste — when you are making comparisons, do you prefer to move your eyes from side to side or up and down? In larger part, it is a matter of convenience, particularly convenience for later typing and publishing of the tables. A very

rough rule of thumb to follow is: whichever *set* of variables, either the independent set or the dependent set, has the more complex and detailed number of categories as a whole is the more reasonable contender for placement in the stub.

48. When it comes to analyzing a set of data, or reading whatever tables are present (in terms of the cycle of science, developing a *ds* description), there are certain general questions to which you would like to have answers: (*a*) What is being talked about, or described? (*b*) What is the general outline of the pattern shown by the data? (*c*) How clear-cut is that general pattern?

49. To get answers to the first question in frame 48, you begin by looking at the table as though it were not yet filled in with data, or in other words as though it were a d_____ table.

(dummy)

50. You want to know the answers to these specific questions: What units are being talked about? What variables, or aspects of those units, are being considered in the table? What specific categories are used for those variables? Which of the variables are cross-classified, and are any joint classifications also used? What relationship(s) is being examined? How is the relationship examined empirically?

51. Therefore, your first job is to look carefully at the table t_____ and the source of the data, and the headings used for the c_____s and the rows, or stub, noting if there are any qualifications explained in f_____s.

(title); (columns); (footnotes)

52. Then you turn your attention to the body of the table. One of your earliest jobs is to make some consistency checks, especially for *internal* consistency.

53. You certainly do not want to waste your time trying to make sense out of data that are not even internally consistent, and so you would check to see that what is supposed to "add up" actually does. Don't be surprised or humiliated if you find errors in a table you have prepared. Always assume that errors can occur — the trick is to build in ways to catch and correct them before you go any further. If a table is given in an article, making consistency checks is usually simple, since the author should already have made them. Sticking to reputable journals lessens the need to worry about the problem, but even so a quick eye inspection never hurts.

54. Here is a simple example for you to practice on. Try to state whether statements A and B below are consistent, giving your reasons for your judgment, if you knew that the sample consisted of 100 eligible voters, 50 males and 50 females:

A. Thirty-seven percent of the males said they were Republicans.
B. Seventy people in the total sample said they voted in the last pres-

idential election and thirty-eight of these were males. Further, more than half of those who did not vote were males.

55. Statement A is the more obviously inconsistent of the two, probably, resting on the fact that with 50 males each counts as 2 percent and so it would be impossible to get an odd-numbered percentage, as the statement claims was true.

56. You may also be able to see rather quickly that statement B is inconsistent. If not, a sure and "mechanical" way to check it is to prepare the table needed, fill it in, and see what you get. The second statement can be shown to be inconsistent as follows:

| | Total | Voted in last presidential election? | |
		Yes	No
Total	100	70	(30)
Male	50	38	(12)
Female	50	(32)	(18)

The numbers in parentheses need to be computed from the information given, and 12 is certainly *not* more than half of those not voting.

57. You may have been able to reason out the inconsistencies for frame 54 without having had to prepare a table to help you, but now let us try a more complicated example. I do not think you will be able to do this one without preparing a table, and so it will also serve as a check on how well you mastered the items covered on table preparation. Check the internal consistency of the following set of data: 1,000 students total; 525 freshmen; 312 males; 470 married students; 42 male freshmen; 147 married freshmen; 86 married males; 25 married male freshmen.

58. The set of data in frame 57 is taken from *An Introduction to Logic and Scientific Method* by M. R. Cohen and E. Nagel (Harcourt, Brace and Company, 1934). The data appear there, but not how to figure out the inconsistency; that you must do for yourself. But as Cohen and Nagel point out, this set of data implies a rather interesting "finding": that the number of females who are not freshmen *and* also not married is a negative number (−57, to be precise). Of course, this is absurd, and the data are inconsistent.

59. To *show* the inconsistency is not so easy. And if you had merely come across the figures and not been told they were inconsistent, you might not even try to check them. If you have not yet managed to prepare an appropriate table and fill it in to show that the figures given imply that the number of not married and not freshmen females is −57, review the frames on table preparation and try again. Perhaps you should turn your completed table in to your instructor and have him check it before you go on, particularly if

you have some difficulty. Let me give you this hint: You will un-doubtedly have to classify some items *jointly* and while there are several ways a satisfactory table might be arranged, if I were you I would use "marital status" in the heading and jointly classify "class level" and "sex" in the stub.

60. Whenever you read a finding, whether stated in numerical form (or quantitative data, for example: 40 percent of the population was at least sixty-five years old) or only in implied numerical form (or quali-tative data, for example: many of the people seemed to be old), it does not hurt to try to prepare at least a mental table and see what some of those "missing cells" might look like. For instance, to stress verbally that "As many as 30 percent do . . ." carries with it what may be even more interesting in light of what you want to know — "as few as" 70 percent *don't*.

61. As well as making some checks for internal consistency, or internal reasonableness, it is a good idea to make some checks for *external* consistency, or reasonableness in light of what else is known on the topic.

62. Of course, even if your results appear to be unreasonable in the face of what is already known, they still might be correct. But you would be wise to check for possible errors *before* developing a new and startling theory to account for your findings. As one example, a pre-liminary tabulation of a portion of the 1960 Census data showed a very high proportion of teen-aged widows among American Indian groups. Census Bureau personnel, many of whom have training in the social sciences, noted this, checked to see if there could be an error in the tabulations and found one. The data were corrected before being released in permanent form, and so social scientists were saved the effort of developing a theory to account for this "peculiar aspect" of American Indian life.

63. Having carefully looked at the table as though it were a dummy table, to see what is being related and how, and having done some checking for consistency, you are ready to turn to the body of the table in detail, in order to try to develop answers to the second ques-tion in frame 48. Begin broadly, picking up details as you go along. First look at the marginals, and then at the rest of the body of the table.

64. You can tell what your entire sample is like with respect to the vari-ables and measures used by examining the m_____ cells.

(marginal)

65. Especially if you feel sure you have a fair sample (depending on the procedures you used to select that sample), then looking at the mar-ginals can tell you what to expect, or the kind of prediction you could make, if you knew *only* that you were talking about units of a certain type.

66. But you would like to be able to do better than that. You want to know whether it was worth while to find out the additional items of information, or the specific v____s and categories used, about those units. As you look at the rest of the table, then, compare what you see with the pattern shown by the marginals.

   (variables)

67. If the pattern in the rest of the table is very much like the pattern for the marginals, then the specific v____s about which information was collected did not aid you as far as knowing what to predict — you could have done as well by just knowing the m____s. If this is true, we say *independence* is present.

   (variables); (marginals)

68. If the specific variables used are not i____ of what you would like to predict, in that the pattern for the rest of the table is *not* very similar to the pattern shown in the marginal cells, then some sort of *association* is present and you need to go on to describe the general pattern of the association and how clear-cut that pattern seems to be.

   (independent)

69. (As an aside, once you *have* described both the general outline of the pattern and the intensity with which it appears, you would go on to interpret the pattern. Especially, you would do some disciplined speculating about what additional information might be needed to understand more fully what is going on. This might be additional information you happened to collect for this study and so you could go on to examine it. Or it might be additional information already available from studies reported by others, and so you could relate your findings to theirs. Or you might very well wind up having to indicate what seems to you to be desirable to investigate in the *next* turn of the basic cycle of science for this topic.)

70. The *particular techniques* you would use to help you identify the pattern in your data depend in part on how extensive your existing knowledge is of possible techniques to try and which might be applicable to your problem.

71. Whatever the t____s used, though, you would proceed in the same general way. You want to describe the *outline* of the pattern (or the covariation present), any particular *clustering* within that outline, and what sort of *spread* there is around the outline, so that you may judge how fuzzy or clear-cut the pattern seems to be.

   (techniques)

72. (As another aside, since I don't want to get into possible techniques here, in that branch of statistics known as descriptive statistics — which is the branch most likely to be of aid to you in this stage of

describing your sample, or developing a *ds* description on the cycle of science — the ways of looking described in frame 71 are respectively referred to as measures of correlation, central tendency, and variance. But the important thing to keep in mind is what you are trying to do, *then* pick from among the various possible techniques or measures according to which of them seem best able to help you do this for the data at hand. Incidentally, the other main branch of statistics, called statistics of inference, contains a number of techniques or measures that may be of aid to you in deciding the extent to which your *ds* description may also be generalized. This task of developing *du* descriptions is related to but still somewhat separate from the task of reading tables, or determining what patterns seem to be present in the data available when they are arranged in a specific way.)

73. Remember that you are limited in your analysis of a particular table by the variables selected for examination, the c_____s used this time for those variables, the relationships looked at, and the empirical way chosen to examine those relationships.

    (categories)

74. These kinds of decisions have to be made for any project, to enable you to see anything at all. But they do also function as a set of blinders, similar to those horses used to wear in heavy traffic. These decisions do permit you to examine some things fairly carefully, but they also screen out other things. To see those things, you would need to prepare a different set of blinders, or make different categories for the variables, or even use different variables, as well as possibly change the relationships examined and how they are examined.

75. If I may change the metaphor, you are engaged in trying to isolate the signal from the noise. By deciding to select certain aspects from the complex reality that appears to us, you have picked one kind of filter to try to locate the signal. You must inevitably do this, but every once in a while you should remind yourself that different filters can give different information about what the signal is like, and sometimes even enable you to pick up seemingly different signals, and so on occasion you should change your approach.

76. To summarize the general ways of proceeding when you are trying to read a table: carefully examine the table as though it were a dummy table, by reading the title, source note, headings for columns and rows, and any footnotes present; then make some consistency checks, especially for internal consistency; then look at the body of the table more carefully, beginning with the marginals and then the rest of the cells, checking for independence versus association as you go along; whatever pattern appears, try to describe it in terms of outline, clustering, and spread.

77. Now let us try briefly to apply these general guides for reading a table to a particular one. I have deliberately put together one using some items I suspect will be unfamiliar to most of you, so be sure not to slight the initial step of reading the title, etc., with care.

78. TABLE NO. _____. FERTILITY RATIOS[a] FOR STATES, ACCORDING TO THE PER-CENTAGE OF THE FAMILIES IN THE STATE WITH THE HEAD OF THE FAMILY COMPLETING FOUR OR MORE YEARS OF COLLEGE, BY COLOR, UNITED STATES, 1960.

	Percentage of family heads completing four or more years of college				
Color	Less than 6.5	6.5 to 8.4	8.5 to 10.4	10.5 to 12.4	12.5 or more
All	587.1	573.9	577.1	533.1	587.4
White	531.0	552.8	561.5	525.4	583.5
Nonwhite	812.5	717.7	705.2	604.0	608.3

Source: United States Census of Population, 1960, *Final Report PC(3)-1E*, Selected Area Reports: Type of Place, Tables 1, 1A, and 1B, just pages 95–109.

[a] The fertility ratio gives the ratio of children under five years old per thousand women aged fifteen to forty-four years inclusive, and is computed as follows:

$$FR = \frac{\text{Number of children under 5}}{\text{Number of women aged 15–44}} \times 1000$$

79. Based on your examination of frame 78, the basic units being considered are _____.

(the fifty states in the United States)

80. On what basis are the states grouped? _____

(According to the proportion of all families within a state where the head of the family has completed 4 or more years of college.)

81. What additional items are noted for the states? _____

(Within each category used to group the states, three fertility ratios: one for the total population of the grouped states; one for the white population of the grouped states; one for the nonwhite population of the grouped states.)

82. Now you need to identify the pattern in the table. To make communication a little easier, I suggest that the following symbols be used. For the proportion of family heads with four or more years of college, I suggest PFH4c. Then, for example, PFH4c/6.5–8.4 would stand for those states where the proportion of family heads with at least 4 years of college was somewhere between 6.5 and 8.4 percent, inclusive. For the various fertility ratio rows, I suggest FR/T, FR/W, and FR/Nw. These stand for fertility ratios for the total population of the grouped states, for the white population, and for the nonwhite population, respectively.

83. To identify the pattern shown, you need to look at the marginal cells

and then the rest of the table. I think you might find it useful to begin with a small sketch, plotting the data according to three curves, one for FR/T, one for FR/W, and one for FR/Nw. For the Y axis, use the size of the fertility ratio, and for the X axis, use PFH4c, according to the various categories shown in the heading of the table.

84. Depending on how you chose your scale for the Y axis, your sketch should be similar to this one:

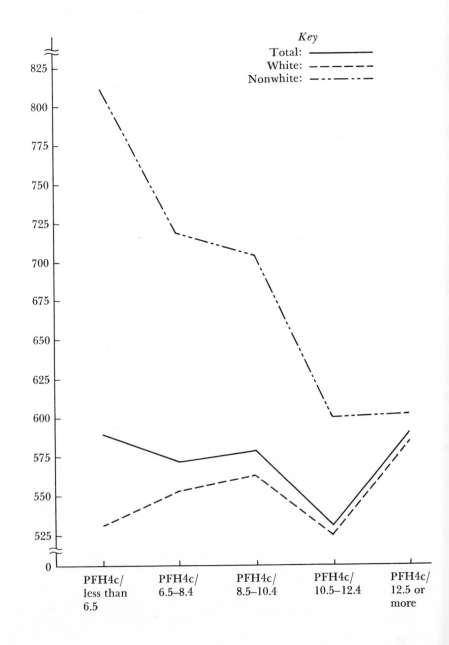

85. Describe the pattern you see for the marginal cells. _____

> (A gradual drop or almost steady for the first three categories for PFH4c, a fairly sharp drop for PFH4c/10.5–12.4, then a sharp rise back up, to equal the level for the first PFH4c category.)

86. When you compare the second and third rows of the table with the marginal cells, is independence or association present?

> (Association, except that FR/T and FR/W are very similar for the top two PFH4c categories: the FRs for the two color categories seem to travel almost *opposite* paths, with the FR/W gradually increasing, with the exception of the one dip for PFH4c/10.5–12.4, and the FR/Nw decreasing in a sort of step-wise pattern: a fairly sharp drop, then level, then a sharp drop, followed by another level.)

87. Now you need to decide what next steps you might take, to see how clear-cut the pattern is and to interpret it. Some of these next steps would not require any information in addition to the raw data from which the table must have been prepared; some might.

88. As one possible approach, you might find out whether each of the states in each of the PFH4c categories used has a proportion that is tightly clustered around some proportion within the range for the category. More formally, this approach could be described as checking the *intraclass variance.* That is, you would like to know whether or not these educational proportion categories represent fairly distinct types, so that within each class or category the clustering is tight. If the intraclass variance turns out to be low, then the clustering is tight and you would have more confidence in using the lines plotted for frame 84 to describe the pattern present — at least the five points on the line for the various PFH4c categories.

89. Another approach, still using no additional information than that needed to prepare the table initially, and feasible since there are only 50 states altogether, would be to plot a scatter diagram. You could use the *Y* axis as given in frame 84, but now the *X* axis would consist of the range of PFH4c, not just 5 summary points. For each of the 50 states you would locate its actual PFH4c on the *X* axis and then locate its fertility ratio (3 scatter diagrams would be needed in total, one for FR/T, one for FR/W and one for FR/Nw, but the procedure would be the same for each) and place a point for the state. Looking at the set of 50 points on the resulting scatter diagram, you would be able to tell whether or not there is an orderly progression (or the "correlation" is high), and to judge to what extent the summary line plotted for frame 84 is a good approximation for the pattern present.

90. Frames 88 and 89 describe possible next steps that might be taken after reading the table in frame 78, to be surer what the pattern *is.*

Additional next steps could be taken to try to figure out why the pattern is as it is. For instance, what about that dip in the curves at FHC4c/10.5–12.4? It represents the low point for all three curves. Why? And why does whatever is operating do so as sharply as it does for the curve for FR/W? What information might you need to find out? Or, to take another possibility, you might speculate on whether or not states with a certain range for PFH4c are also states with a certain range for the proportion of inhabitants living in large metropolitan areas. That is, based on other knowledge you might have, you might feel that the more metropolitanized a state is, the lower its FR might be, and so you might try to classify states both according to PFH4c *and* according to degree of metropolitanization (a joint classification) and take a look at the FR pattern that shows up then. It might turn out either that the pattern would become sharper *or* that degree of metropolitanization alone is capable of accounting for what is going on more satisfactorily than PFH4c. Still another possibility is that you would stop trying to look for additional information to help you predict FR patterns better, but would decide that if looking at states classified according to PFH4c could do a passable job of predicting FR patterns, then what *else* might it help you to predict about states?

91. As is not at all rare, once you read (or analyze) a *particular* set of data, you are not likely to end up with what you feel are definitive answers, but instead wind up with many more questions to be investigated.

92. Finally, how do you interpret "lucky finds" in a set of data, or things that turn up that you did not systematically note?

93. To take a purely hypothetical illustration, suppose you did a questionnaire survey and among other things asked about the money income of the head of the family. Further suppose that some of the heads of families volunteered, even though you did not ask this — whether you *should* have is a separate question — that total family income is considerably higher because the spouse too is employed. And, suppose that it turned out to be among the family heads with either the highest or the lowest educational attainment that this information most often was volunteered.

94. Are you justified in generalizing, from the data you have, about the relation between *total* family income and educational level? Unfortunately, no.

95. This "lucky find" can be used to guide further studies, but if you had wanted this information you should have asked for it from everyone in the sample. It *might* be that husband and wife both are most likely to be employed when educational level is either high or low. But it *might* be that actually having both spouses employed is most common on the middle educational level while volunteering such information to a stranger is most common to educational levels

at the extremes, and you have observed only the *volunteering* behavior. If you want to generalize about certain kinds of volunteering behavior and educational level, fine, but if you want to use the content of the information volunteered to generalize about your entire sample and the relation between educational level and employment of both husband and wife, that is not cricket. More formally, such generalizations are known as the fallacy of reasoning from selected instances rather than from a fair sample.

I-2. APPRENTICE-TYPE PRACTICE: A SIMPLIFIED PREVIEW OF THE ENTIRE RESEARCH PROCESS

FIRST PORTION OF THE PROCESS: FROM AN IDEA TO A RESEARCH PROPOSAL

Suppose you are on your way to attend a concert, or a hit musical, or some such event. Once inside the building you pass a crowded stairway. You note that most people are passing on the right and the occasional ones who do not are glared at or even spoken to angrily, with various mutterings about people who don't watch where they are going. You may have seen similar situations before without giving them a second thought, but this time for some reason your curiosity is aroused and you begin to wonder why what you have observed should be as it is.

Suppose further that you get to the play a few minutes before curtain time and notice that most seats are already occupied. After the play starts a few people come in late, are glared at, and if they talk on the way to their seats are loudly shushed. Again, you wonder why.

In trying to answer your own question you would like to develop some description of what is going on that is more generally applicable than the two specific situations observed, and if possible explain that more general statement. You might — if not already too absorbed in the play — think to yourself that despite their many differences the two situations have the common feature that most people are behaving in the same way and the few who are not have their behavior reacted to in an unfavorable manner. How might this common feature which you have mentally abstracted from the two different particular situations be accounted for? And, of the possible explanations that may occur to you, how could you go about finding out which of them seems most probable?

A number of possibilities, or explanations, might occur to you if you stopped to think consciously about the matter. Some are listed below.

E1. Most people are behaving in the same fashion because they have been taught the right thing to do and no longer question its rightness.

E2. Most people are behaving in the same fashion because they wish to avoid the unpleasant reactions of others that deviation seems to call forth.

E3. People are behaving at random and it is just happenstance that on the particular occasions observed most behaved in the same way.

E4. The particular places observed are critical, and in other places people would walk on the left or the middle, or stand up during the performance, or all arrive in the middle of the play, or whatever.

E5. The particular times of observation are critical, and at other times (hours, days, and so on) people would exhibit other behavior than that you observed.

The list could of course be extended, perhaps even to include combinations or mixes of those mentioned, but these will do for illustration. For any explanation added to the list, however, you would want to check that, as in the list above, if true each could account for what you have observed so far.

Some rather simple procedures, although on occasion time-consuming, could eliminate some of the explanations on the list. For instance, consider E3, E4, and E5, which refer to randomness, particular places, and particular times, respectively. You might feel justified in thinking that the two different situations already observed suffice to make E3 improbable enough to be discarded. To try to eliminate E4 and E5 you could observe at different locations within the building and at different times during the forthcoming week.

But, perhaps behavior is generally random and the two cases observed are both atypical; perhaps different places in the same building are not important but different kinds of buildings are; perhaps different hours or days of the week are not crucial but different months or years are. These broader possibilities could be checked in a similar way as their more specific counterparts, although the checking would take a little longer to do.

However, suppose you are satisfied that you have enough informal evidence from casual observation (which you have deliberately tried to recall) to eliminate E3, E4, and E5 as "reasonable contenders" for what is going on and so you focus on those left, E1 and E2. How might you choose between them, or at least try to assess their relative contributions?

First, though, let us put the description and explanations in terms a sociologist might use. The common feature you abstracted from the two particular situations can be called conformity to norms, or standards of behavior. E1 can be called an internalized norms explanation and E2 a fear of sanctions explanation.

Norms are said to be internalized when they have become so much a part of the "blood and bones" (or more precisely, of what is usually referred to as the conscience) that behavior occurs without any thought of questioning the rightness of the norms and so sanctions are essentially unimportant in affecting behavior. Sanctions can be either positive or negative, either rewards or punishments, although each of the sanctions you have so far observed has been negative. Incidentally, an obvious extension of E2, which would still claim that behavior was sanction-oriented, would be that most people behave so as to receive positive sanctions and avoid negative ones.

If either E1 or E2 were the sole important factor in explaining conforming behavior, some quite different practical consequences could be derived. On the one hand, if E1 were correct in extreme form then society needs no policemen — everyone would conform because he thought it the unquestionably right thing to do. But if E2 were correct in extreme form, society needs as many policemen as it can get and it needs them everywhere — everyone conforms solely because he fears getting caught deviating and being punished for his behavior. Since the two explanations have some radically different policy implications, you might feel that these two are worth some further effort on your part.

Now you are ready to begin developing a research proposal. Unlikely as it may seem, the best place to begin planning is at the end. First determine what kinds of generalizations you would like to be able to make at the conclusion of your project. Then work backward. Determine what kind of pattern would have to be present in the evidence if your generalization is to be supported and then determine what you would have to do to enable yourself to see the pattern if it is there.

You would like to wind up with generalizations of this type: There is thus and so amount of conforming behavior present and it seems to be occurring for such and such reason. Within the limits of the kind of generalization desired, you would like to make things as easy for yourself as possible in making your observations systematically. With all this in mind, you would like to find cases where (a) it is clear both what the norm is and what is considered to be conforming behavior; (b) the situations are of the same general type but the sanctions differ in severity between situations of the same general type; and (c) the kinds of behavior that might occur could be placed into categories according to degree of conformity in each situation.

As an aid to your thinking, you might sketch a rough diagram, using such vague categories as high or low:

Severity of sanctions	Extent of conformity				Total
	High	• • •		Low	
High					
•					
•					
Low					
Total					

As you learned in Exercise I-1, a diagram such as this is called a table. Tables are often filled in with numbers, or quantitative data, although they need not be. Tables display relationships between variables — any kind of variables. As an aid to developing and refining your plans, they can be invaluable. Eventually, of course, you will want to make the diagram less vague.

Once you have your diagram roughly sketched, examine it to see whether you have left out anything critical to answering two questions: (1) Is it true that most people conform? That is, you want to know if the generalization developed for the previous two situations observed holds true in other situations. (2) If it is true that most people conform, do they seem to be doing so because E1 is true or because E2 is true? That is, does conformity occur because norms have been internalized or because sanctions are feared?

Try to visualize various patterns of X's which could occur in the cells of the table and decide how each pattern might best be interpreted. Visualize patterns according to both shape and intensity, or in other words, general outline and extent of clustering or concentration within the general outline. It is best to think of clear-cut patterns first and how they might be interpreted, so that when you examine your data later you will have some "standard" patterns to compare with the actual patterns appearing.

If it is true that E1, internalization of norms, is all that is operating, what pattern of X's in the table would you hope to find? Write your answer on a separate sheet of paper, and *after* you have written it turn to page 76.

If it is true that E2, fear of sanctions, is all that is operating, what pattern of X's in the table would you hope to find? Write your answer on a separate sheet of paper, and *after* you have written it turn to page 77.

The next task is to develop a specific research plan, to enable you to collect data and see whatever pattern actually occurs. Several criteria guided my choice of a particular research design for the problem involved. As general restrictions on this exercise to illustrate the kinds of decisions involved through the entire research process, from idea to report, I wanted to pick situations (a) that occurred fairly frequently, so not too much time would be devoted to just this exercise; (b) that were accessible to observation by anyone; and (c) where the observations could be easily made without much prior training.

As specific restrictions because of the content of the exercise, I wanted to pick situations in which the same type of norm was present, in which it was clear what the sanction was and what was called for in the way of conforming behavior, and where both what the sanction is and what constitutes conforming behavior were likely to be widely known. These specific restrictions, or controls, were placed for the same reason any controls are imposed in any research project: to try to eliminate as many as possible alternative and legitimate interpretations of the results when the project is completed.

For instance, there is considerable difference between the kind of norm involved in the prohibition against taking another's life and the one in the prohibition against entering a queue in a place such as a bank at other than the end of the line. You would like to be able later to discount such matters as that perhaps the difference in the *kind* of norm from situation to situation accounted for differences in the amount of conformity; or that perhaps the *vagueness* of the sanctions and definitions of what constitutes conformity made the reliability of the classifications of the observations questionable; or that people might have behaved differently except that they were not sure what the sanction was ("ignorance of the law") or were not sure what was expected of them ("stranger in town.") To avoid these potentially obscuring factors when trying to see whether fear of sanctions or internalization of norms seems to guide behavior, the restrictions were imposed.

I make no brief that the situations I have picked are optimum. But I do plead that the restrictions are not *all* easily met and that on balance the situations picked do meet them reasonably well. (If your ingenuity enables you to think of situations that meet all the various restrictions more satisfactorily, by all means use them instead. Your later decisions will then be different from those suggested below, but the same *kinds* of decisions will still have to be faced.)

Legal situations are quite clear-cut. For these situations it is usually clear that if behavior is thus and so then the penalty is such and such. Because they are easily observable, traffic situations were selected. In particular, I chose extent of conformity with respect to symbols of differing degrees of obviousness in indicating a car should stop, namely a red light and a two-way stop sign.

I tried to find situations of the same type in which the extent of conformity could vary *and* in which the severity of the sanctions imposed for nonconformity varied. I have not been able to think of ones where this is true and which also meet the restrictions stated above. Instead, I have settled for situations where the symbolic reminder is more and less obvious. (At least in the area of California where I teach, the penalty is the same for going through either a red light or a stop sign, although when discussing this exercise in class I have found that some students, especially those without a driver's license, had the impression that running a red light carries a more severe penalty. A few even thought that going through a four-way stop sign was more severely sanctioned than going through a two-way stop sign. In light of the design I would like to have used, it is unfortunate that this impression is erroneous, but it is, and almost all students in class were aware of the actual sanction.)

As it is, the design does not permit a choice between E1 and E2, but it does enable some determination of the amount of support for E1, especially when additional restrictions are imposed, as you will see in a moment. I still felt it worthwhile to stress both explanations and discuss the kinds of *theoretical* situations one would like to observe and then point out the compromises sometimes necessary because of *feasibility* considerations. Every investigation must always strike some kind of balance between theoretical relevance and feasibility when the actual empirical design is finally being specified. Neither can be ignored.

If you glance back at the rough table shown earlier, some of the specifications needed should now be fairly obvious. The label for the stub needs to be changed to something like "Traffic symbol indicating stop," and the categories in the stub would become "Red light" and "Two-way stop sign." The heading can remain the same, but now it is necessary to come to grips with what such vague terms as high or low will mean for this particular study.

"A full stop" is a natural choice for the term high, and "Failure to slow speed at all" is a natural choice for the term low. Note that if a car actually speeded up when going through the symbol, it would still conform to the choice for low. A choice for the middle is not so obvious. There are all degrees of slowing down and the problem is how to divide them into usable categories. It is not rare, by the way, that the extremes of what you want to see are clear-cut and the middle ranges are troublesome.

In the past, when I have posed to students the question of how best to set up the middle categories between a complete stop and no slowing, they have had little difficulty in recognizing there is not much problem in stating clearly what one might want to observe but there may be great practical problems in observing it. For instance, you might decide to divide the middle into just two categories: slows down at most five miles per hour slower than was traveling; slows down more than five miles per hour slower than was traveling but does not stop.

Other possibilities might occur to you as well, but these will do to illustrate the observational problem. How accurately can the average observer distinguish these amounts of slowing by watching at a street corner? A particular observer would probably have difficulty in deciding which of the categories is applicable, and that means "intraobserver reliability" is likely to be low. And, if any particular observer would have trouble deciding, then agreement between observers — or what is usually termed "interobserver reliability" — will be low. The observers are performing the role of recording instruments. As with any instruments, you want reliability or comparable results under comparable circumstances.

The difficulty in achieving minimal disagreement between observers, which is necessary if we are to muddy things up as little as possible for ourselves, might lead to the following decision rule. Use three categories for extent of conformity: high, medium, and low. Operationalize them as follows: If car comes to a full stop, check high category; if car does not slow down at all, check low category; if car speed does not meet the criteria for either high or low, check the medium conformity category.

(As an aside, if you decided to ask the various observers to note such additional characteristics as whether the driver is "young/middle-aged/old" or is "male/female," interobserver reliability would undoubtedly be lower for these items than for stopping behavior classified according to the decision rule given above. Just as in the case of stopping behavior, you would need to establish rules for determining which age and sex categories a given driver should be placed in. In these days of increased acceptability in many places of long hair for either sex and with the likelihood that an observer will often have just a fleeting glance at the driver, developing decision rules for noting age and sex that are practical in a street corner observational situation will be none too easy. You might want to check this for yourselves by having two observers at a few of the corners who would each try to note these additional pieces of information as well as stopping behavior. Later, compare the amount of agreement between the two on the number of drivers independently placed in various age and sex categories relative to the agreement on the number placed in the stopping categories. Besides the problem of setting up workable decision rules, there is a limit to the *amount* of information that can be reliably noted by an observer during a briefly occurring incident. Therefore, for the purposes of the rest of this exercise be sure the observers first note stopping behavior and then whatever else you decide to have them try to record.)

The situations to be observed are still not yet specified precisely enough. Will any car coming up to a stop symbol do for inclusion in your sample, or would you like to impose additional restrictions? For instance, you could include a car coming up to a red light where other cars are already stopped, but on reflection you would probably decide this is not a fair test. The car might stop to avoid a collision, regardless of any fear of a fine if caught not stopping, or any feeling that stopping when there is a symbol indicating you should is the morally right thing to do. So, you would like the driver of the car to have an opportunity to choose on *these* bases, unhindered by fear of a collision. As a practical matter, then, you would be wise to avoid the rush hour as a time for taking observations. Similar reflections would probably lead you to place additional restrictions: a policeman should not be conspicuously present; school crosswalk stop situations should be avoided.

And one other control is essential as a practical matter. You, as observer, serve as a recording instrument. Whenever using any recording instrument you need to either measure the effect of the instrument itself on behavior so that you can discount its effect when drawing conclusions, or else at least minimize its effect. Thus, you should not be obvious in your activities. Unless you are unobtrusive, your very presence and activities may alter the behavior of the car drivers. They may slow down out of curiosity. Or, since they do not know who you are and for what purpose you are noting something about their behavior, they may be extraordinarily conforming in their actions, just to "play it safe."

These various restrictions help make any conclusions you later draw stronger. You have minimized the chances that conformity occurs because of fear of hitting a schoolchild or a car. And, by insisting that a policeman not be noticeable and that you be unobtrusive, you have minimized the chances that behavior conforms because of fear of detection of nonconformity. Hence, if behavior does conform, it is more likely that it is *not* because of these things. This makes any inference you might make that conformity occurs because of internalized norms just that much stronger.

As is typical, setting up controls has affected sample selection. But there are still a few more decisions related to picking your sample. You need to decide whether any situations meeting the restrictions already imposed will do for inclusion in your sample, or portion you do observe of all the relevant observations you could have made, or whether you should pick them in some particular way, such as a random sample of the available red light and two-way stop sign corners.

Making this decision hinges on whether you feel justified in thinking that the distribution of behavior from one red light setting to another or from one stop sign setting to another will be similar, or will vary. You might feel that the distributions of conforming behavior may vary, depending on, say, whether a red light is present in a congested area compared to a semirural one. But partly for feasibility reasons, for this exercise we will assume that the critical aspect is the type of symbol present.

We will assume that while the distribution of behavior may differ from a stop sign compared to a red light setting, those distributions will be similar from one red light to another and from one stop sign to another. This is a *uniformity* assumption. We are assuming that whatever the distribution of conforming behavior may be in a situation, that distribution will be essentially the same (or uniform) from one red light setting to another and that the distribution in one stop sign setting will be the same compared to another stop sign situation. This assumption of homogeneity or uniformity of behavior within the same kind of symbol setting is used to justify a kind of "grab-bag" sampling procedure — include in your sample *any* red light or stop sign setting that meets the restrictions imposed earlier. (If, when comparing results later, this uniformity assumption does not seem justified, then in your report you should warn others that future research on the topic will not be able to get by with anything as simple as a grab-bag sample; better sampling techniques would be needed.)

In addition, you need to decide on the size of your sample. You need to decide on the number of observations to make in each kind of stop symbol setting. You could observe for the same length of time in each kind of situation, regardless of the number of cars noted. Or you could decide to note the same number of cars for each situation, regardless of the length of time involved. Later computations will be easier for you if you pick the same number of cars, so for this exercise we will choose that option. Somewhat arbitrarily, we will decide that twenty-five cars in each setting, or fifty observations altogether, will be a sufficiently large number to reveal whatever patterns are there.

Finally, you need to decide how to record and manipulate your data. With only fifty observations, it is feasible to use the simplest method of recording them, a hand tally. Use a slash for each observation and after four slashes are made, place another slash through them to indicate five. For example, $\cancel{||||} \ //$ would stand for a total of seven observations of the same type.

If you prepared a large copy of the dummy table specified, you could enter the tally marks at the top of the appropriate cell and still have room to enter the actual number in parentheses below the tallies and enter a percentage after it has been computed. You should convert each row to a percentage distribution before beginning later analysis. For example, a cell might look like the one below when you are ready to begin analysis:

$$\boxed{\begin{array}{c} \cancel{||||} \ // \\ (7) \\ 28\% \end{array}}$$

The 7 comes from the number of tallies made and the 28% comes from dividing the number in the cell by the total number for the row. The total for a red light or for a stop sign row has been fixed at 25 for this exercise, and 25 divided into 7 gives 28 percent. (A dummy table, to be copied and filled in, appears on page 72.)

A brief summary might be in order by now:

Problem: Broad problem of conformity to norms has been narrowed to conformity to a particular norm, namely that a car ought to stop when there is a symbol indicating it should stop. Conforming behavior will be examined according to percent distributions of the extent of conformity shown in different situations, and the resulting pattern will be examined to see how much support it lends to the tentative explanation that conformity occurs because of the internalization of norms. To do this, situations have been restricted to those where there is little likelihood that conformity occurs because of fear of detection of nonconformity by a policeman or a suspiciously behaving stranger — you — or because of fear of a collision or hitting a schoolchild.

Situations to be observed: Traffic at a red light and at a two-way stop sign, each kind of situation subject only to the following restrictions:

1. A school crosswalk is not involved.
2. No policeman is obviously present, on foot, in a car, or on a motorcycle.
3. Situation must not be one in which car must stop to avoid collision (therefore, avoid rush hour).
4. Your behavior is as unobtrusive as possible (and should car drivers show curiosity about your activities, cease and observe somewhere else).

Number and type of observation to be made: Observe 25 instances of car behavior in each of the two types of symbol setting, and classify according to three categories of conformity:

1. High: car comes to full stop.
2. Medium: car behavior does not fit categories 1 or 3.
3. Low: car does not noticeably slow its speed at all.

Manner of recording: Hand tally in cells of table.

TABLE 1. CAR BEHAVIOR IN TRAFFIC SITUATIONS, ACCORDING TO SYMBOL INDICATING STOP AND EXTENT OF CONFORMITY[a]

Symbol indicating stop	Extent of conformity[a]			All cars
	High	*Medium*	*Low*	
Red light				(25) 100%
Two-way stop sign				(25) 100%
Both situations				(50) 100%

Source (street location and day and hour of observation):
  Red light setting(s) _____
  Stop sign setting(s) _____
  Observer's name _____
  [a] High: car came to full stop; low: car did not slow speed; medium: all other cases.

To complete your research plans you need to decide on the allocation of your resources (in this case, "time") for collection and analysis of data, and for writing a report on the project. Then you would be ready to move on to the second portion of the research process, evidence collecting to report writing.

SECOND PORTION
OF THE PROCESS:
FROM COLLECTION
OF DATA TO
REPORT WRITING

Now collect your observations and convert them to percentages. If you are working alone with this book, try to get at least five different samples of fifty observations each. If you are working with this book in a class, you can later compare your sample results with those of your classmates.

In general, you should follow the guides to table reading indicated in Exercise I-1. First make some minimum accuracy checks. Everyone makes mistakes. The trick is to build in ways to catch and correct them rather than just hope you did not make any this time.

The numbers in the rows should add to 25 except that the "Both" row should add to 50. If they do not, you should take another sample of observations. Once the percentages are computed, each row should add to 100 percent. Further, percentages in the "Both" row should be a multiple of 2 and the percentages in the other rows a multiple of 4. If you have an odd percentage anywhere you have made a computational error and need to correct it, since with 50 observations any single one is worth 2 percent and with 25 observations any single one is worth 4 percent.

You now have a number of samples available to you and each can be considered a replication, or repeat, of the same project. For your final analysis, use a pooled estimate of the percentage for each cell as your "best guess." To obtain a pooled estimate of what is going on, either combine the numbers for each cell and recompute percentages based on the total now available for each row, or add up the percentages each of you obtained in a given cell and divide by the number of samples, or sets of 25 observations each. Again, make some internal consistency checks.

Compare your results for a single sample with the pooled estimate. Some variation from sample to sample is to be expected and replication in a number of cases is one good way of enabling you to set bounds on how much deviation can be expected simply because just a portion or sample of the observations that could have been made were made.

Suppose that in making the pooled estimate, for some cell you had a series of percentages such as 68, 72, 72, 76, 74, 76, etc., and then one showed up that was 40 percent or less. How might you interpret this "deviant" result?

This would seem to be a bit more deviation than could be expected just because you are looking at samples. So, you would first check if the observer was following the definitions and procedures he should have. If he was, then check whether there was anything unusual about the traffic situations observed which could account for the deviation somehow. In other words, try to determine if the deviation is "real" or an illusion because agreed-on procedures were not actually followed.

The game of science is completely dependent on the honesty of the players. When something unusual occurs, unless and until there is strong evidence to the contrary, always assume that the peculiarity is real and therefore something to be explained. One of the reasons replication is so very important (as is keeping up with the literature to know what others have done) is that it enables scientists to get to know what to expect and so to spot a result as truly unusual. If any deviation cannot be explained it takes its place in the store of anomalies or "puzzles we hope to explain some day" that every scientist in any discipline tends to carry around in his head and occasionally worry over. So-called accidental discoveries that may later provide the key to unlock various scientific "black boxes" are most likely to be spotted by the scientist with a prepared mind. By being aware of what has been done by others he knows what is likely and what is not, and he knows what remains to be explained.

Once you have the pooled estimate, enter it in your table. You might use a different color, or underline the pooled percentages, or use some such distinguishing device. (Unless, of course, you want to prepare a new table, with a title beginning "Pooled estimate of" and prepare a different source note.) In analysis and write-up of your report, use the *pooled* estimate.

You know how and why the table was put together, so you begin analysis by taking the table apart. Look at the row marginal to tell you how the entire sample behaved as far as degree of conformity. Then look at each row to see how much difference in the general pattern shown by the total sample each kind of symbol setting makes. If the percentages in each row are very similar to the percentages in the column marginal cells, then the kind of symbol setting is irrelevant to (or independent of) the extent of conformity. Knowing the additional information, kind of symbol present, would not enable you to improve the prediction you could make knowing only that *some* kind of symbol indicating a stop was present: the percentages in the "Both situations" row.

Compare the shape and intensity of the pattern shown in the table with the pattern you would most like to see, concentration in the "High" column, to see the correspondence between the two. Deciding how close the pattern turned out to be determines the kind of answer this study can provide to the two questions you wanted to answer: (1) Is conformity typical, especially highly conforming behavior? (2) Is the pattern such as to indicate that whatever conformity is present is congruent with, or does not contradict, E1, namely that norms have been internalized?

Now prepare a short paper on this project, no more than five double spaced, typewritten pages for the verbal portion. (You have deliberately been asked to prepare a short paper. In general, short papers covering the same information are harder to do than long ones, because you must get to the point quickly.)

Assume you are writing for an "intelligent layman." Since he is a layman, you will have to be clear, and cannot assume he knows sociological terms without definitions, but since he is intelligent, do not belabor or bore him. Remember that the reader is not interested in doing the researcher's job of analysis. He wants to read your considered distillation of what you wanted to do and why, how you tried to do it, what you learned, why the pattern you say is in the data is there, and why the more general implications of that pattern are likely to be correct.

For this Exercise, use the following major headings in your report: Problem, Method, Major Findings, Implications. The first section should contain a statement of the general problem, the specific portion of it you actually investigated, and why the problem was narrowed as it was. Normally, this section would contain some review of the literature used to aid you in establishing and narrowing your problem. For this practice exercise, no "review of the literature" was done other than what might have been in your memory from your general reading. The second section describes your procedures, along with some justification for them. The description should be clear enough that if someone else wanted to repeat the study in his own area he would know what to do to match his procedures to yours. The third section tells what generalizations you feel can be made, based on the specific data obtained for *this* study. The last section discusses and attempts to justify the broader generalizations you feel can be made.

The first section places your specific problem in perspective according to what was known on the general problem when you began. The last section again provides perspective, this time in light of what is known now that your project's results have been added to the pool of knowledge.

If the project had been a complex one, the last section might also contain a brief summary of the preceding sections, but the project is so simple this seems unnecessary. Nor is the project complex enough to merit a final section, or appendix, containing detailed data, definitions, and references. If you had needed such a section, then highlighted portions from the appendix data would appear in the third section, in the form of short text tables or pie charts or bar charts or other graphic devices. Instead, the table used to collect and analyze your data is quite short, so somewhere in the third section (Major Findings) the table should appear in its entirety.

Once you have completed your report, reread it as though it were a report on a project you knew nothing about. Check it for clarity, and especially check it for the quality of the more or less explicit reasoning underlying what you say, and make any revisions needed.

Exchange your completed report for someone else's on the same project and read it as though the project were initially unknown to you. Check that the items that are supposed to be covered in each section are, and check the quality of the reasoning. Briefly write your evaluation of the report you have just read.

Now look over the evaluation done on your report by someone else and see to what extent criticisms were made that seem merited enough that you should revise your report. Write your response to the evaluation of your report. That is, if you feel criticisms were made that are unjustified, indicate why you feel so, while if you feel some portions of your report should be revised, revise just those portions.

Items to be turned in: (1) your original report; (2) the evaluation prepared by someone else; (3) your response to the evaluation of your report.

As shown below, the most desirable pattern is one of X's in the High column:

Severity of sanctions	*Extent of conformity*					*Total*
	High	•	•	•	*Low*	
High	X					
•	X					
•	X					
•	X					
Low	X					
Total	X					

The pattern is a "constant" one, or similar proportions of the total clustered in the same kind of cell for each row. The pattern tells you both that it is true that most people conform and that they appear to conform irrespective of the severity of the sanction. Since the fear of sanctions explanation, E2, would be discounted as improbable based on the pattern shown, it is now more probable that your remaining explanation is correct, E1, or internalization of norms.

Suppose you found some other, less desirable, constant pattern, such as uniformity in the Low or in one of the middle columns? If any of *these* possibilities occurs, it is still true you can discount E2 as a possible explanation, since it would seem that behavior is occurring without reference to the severity of the sanction involved. But such a pattern would cast more or less doubt both on the generalization that most people tend to conform and on the possible explanation that whatever conformity is present occurs because of internalization of norms.

Before making some kind of judgment about how *much* doubt would be cast, you would first check to see whether the specific design used to obtain observations somehow inadvertently muddied the water for you. In other words, in trying to decide whether or not you were wrong, you try to determine whether the results might have occurred (1) because of inadequacies in your design for collecting observations, or in some other way such as carelessness of some sort, so that your *method* is at fault; or (2) because your *theory* is incorrect and the model you developed to correspond to what is going on "out there" is a poor correspondence, and so you had better try again.

A so-called left-to-right diagonal pattern would be most desirable. In outline, the pattern of X's goes from the top left cell to the bottom right one, as shown below:

Severity of sanctions	Extent of conformity					Total
	High	•	•	•	Low	
High	X					
•		X				
•			X			
•				X		
Low					X	
Total						

As far as intensity, either a pattern of equal concentration in each of the cells along the diagonal, or a pattern of more concentration as one moves up and to the left would be acceptable, although the former would give more clear-cut evidence against E1 and for E2.

The left to right diagonal pattern would be interpreted generally by saying that the more severe the sanction in a situation, the greater the extent of conformity shown. Patterns like this are also called *direct* correlations, or a covariation such that the more of one variable the more of the other, and conversely. In other words, the variables tend to travel the same path.

Suppose you found a different diagonal pattern, a right-to-left one, where the variables travel opposite paths (the more of one the less of the other, or *inverse* correlation)? How would you interpret this? This pattern would mean that conformity tends to be greater when the sanction is less severe. It is still true that prediction would be good based on a knowledge of the severity of the possible sanctions, but the predictability is *opposite* from what you hoped to find.

As in the case for patterns for E1, before deciding you might be wrong as far as the model proposed, E2, you would first examine your method to see if there are difficulties there. If you decide there was nothing in your method that might have produced a right-to-left diagonal pattern that was not "really" there, then you would have to question not only whether E2 is wrong but also whether your generalization that most people tend to conform is wrong. Both explanations, E1 and E2, were developed on the assumption that generalization was correct.

After thinking about the kinds of patterns you would like to see in order to make either E1 or E2 less probable and the remaining one more probable, you also have to consider the unhappy possibility that the actual pattern obtained will not be "close enough" to *any* of them. Unfortunately, it is not as rare as one would like to have none of your tentative working models either supported *or* eliminated satisfactorily. Such occurrences are known colloquially as back-to-the-drawing-board situations.

I-3. On Your Own: Begin Problem Selection

Now that you have read Part I of the text and through the exercises so far have gained some skill in table preparing and reading and some apprentice-type practice on a project from idea to completed report, you might try to develop a project of your own to do. First, you need to pick a topic that interests you and then narrow it to a form manageable enough that you can examine it and complete writing a report on the entire project by the time the course is over. So, you might start by deciding on a rough allocation of the time and effort you can afford to spend on the various stages of the research process.

Perhaps the best way to do this is to begin with the time the course will end and to work backward. You will want to have enough time to look over the first rough draft of your report and then make any final revisions you might find desirable. After subtracting this amount of time, allocate some time for collecting information, specifying both beginning and ending time points for data collection. In the time you have left, review the literature and get your plans in good shape.

Remember that the game of science is a never-ending game: any particular project is a part of the "work in progress," and every report on a project is in a sense just a progress report. Undoubtedly, whatever you do, you will find there are a few more items you would like to know about before writing your report. While a certain amount of flexibility is both necessary and desirable, do not fall into the far too common trap of pursuing what must inevitably be a never-ending trail of promising leads to the point that you have inadequate time left to do a satisfactory job of analysis and report-writing.

Keep both theoretical relevance *and* feasibility clearly in mind. Neither should be slighted. When you begin to speculate on what you might do, *of course* let your imagination roam freely over what you consider are the most significant questions, but after this "thinking big" try to "think small" (although also, of course, not too small) when it comes to the piece you will actually do.

It is much more important, both in what you might learn from what is, after all, still a kind of practice exercise and in what might be any possible contribution you can make to our general supply of scientific knowledge, that you do a good job on what you do decide to undertake than that you cover "all" variables that might be relevant. You need both humility and self-confidence. You should have the humility to realize that you cannot do everything and that you will make mistakes (otherwise, you certainly do not need this book and might as well close it right now); but you should also have the self-confidence to recognize that your reasoning ability is likely to be as good as the next fellow's and with some care and a clear grasp of what seem to be useful guides for proceeding, the mite you are able to add to the store of verified scientific understanding will be a worthwhile addition.

By the time Exercise Set II is scheduled to be completed, if not a bit before this, you should have a detailed research proposal ready, covering both the broad problem of interest to you and the specific part of it you actually intend to investigate, as well as some fairly detailed plans for collecting and analyzing information. By the time Exercise Set III is scheduled to be completed, your report should be in its final revision stages.

Therefore, you should immediately begin to try picking a topic and narrowing it. As far as anything that might be turned in at the end of this first stage, a brief statement of your broad topic, along with some indication of how you propose to narrow it, should suffice. But your instructor may also want you to turn in your review and evaluation of whatever literature you peruse, and certainly by the time Exercise II-1, covering locating and evaluating the literature, is completed, you should also have pretty well completed your literature review for your project.

As some rough guides, select a minimum of *ten* items and a maximum of *twenty* for review. Do not use popular journals, at least for articles you will turn in an evaluation on. No more than three of the twenty items on your list should be books and no more than three should have appeared earlier than twenty years ago. Read and evaluate at least *five* items on your list.

PART II

First Portion of the Research Process
from getting an idea through developing a plan

How odd it is that anyone should not see that all observation must be for or against some view, if it is to be of any service.

CHARLES DARWIN

1. Introduction

Paradoxical as it may seem, the most useful place to begin planning an investigation is at the end. Decide on your objectives, on the kinds of statements you would like to be able to make when you complete your project. Then mentally work backwards. Decide what patterns would have to be present in what collected observations if your desired generalizations are to be supported or else to be denied. Then decide what you have to do to collect those observations and to enable yourself to see the patterns that are there. This set of decisions becomes embodied in your research proposal, or plan, and the first portion of the research process involves developing a plan from an initial idea. The second portion consists of carrying out your plan for collecting data and your plan for analyzing, interpreting the results, then writing a report on the entire investigation.

Determining what you want to know about which units and how accurately you want to know it, what information you will need to find out, how you plan to obtain that information, and what you plan to do with it, is the first main thinking stage in the overall process. Making sense of your observations once they are obtained and determining their broader implications is the other main reasoning stage. It is these thinking stages that are the most absorbing and enjoyable in the game of science.

Between these two stages there is an interim period of actually gathering and manipulating your data. It is only fair to say that during this period there can often be some undisguisable drudgery. Various technological devices, from tape recorders to computers, tend to lessen the drudgery involved, often substantially. The best way to minimize boredom during this interim phase, however, is to pick a topic that truly interests you. This requires getting an idea. Once you have an initial idea, there is a common set of general decisions for any project.

Your problem needs to be placed in perspective. Actually, perspective should be provided at two points, the beginning and end of your project. That project will fit into some part of the basic puzzle and so you need to provide perspective on where we are as far as what is already known about that part. Later, you need to provide perspective on where we are now that your results are available.

Placing your problem in perspective involves locating, evaluating, and using what is already known. This aids you in deciding more clearly on your underlying objectives, or the level of your study and its basic emphasis.

On the one hand, you may choose either a reconnoitering or a reconnaissance level. Such studies emphasize collecting observations in order either to locate or to specify more clearly the outlines of pieces that might be useful in eventual explanation or theory construction: preparing a tentative fit of the pieces. On the other hand, you may choose a testing level for your study. Here the emphasis is on collecting observations in order to check some existing fit, or theory. The difference between studies with one or another set of underlying objectives lies more in what you plan to do with the observations obtained — how you plan to reason with and about them — than in how you plan to obtain them. The details of procedure will not necessarily differ greatly.

With either emphasis you need to answer a number of similar questions. What will your basic strategy be? That is, will you take your observations as of one point in time (yielding cross-sectional, or "state" descriptions) or try to observe through time (yielding longitudinal, or "process" descriptions)? Will you observe naturally occurring situations or attempt to manipulate situations, and if the latter how much and what kind of manipulation will you do? Will you observe directly, or indirectly through one or another index? Will you use data generated for the purposes of the study, or will you use data already collected, perhaps for some other purpose? How can you ensure adequate controls so that when you are through there are not a great many alternative interpretations that might be made of the same evidence? How can you ensure that you really do get an adequate sample from the parent class you want to generalize to?

These sorts of questions, related to procedures for observing as well as you can, are similar for studies with either emphasis. In either case, observations need to be collected and described and you need to be concerned with separating "evidence" from "interpretation." With either emphasis, at some point you are observing, and would like to "see" as well as you can.

Once your problem is in perspective and you have decided on your underlying objectives, you need to develop a plan for investigation. You will need to choose your basic strategy — cross-sectional or longitudinal — and set up an initial analysis plan, indicating what variables you want to relate and how the relationship will be studied. You will also need to decide on a specific plan for collecting observations. This includes deciding on the situations to be observed, on the source and form of the observations to be made, on what controls will be placed on those observations, on what procedures will be used for selecting your sample, and on how you will allocate your resources (time, money, personnel, equipment) available for completing this investigation. When all this is done, you will have "operationalized" your problem and will be ready to move on to the second portion of the research process.

The first portion, then, involves getting an idea, specifying what you want to know and deciding on a plan for finding out. The following sections are intended to provide some guides for doing these things.

2. SELECT PROBLEM

Problems are either given to you or you more or less systematically pick them for yourself. In other words, you may systematically examine the puzzle of concern to your discipline with an eye to finding some worthwhile project to do, or you may note something that arouses your curiosity and decide to investigate it further, or you may be asked to work on a problem by someone else.

Roughly speaking, problems tend to be either application-generated or discipline-generated. For application problems, you may primarily apply either content knowledge or technique knowledge. You may try to apply content knowledge, or knowledge of those aspects of your discipline's puzzle that have already been deciphered, in order to explain what is going on in some concrete situation of practical importance. Or, you may apply certain techniques for finding out.

For instance, if a sociologist you might be asked by some planning agency to apply your knowledge of general population trends and their implications to a particular area such as a state or county, describing specific population trends in that area and discussing the probable implications of those specific trends for certain interests, such as health or education. Or perhaps you might be asked to apply your knowledge of techniques of questionnaire construction and sampling, to learn the reactions of members of different parts of some metropolitan area to alternate proposals for regional government, or to ascertain the amount and severity of illness during some period that was never called to the attention of any medical doctor, or even to get information about which kinds of people repeatedly watch which television programs.

However, there may be no adequate general knowledge or no satisfactory techniques available for application, and so solving a practical, or supposedly "applied" kind of problem may lead to the development of such knowledge or techniques. It is not rare for various application-generated problems to yield information furthering basic understanding, just as it is not rare for solutions to discipline-generated problems to have practical applications.

As far as primarily discipline-generated problems are concerned, more or less systematically going back over the fundamental questions related to your discipline's puzzle should provide you with a wealth of topics to study further. Sociology, for example, is the study of the group aspects of life. Basic questions include: What kinds of groups are there? How are they organized? How do they operate? How are they related to one another? How do they change in organization, operation, or interrelation? To what extent *must* the group aspects of life be as they are or change as they do?

In sociology's puzzle, as in the specific puzzle for any discipline, there are some areas where there are gaps and some areas that are vague or little confirmed. Nor is it rare to find that proposed explanations are to some degree apparently inconsistent. For your project, then, you might decide that some existing explanation could be broadened to include additional kinds of situations, or deepened to include additional kinds of relationships, or even that some alternate explanation seems more promising to you than those in current use and should be examined further.

Selecting a broad discipline-generated problem and narrowing it to a particular problem for further study depends on the basic puzzle of interest. Selecting a broad topic is bounded by the kind of puzzle the discipline is attempting to solve and shaped according to the major segments of the puzzle. Narrowing the topic is guided by how much is known and how much remains to be known within each segment.

Whenever your mind is not already prepared enough that a number of worthwhile projects occur to you, taking any one of the fundamental questions for your discipline and systematically locating and evaluating existing knowledge related to that question should do the trick, and a good introductory textbook is an excellent place to begin. No matter what the field of study, a good introductory textbook is a worthwhile starting base, especially if you are temporarily stymied for ideas. An introductory text represents one of the few places you get (or should get, if the text is a good one) a systematic view, in broad outlines, of what people calling themselves "—ists" would like to know, how much of this they think they already do know, and the major evidence underpinning the degree of likelihood they feel that various "known" items are "true." A review of such a text should enable you at least to settle on some segment of the puzzle that intrigues you, and you can go on from there.

If you get started on your problem by taking one of the broad questions for your discipline to investigate further, you are essentially beginning at the top of a turn of the basic cycle of science. If you are to proceed efficiently, you will need to find out what is already known on the topic picked and then continue along the right side. If you get started by rather accidentally noting something that arouses your curiosity (as was the suggested starting point for Exercise I-2), you will usually need more or less quickly to go up the left side of the cycle, by trying to generalize what you have noted and to develop some tentative explanations. Once this is done, then here too you will proceed more efficiently if you try to find out what others have done that is related to your problem, as part of continuing down the right side of the cycle. Even for those times when your project gets started because you want to apply available knowledge or technique, to proceed efficiently you need to be aware of what has already been learned as far as detailed knowledge of either content or technique.

For any of these starting points, then, you will rather quickly find it desirable to place your project in perspective. This requires locating, evaluating, and using what is already known.

2.1 LOCATE WHAT IS KNOWN. If I were limited to just one piece of advice for the beginner, it would undoubtedly be to make friends with your local librarians. Some less personal aids are available too, however.

The card catalog in any library is alphabetically arranged in three ways: by author, by title, and by subject. This card catalog can be used to find books and monographs located in the library, but it cannot be used to locate journal articles, or what is called "periodical literature."

Nor, of course, does it contain a listing of books and monographs that are available, but not in that library. Once you know what to ask for, your librarian can arrange an interlibrary loan, although obtaining a book from another library may take several weeks. The reference volumes, *Books in Print* and *Paperbound Books in Print,* can be used to locate promising titles for an interlibrary loan request.

Before staggering home with armloads of books, however, you would be wise to try to locate book reviews and read them first. A good place to start is with the *Book Review Digest.* These volumes contain excerpts from reviews of books that meet certain criteria. Paperbound books are not included, the book must have received at least two reviews within a certain time period after publication, and those reviews must have appeared in certain journals. Approximately two major journals are monitored for a given discipline, such as sociology or anthropology.

Here is an illustration of the kind of information you can get from the *Book Review Digest,* picking an item I think might be of interest to several disciplines. Under the listing by topics in the 1968 volume, there is this item:

Urban research and policy planning. Schnore, L. F., ed. (Ag '68)

Turning to the appropriate pages elsewhere in the volume, this is what appeared:

SCHNORE, LEO F., ed. Urban research and policy planning (Urban affairs annual reviews, v 1) ed. by Leo F. Schnore and Henry Fagin. 638p il $20 Sage publications
301.3 Sociology, Urban. Urban renewal
68–8131

A "series of original articles by specialists in all the disciplines encompassed by urban studies, urban affairs." (Choice) Bibliography

Reviewed by Frank Smallwood
Am Pol Sci R 62:620 Je '68 900w
"Whatever faults that (this volume) may have do not appear to be the responsibility of its editors. . . . First, they offer a volume that parallels the needs of contemporary urban research by cutting across disciplinary boundaries in both of its major parts. . . . In addition, the readings are organized in pairs. Usually, the first selection in each pair deals with general problems centered on a single discipline or a common theme, while the second deals with specific research interests. . . . This procedure deserves praise, since, at its best, it enables the reader to examine in depth one aspect of a problem that has just been treated in breadth. . . . (However, the selections) range from the banal to those which deserve wider attention."

P. G. Marden
Am Soc R 33:328 Ap '68 700w
"Although possibly regarded as a companion to (P.) Hauser and Schnore's The Study of Urbanization (BRD 1966), this volume performs an important and somewhat unique service by emphasizing policy issues. The difficulty of relating academic research and programmatic interests is illustrated by the separation between Part I, which evaluates the literature in each of the traditional disciplines, and Part II, which focuses on policy planning. The articles are uneven at times, but many represent outstanding analyses and most provide comprehensive descriptions of the state of present knowledge about various urban problems. Excellent bibliography. Should be of considerable value for general reading as well as reference purposes to all social scientists interested in urban affairs."
Choice 4:1140 D '67 150w

As you can see, the information contained in this abstracted form is far more useful to you in deciding what to read thoroughly than a simple listing of book titles would be. Even for a book that does not meet the criteria for inclusion in the *Book Review Digest,* for instance an original paperback (such as the one you are reading now) rather than a paperback edition of a book that originally appeared in hardbound form, you may still be able to locate a review of it by searching the most likely professional journals. This gets us into locating the periodical, or journal, literature.

Several kinds of indexes to articles in journals are available. You may already be aware of the most general and widely used one, *Reader's Guide to Periodical Literature.* Less general but still covering several fields are those such as the *Social Sciences and Humanities Index.* As far as specific journals are concerned, at the end of the year each is likely to have an index as part of one of its issues. Sometimes a cumulative index is available separately, covering a number of years. These cumulative indexes usually have at least three alphabetically arranged sections. One is devoted to authors, another to subjects, and the third to book reviews.

Few indexes contain much information on an item besides the author, title, name and date (and/or volume number) of the journal, and the pages on which the article is found. But, for some disciplines journals are available which contain solely abstracts of recently published articles. For the same reasons that the *Book Review Digest* can help you decide which books to read, these journals containing abstracts can help you to decide which articles to read.

Usually a subscription to at least one journal is included in the yearly membership dues for a professional association. At a minimum, you should find out the names of these "official" journals in your own and closely allied fields. Try to learn the names of any other major journals as well. Since researchers will try to publish in these if they can, it is well to keep their names in mind when trying to decide which articles to read from your list of potentially promising ones.

And you should not overlook such cross-cutting kinds of journals as *Science* and the *Journal of the American Statistical Association*. The latter contains many articles that may be useful methodologically, and sometimes for content as well, in a number of disciplines. A subscription to the former is included with the dues for the most broadly based association of scientists in this country, The American Association for the Advancement of Science. Since scientists are very *human* beings, they like to reach a broader audience as well as try to publish in the major journals for their specific disciplines.

If you have access to a fairly large library, such as a college library or the main one for a big city, it is worthwhile to investigate the government documents section. (Small libraries are not likely to contain much in the way of government documents beyond the latest Census volumes for the United States as a whole and for the state in which the library is located.)

Government documents can be invaluable. Not only do they typically contain some basic descriptive data which the reader can analyze as he chooses, they often contain helpful analyses and summaries of interest to several of the social sciences — especially in those documents published on an intermittent basis.

Trends in the labor force, in growth and composition of metropolitan areas, in characteristics of minority groups, and in family characteristics, are just a few of the topics covered with some regularity by our national government. On a more macroscopic level, publications by the United Nations (especially UNESCO and its subdivisions) such as occasional reports on "the world social situation," can be absorbing reading for specialists and generalists alike. On a more local level, individual state governments and even some counties and cities publish reports off and on. Those put out by departments of social welfare, public health, industrial relations, and education are likely to be of most interest to social scientists.

Listings of government documents are available in catalog form in most libraries, at least for the national level of government. Your library may be able to borrow them or, since the cost is usually modest, you may wish to purchase them from the Government Printing Office in Washington, D.C. For publications by levels of government less broad than this, you may have no choice but to rely on the librarian for assistance. However, if the library is large enough to have a separate government documents section it will usually have a librarian with special government documents training. Beginning to find out what is available and pertinent in the myriad government publications can be something of a headache at times, but one well worth suffering.

Another kind of catalog is available useful, and likely not to be known to the novice. I refer to catalogs issued by publishing companies for various reprint series. For instance, the Bobbs-Merrill Company publishes reprint series for which leading professionals select not only articles but portions of books that they consider merit reprinting. Looking over the catalogs of available reprints (primarily designed to give instructors flexibility in selecting reading material to be purchased by students) gives you in handy form a sort of minimum list of those items experts on a topic feel "every young ——ist" should be acquainted with for that topic, although of course quite recent publications are not included.

You should make a notation in some standard form of any item you decide might be worth finding and reading. A common method is to use five-by-eight inch index cards. Enter the reference at the top of the card. Book titles should be underlined, and you should include the name of the publisher and the date of publication. For example:

Cohen, Morris R. and Ernest Nagel, *An Introduction to Logic and Scientific Method*, Harcourt, Brace and Co., 1934.

Here are two examples for journal articles, the second with more than one author:

Rodman, Hyman, "Family and Social Pathology in the Ghetto," *Science,* vol. 161, no. 3843 (23 August 1968), pp. 756–762.

Thomas, William C., Jr., and Herman E. Hilleboe, "Administrative Centralization Versus Decentralization and the Role of Generalists and Specialists," *American Journal of Public Health*, vol. 58, no. 9 (September 1968), pp. 1620–1632.

Your notes can then be added to the card when you read the material, using additional cards as needed.

Once you have a list of items, your search strategy will be more efficient if it proceeds according to the following guides. (*a*) Begin with more recent literature and then work back in time. This way, some of the important earlier material will already have been located (check the footnotes) and even partly digested for you. (*b*) Especially if they are recent, articles that amount to a summary and hopefully also a critique of major items on a topic can be a helpful starting point. I have in mind articles with titles something like current issues in medical sociology, or stratification literature in the sixties, and so on. (*c*) Begin with broader treatments and work toward narrower ones. (*d*) Read for both content and method. Even if something that sounded promising for content turns out not to be, the method employed may give you some ideas for your own project.

Once located, published material must be read and evaluated in order to aid you in narrowing your topic to a manageable form. The next section contains some guides for evaluating reports.

(Of course, after locating and evaluating what is known so far, you might decide that what is currently most needed is not a research project resulting in a research report but work resulting in some other kind of report — perhaps pulling together and giving a critique of what is known, or else constructing and presenting a more systematic explanation of what is known, or a more systematic development of existing explanations. You must inevitably do at least some of this kind of pulling together, criticizing, and developing for any research project. Still, the rest of this book assumes that as a beginner or a consumer it is a project with a research focus that you most need guides for doing, and hence for evaluating reports of research projects done by others. In any event, evaluation of the other kinds of reports is much harder without an understanding of the research process underpinning the empirical results whose description and interpretation must form a major part of the foundation for such other papers.)

2.2 EVALUATE WHAT IS KNOWN. No matter what its underlying emphasis, every research report should at least touch the main points in a full turn of the cycle. Some model or idea, even a vague one, is used to guide the selection of observations and so some attention needs to be given to the right side of the cycle, or theory elaboration. Once observations have been obtained they need to be described and interpreted and some attention given to the implications of this with respect to the initial tentative explanation, that is, to the left side of the cycle, or theory construction and revision. However, in addition to research reports you will encounter reports that contain information relevant to just a portion of the cycle. Among these, major types are: survey kinds of articles, which amount to summaries and/or critiques of existing papers; articles devoted just to theory construction and/or elaboration.

Regardless of the type of report (research, survey, or theory), once you have located it you need to evaluate it. In order to evaluate it you need to know what is in it, or summarize it. In fact, one aspect of evaluation is to check for completeness: check to what extent items that should be covered in a report *are*. Along with this you also check the quality of the items present.

A sort of checklist can be used with respect to both completeness and other aspects of quality. Of course, it is just a memory device, but habitually using this guide will almost automatically ensure that you do not overlook items merely because you are temporarily swayed by either the grace or the ponderousness of the language.

The guide suggested here contains both a topical outline, which is a set of "pigeonholes" to check for completeness, and a set of related questions to ask to check on other aspects of quality. (The questions suggested are adapted from those used by Darrell Huff in the last chapter, "How to Talk Back to a Statistic," of his book, *How to Lie With Statistics* [Norton and Co., 1954]. Mr. Huff's questions are these: Who Says So? How Does He Know? What's Missing? Did Somebody Change the Subject? Does It Make Sense?)

The content you place in the set of pigeonholes will vary somewhat, not just because of the specific article involved but also because of the type of article it is. However, the same general set can be used and can be thought of as a broad outline both for summarizing the work of others and for preparing a paper of your own.

The order of topics given below may not be followed by an author, but *where* material appears in a report is not nearly so important as *whether* it appears. Somewhere in the report material should appear that can be used to complete the outline. It is in the poorer quality studies that material will be missing. For those studies you may find yourself wondering why the author wanted to study the topic anyway, or where this study is supposed to fit in with anything else on the general subject, or just exactly how he obtained a particular result, or whether a statement made is based on data examined in this study or on greater or lesser navel contemplation, or "umbiloscopy."

The major headings in the topical outline are: Problem; Method; Major Findings;

Implications. A section labeled Appendix may or may not be present for some reports.

The first pigeonhole contains what the author wanted to do, the second contains how he went about it, the third what he found out, and the fourth his judgment of the implications of what he has done and learned. Much of the material you are looking for may be covered briefly, but it should be there.

Information covering both the broad topic of interest and the piece of it actually investigated comes under the first heading, Problem. You want to know what segment of the puzzle is under consideration, as a kind of orientation, and then what specific part of that segment is actually going to be looked at in this report. Some justification as to why the problem was narrowed as it was should appear in the report and you would place it under this heading.

If the report is a survey or assessment type, it should be clear for what portion of the puzzle existing material is to be summarized or criticized *and* what the major categories are according to which the summary will be described or the criticisms made. If a theory paper, it should be clear what portion of the puzzle is to be accounted for or elaborated. And if a research paper, it should be clear on the *particular* variables and relationships used in the narrowed problem actually investigated.

Under the second heading, Method, you are concerned mainly with the way the sample was picked and with the kinds of restrictions, or controls, used. If a survey paper, you want to know about spatial and temporal coverage. That is, you want to know which authors, journals or books, and which countries were included, over what time period. (You have already learned the

scope of the content coverage for the first heading.) Here your interest is in learning the author's justification for his sample and controls and whether you feel his justification is adequate. On the one hand, you ask yourself whether his method is well enough described that you feel sure you know what he did. On the other hand, you ask whether his method is adequate for his problem or whether something critical is missing from the report solely because of the method used. For instance, you need to judge whether the time period selected, or other aspects of his coverage, amount to serious omissions if the summary or critique is to be satisfactory.

For a theory paper emphasizing constructing or revising explanations, the second topic heading should contain information on what described observations are to be accounted for and how confirmed these descriptions are, as well as anything else used in theory construction — such as analogy with other explanations able to account for similar kinds of items. These other explanations used in analogous reasoning could come from other disciplines, not necessarily solely from the discipline of the author. For a paper emphasizing theory elaboration, you want to know where the premises come from and how well confirmed they seem to be, as well as what kinds of elaborations are intended.

Probably you will find that descriptions of the method used will be implicit for survey and theory papers and you will have to do some rereading and rearrangement before you are sure what was done and can judge the adequacy of the method. Such "implicit" descriptions of method should not be present in research reports in professional journals. In fact, one of the difficulties with reports that appear in popular and semipopular media is that the method is often not described explicitly enough to be of aid to you in judging the report and in developing a plan for your own project. Research reports in professional journals are not as likely to be guilty of this kind of vagueness.

As in the other two kinds of reports, under this topic heading you are concerned with the plan for collection and analysis, or use, of information. Again you ask yourself about adequacy, both in the sense that the description of the method is clear and in the sense that the method used is an appropriate one for the topic. Under the latter point you particularly look for any critical omissions because of the details of the specific method used. Authors of research reports, especially those published in the better journals, will typically tell you any omissions because of the method used and what they feel are the implications of those omissions for the interpretation of the results. You need to judge both what they say and whether they have overlooked any other omissions you feel might be critical.

It should be a little easier for you to judge the method used after we have discussed selecting a general strategy and selecting a specific design, but let me give just one example now. Suppose an interview survey were taken which inquired about political preferences and behavior of adults and used as acceptable respondents any adult at home at the time the interviewer came to the door. If the survey were done during the daytime, as is likely, most respondents would be housewives, or at least not employed on the day shift. If the intention is to describe the political behavior of *all* adults, male as well as female and employed as well as not, you might consider that the specific details of the method were not appropriate. (In a sense, when you ask whether the method is appro-

priate, you are asking: Depending on where you want to get, can you get there from here with the means you have chosen?) On the other hand you might feel that a similar procedure for admissible respondents used in a survey of major purchases during the past year, even though it would still include nonworking housewives as the prime source of information, would not result in a serious omission. Or at least you might feel that the generalizations made would not need as serious qualifications as those based on the preceding survey.

The third section, Major Findings, refers to interpretations made based *solely* on information for the study at hand, while the following section refers to broader interpretations using the major findings and perhaps other information as well. For the third section, you ask yourself whether or not the author has changed the subject in some way.

For a summary or critique paper, this amounts to asking whether the summaries or criticisms covering what was examined sound as though a *different* sample was obtained. For instance, do they sound as though a broader sample was covered, such as one containing all countries rather than just the United States or all relevant journals rather than those actually examined?

For a theory paper you want to know what explanation(s) was constructed or what developments and elaborations were made of some existing explanation(s). As far as changes of subject, you note whether the explanation provided is stated as though it accounts for different (typically for more confirmed) described observations than those actually used and whether the arguments are claimed to be stronger and sounder than they are.

For a research paper, you particularly want to know whether the descriptions are stated as though a different *sample* or different *measurements* were used than those that were. For example, does an author use a sample of college sophomores in one college and then generalize, without sufficient justification, as though he had a sample of all adults? Or does he use measurements based on what people say they do and then change the subject and generalize as though he had used measurements based on how people actually behave?

Under the last heading you want to know what broader implications are stated and how reasonable they seem to be. For any of the kinds of papers, you ask yourself whether these broader inferences seem to make sense.

In part this amounts to asking whether any background kind of information that would help in judging the interpretation is missing, and in part to asking about the strength and soundness of any arguments used to make the broader inferences stated. To take one rather extreme example, suppose a study showed that chronic diseases, such as heart disease and cancer, are now a large fraction and acute illnesses a small fraction of all illness in the United States whereas the reverse was true around 1900. To judge any possible claim that this implies we are now having an "epidemic" of chronic disease compared to the past, it would be helpful to have some background information. In particular, you would like to know whether the level, or rate, of acute illness is the same now as it was earlier, or whether chronic illness is now a large fraction of the total simply because other kinds of illnesses have been eliminated or substantially lessened.

Often the hardest part of filling in the pigeonholes even in good reports is separating generalizations that are really part of the major findings from those that are implications. Many authors tend to follow or intermingle with each major finding

some speculation about its broader implications. This is a matter of taste and often makes for a more readable report. However, even if intermingling is present it should be clear which is which: which interpretations are immediately founded on evidence examined for this study; which interpretations are rather more remotely founded. Authors are not always as careful as the reader might like in distinguishing between the two kinds.

Typically, a summary is present in a report. Its quality only indirectly affects your judgment of the overall quality of a published report. But to use the topical outline or set of pigeonholes to prepare your own papers, you need a place to put the summary.

In the past a summary was almost always put near the end, either preceding or just after a discussion of implications. But there is a growing trend to put the summary earlier. Some even place the summary first. More often, if it is early it appears after the introductory (or Problem) section, or else after the Method section, but in any case before a detailed description of findings. Then the reader can more quickly discover what was done and why, and what was found out, in order to decide whether or not he wishes to read the rest.

Appendix-type material, if any, is used to aid making judgments about other parts of the paper, and sometimes even to permit some reanalysis of the results. Here is where you would place material too detailed or complex to appear in the general text except in summary form. Footnotes giving unusually complicated definitions for which shorthand terms are used in the text, or any other detailed qualifications on what appears in the text, are candidates for an appendix. The bibliography would also be in some appendix section, whether explicitly labeled as such or not. And the basic data used, if it is a research report, appear here in at least some summary form.

Figure II.1 can serve as a recapitulation. In the left column, the headings for the Topical Outline appear and the major items that generally should be included are listed under each heading. Suggested questions to ask to check on other aspects of quality besides completeness appear in the right column.

Attaching specific questions to specific topic headings is just a device to ensure that you do not omit any. For instance, reasoning is of course used throughout any report and asking about soundness and strength should be done all along the way, as a kind of overall check on quality. Another, and closely related, overall check on quality is the question about bias.

Some of you may recall a certain television advertisement demonstrating that cars got better mileage using gasoline with platformate than without it, leaving the clear implication that therefore the advertiser's brand of gasoline is superior to others sold. As was pointed out in the *Wall Street Journal* and elsewhere, the better mileage was real enough but the advertiser had neglected to mention certain background information: For purposes of the demonstration the advertiser had had to carefully remove the platformate from the gasoline used by one of the cars, because virtually all brands of gasoline sold in the United States already contain this ingredient. Whether this example should be tied to the question about bias (especially deliberate bias) or whether it should be placed under the question about missing but needed background information would seem to be a matter of taste.

Similarly, some of the other questions listed as applicable to one topic heading might be asked about other topic headings as well. If you remind yourself to ask the *set* of questions sometime, that is what counts.

3. Begin Plan for Investigation

Now that you have settled on a broad topic and done some reviewing of the available literature, you are ready to begin to settle on a specific problem you will try to investigate. To do this, you need to use what you have summarized and evaluated, as well as your own creative imagination, to develop your understanding of the implications of what is known on the topic.

As you do so, you will be deciding on the level, or underlying objectives, of your study: exploratory, or reconnoitering level, to try to locate pieces of the puzzle that seem promising; systematically surveying, or reconnaissance level, to try to delineate more specifically the outlines of pieces already noted as promising; or testing level, to check how well some proposed fit of the pieces, or explanation, holds up under empirical observations. And you will be developing an initial analysis plan, to be used to aid you in making sense of your observations later and to aid you in more carefully deciding now what observations you will try to collect.

Along with all this, you will quite likely find that you are not as through "reviewing the literature" as you thought you were, and you will need to go back occasionally to find more specific information on one or another point related either to content (what is known) or to method (how to find out). Further, your analysis plans, as well as your later plans for col-

FIGURE II.1. GENERAL GUIDE FOR PREPARING, SUMMARIZING, AND EVALUATING REPORTS

Topical outline	*Suggested questions*
I. *Problem* Broad problem (including review of literature) Narrowed problem actually investigated in this study	A. How good is the justification used for narrowing the problem? In particular: Does any deliberate bias (intent to mislead) seem present? Does any unconscious bias seem present, such as a "pet theory" that might distort what researcher will see in his data, even though he may have the best of intentions? (If you spot either kind, proceed with extra caution in reading paper.)
II. *Method* Plan for obtaining information to be employed in this study Plan for analysis, or use, of information obtained	B. Is method adequate, both in description and for solving problem? In particular: Is it clear what was done? Is the method appropriate, or are there critical omissions resulting from the details of the method used?
III. *Major Findings* Main generalizations based on *this* study's data (Optional but desirable, especially for research reports: graphic material to illustrate findings)	C. How justified are the generalizations comprising the major findings? In particular: Has the subject been changed with respect to the sample? Has the subject been changed with respect to the measurements (using measurement in a broad sense of the term)?
IV. *(Summary and) Implications* (Brief summary of information under other headings. If it does not appear here, place after first or second heading) Disciplined speculation on the broader implications of this study's findings	D. How reasonable are the implications? In particular: Is any background information needed for assessment of the implications missing? Are the arguments (logic) used both as strong and as sound as possible?
V. *(Appendix)* (Details of complex definitions and other kinds of footnote-type material Bibliography Basic data, if research report, at least in some summary form)	

lecting information, will be guided both by trying to choose the best *dt* descriptions to work with from among those possible and by trying to anticipate how you can later develop the most accurate *ds* and *du* descriptions you can.

3.1 PLACE PROBLEM IN PERSPECTIVE: USE WHAT IS KNOWN. As you summarized and evaluated what was known on a topic, you probably tried to fit the information into a coherent picture. Even so, it is a good idea consciously and deliberately to take time to sift what is known and systematically to try to develop a kind of where-we-are-as-of-now model.

For any topic in any discipline, you will likely find that for some parts of the model you develop, there are some good fits, some parts that are virtually blank, some that are fuzzy or ill-defined, and some parts where there are alternate fits possible. When you try to decide on what you should do for your project, then, you look back at the model developed and determine what you think would be the best way to try to *improve* it.

Depending in part on your temperament and in part on what the model looks like, you may decide to try to fill in some of the blank spots, or explore; you may decide to try to make some of the fuzzy portions less so; or you may decide to check some of the proposed fits of the pieces. While it may seem obvious that exploring and surveying level studies can lead to matters that are then in need of testing, it is not at all rare for testing level studies to open areas that need to be explored and surveyed. No one level of study is inherently better than another. All are needed from time to time, if progress is to be made.

As you work the pieces of your model back and forth to see what you might use-

fully do, it is often helpful to try to vary your approach, as suggested in Part I. To refresh your memory briefly, four main variations in approach are commonly used: trial and error; divide and conquer; work on a related but more accessible problem; use analogy.

You might ask yourself questions such as the following, as you work with what is already known and bring your own creative imagination to bear on it. Of the various trial and error possibilities that seem reasonable, which of them have already been explored, and do the results indicate that it might be productive to continue with some of these possibilities, or is it time to move on to other possibilities, and if so, which ones appeal to me? What pieces of the puzzle have already been fitted together and what now remains to be known, and of what remains to be known, which part might I like to fill in? Has existing work raised some questions I would like to answer, and if so can I try to answer them directly, or will I find this too tough and so should I try to work on a more accessible question, and if so, which one? Have analogous problems to one that appeals to me been worked on, and if so can I use either the content or the method to try to make sense of what is already known and to guide me as to what I should try to add by my project? This self-questioning about what you have read and evaluated often can lead to the unexpected and happy discovery of some "key element" or else a new way of looking at the problem, and so enable you to think of a project to do.

A related consideration to aid you in developing your model of the existing state of knowledge about some phenomenon that piqued your interest and got you started trying to find out what is already known about it, is that we are usually concerned with knowing two matters about some phenomenon: What can it account for? What accounts for it? Again, depending both on your temperament and what the model looks like, you may find that you want to work on one of these two halves of the task of understanding what is going on. The four approaches and the kinds of self-questioning suggested in the previous paragraph may, of course, be used to help you for either half.

3.2 INITIAL ANALYSIS PLAN. Now that you have some kind of where-we-are-as-of-now model (or *expl* on the cycle) you need to develop it further (or move to *dt* on the cycle). Any model, or explanation, will carry with it a number of implications. The shorthand reference on the cycle to *dt* covers the host of implications of the various explanations available, and some one or more of the possible *dt* will be what you will focus on to investigate more carefully in your project. How can you find out what these *dt* are? Which should you focus on?

Some of the *dt* may already be in the reports of others, especially in the implications sections of those reports, and some will be developed by you. The stage of moving from *expl* to *dt* is one of those most particularly calling on your imagination and creativity. Here is where you play with various versions of "I wonder what would happen if. . . ." You do some speculating on what would happen if thus and so were true or false; you speculate on what would happen if this or that were changed in some orderly fashion, either increased or decreased or some other systematic variation.

As you might anticipate by now, there are rules and guides for this play. You are engaged in reasoning, or developing arguments in which you use certain proposi-

tions (premises) to justify certain other propositions (conclusions). Deductive arguments, inductive ones, or both, may be used, but their use is guided by the desirability of obtaining strong and sound arguments.

While you are free to consider any premises and conclusions that please you when you begin play, you are limited to ending with those that can be used in adequately strong arguments, or ones in which if the premises are true, it is unlikely that the conclusions would be false. Whatever training and skill you have in the use of reason generally, and in the use of symbolic logic and mathematics in particular, will no doubt be helpful, and difference in this kind of skill from player to player is another of the reasons why some play the game of science better than others.

As far as which consequences should be picked for more detailed consideration, remember that we confirm a possible explanation by eliminating competing ones, and that this is done by checking the consequences (*dt*) of the various explanations against empirical observations. The set of *dt* you manage to wind up with can be thought of as a *sampling* from the set of all possible consequences of the explanations.

In this sample, if you can discover consequences that are not compatible with two or more explanations (and there must be some, otherwise the explanations would not truly be different — the trick is to locate them), each of which seems otherwise promising, then such consequences are likely candidates for investigation. Or, if you can find consequences that are relevant for some facet of the topic that seems important but you feel has not been adequately explored or confirmed so far, then such consequences are likely candidates for you to investigate. And in either case, whenever you are lucky enough to uncover consequences that can confirm or deny *several* explanations, not just one, then you will proceed more efficiently (or make a better move in the game) if you work with one of these consequences.

You are in one of the principal thinking stages of the research process. If your thinking is not done well here, while you are trying to decide what might be worth the effort to investigate it, what specific variables should be used in the investigation and why, as well as how they should be related and why, then the rest of your project will be just that much less useful as a contribution to knowledge. Concentrated thinking can be hard work. So, it never hurts to take some time-and-experience-honored advice: take a break; try.

If you do something else occasionally, and in particular follow the very old advice to "sleep on your problem," you give your unconscious mind a chance to make its contribution. The manner in which your unconscious mind sometimes manages to come up with a needed bright idea is still a mysterious process, to be sure, but giving your unconscious a chance works so often you should take advantage of it. However, both your unconscious and your conscious mind are not likely to come up with bright ideas unless they are engaged in a problem you really care about solving. This is the basis for the advice to *try,* preferably as hard as you can and preferably more than once, with some kind of respite between tries.

Developing an initial analysis plan takes you part of the way along the cycle from *dt* to *do*. Deciding on a basic strategy and deciding on the specific design you will use to collect the observations needed to carry out your analysis plan takes you the rest of the way toward completing an empirical interpretation of your problem.

From among all the variables you think might have some important bearing on your problem, you need to settle on those you will actually use. For each variable picked, an empirical counterpart will be needed, including the categories to be used for each and the specific procedures to be employed to decide when an observation belongs in one category rather than another.

The variables and categories may be vague to begin with, such as high socioeconomic status, or moderately conservative political behavior, or somewhat authoritarian pattern of interaction, or whatever. Eventually, though, you need to be as clear as you can on how such variables as political behavior and such categories as high or somewhat are to be interpreted for your study.

After this, or more likely along with selecting variables, you need to determine which of them will be cross-classified, or related to one another, and how the relationship will be examined. This means you must decide which relationships are of theoretical interest to you, for this study what will constitute an empirical counterpart to them, and what procedures you will use to determine whether and to what extent the relationship is present.

Along the line you should make some decisions about criteria you will use to determine the extent of two kinds of significance. Roughly speaking, one may be called statistical significance, or whether any patterns in the data are "real" rather than due to chance. The other may be called theoretical significance, or whether the patterns "matter." You need to make at least tentative decisions about both.

If the patterns are not due to chance, then they are real in the sense that they probably exist in the parent class as well, while they might be considered illusory if the probability is high that the operation of chance alone in the selection of observations produced the patterns. If the patterns matter, then depending on the level of the study they should fill in a gap in knowledge, or make knowledge more precise, or confirm or indicate that revisions are necessary in some initial tentative explanation.

The set of decisions, then, amounts to preparing an analysis plan. You need to specify what variables you will look at, how you will relate them, how you will try to see the relationships between them, and on what basis you will decide whether what you see is likely to be illusory or not, and if not, whether and how much difference it makes for the problem with which you began.

It is often helpful simply to list as many factors as you can, based on your reading and your disciplined speculation, that you think might be importantly related to your topic. You will not be able to examine everything, and if you try to, you will likely have to do such a superficial job that you will wind up with little more than material for anecdotes. Your task is to do some cutting and narrowing, in order to settle on a list of items that are both important and manageable, and then choose from among them.

Arranging items into clusters of similar ones can usually be done and is often useful, as is even a very rough indication of the form you think relationships might take. Again do some disciplined speculating. For instance, speculate about what would be likely to happen if the items in one cluster were somehow allowed to vary, perhaps increase or decrease. Would there be an increase, or a decrease, or some other systematic pattern of change in other clusters of items, and if so, which ones? About how intense or pronounced do you think

the pattern of change would be, and why?

Rough sketches can help, even some arrows pointing in the direction of supposed change resulting from one or another alteration. Along with this, try to rank order variables and relationships according to relative importance, even if the ranking is far from precise, and then try to decide how many of these you could satisfactorily handle in this specific project. Once this is done, think about the categories you would like to use for your now shortened list of possible variables and relationships.

As you do this thinking, try to settle on which variables will serve as dependent variables and which as independent. That is, if you are tentatively saying A is related to B, how do you want to observe the relationship? Do you want to see what happens to A as B varies or do you want to see what happens to B as A varies?

This amounts to asking whether variation in A is to be accounted for by variation in B, or conversely whether variation in A will be used to account for variation in B. The one you decide to account *for* is termed the dependent variable and the one used to do the accounting *with* becomes the independent variable. Of course, you might want to look both ways in sequence, even in the same study.

For instance, you might let A stand for occupational level and B stand for educational level. Using the *same* set of basic data, you might use each as dependent variable, in sequence. You could examine the percent distribution of occupational levels according to certain educational level categories. Then occupational level (or A) would be your dependent variable and educational level (or B) your independent variable. Or you could look at the percent distribution of educational levels for various occupational categories. Here B is the dependent variable and A is the independent one. While the needed computations would be made slightly differently, the same basic observations could be used. Depending on how much you know about your problem already, variables may be selected to serve as independent or dependent variable only, and not as each in turn. If so, you would analyze only one way rather than both and set up your analysis plans accordingly.

For the illustration just given, each of the variables (occupation and education) would have to be divided into categories and a procedure would have to be set up to decide which concrete observations belong in which categories. Further, a specific way of examining the relationship empirically would have to be determined: in the example, percent distributions were used. And in general, all three items need to be settled: the categories to be used for variables; procedures for placement of observations in particular categories; specification of the empirical way(s) in which the relationships will be examined.

Sketching that kind of diagram called a dummy table (see Exercise I-1) can greatly aid you in clarifying much of this for yourself. In fact, sketching rough diagrams of this sort, tentatively deciding what kinds of patterns might appear in the table and how they could be interpreted, then deciding how feasible it might be to get the information needed to fill in the table, can even aid you in narrowing your list of initial variables you *might* examine to a list of those you feel merit the effort and are practicable for you.

The diagrams can be vague at first, becoming more precise as you sharpen your thinking. Diagrams of this type are not limited to usefulness to studies where you think you might be able to gather quantitative observations. They are pictures of possible relationships between variables —

any kind of variables. The very act of preparing such diagrams and trying to make them more precise seems to make it harder to overlook such questions of theoretical relevance and feasibility as: Which variables should be cross-classified and should the effects of certain ones be looked at singly or should joint classifications be used? Given the resources available for this project, what kinds of compromises seem desirable, such as more detail for a narrower range of items or less detail for a broader range?

In making up and refining your analysis plans, it is always good strategy to decide on the maximum number of cross-classifications and joint-classifications you want to examine. No matter what the level of your study, this is a useful thing to do before collecting information. The degree of precision you achieve may vary, but this prethinking is of great aid in blocking out what you want to observe. Especially in exploratory level studies, where you may not be able to set up in advance anything but rather vague categories for broad variables in your dummy tables, this process helps ensure that you not overlook items you later wish you had noted. You simply cannot observe everything. What you do observe will necessarily be guided by what you think is worthy of note. The more you have forced yourself consciously and deliberately to reflect on this before you are caught up in the sometimes hectic activity of actually carrying out a study, the more useful your observations are likely to be in later analysis.

As with virtually everything else in the research process, setting up analysis plans is guided by both feasibility and relevance. Your aim is to maximize your chances of remaining within the bounds of feasibility — so that you do not wind up with no resources left to complete the project — while minimizing your chances of overlooking pertinent variables, cross-classifications, and joint-classifications. The act of preparing dummy tables with as much precision as you can manage helps. So does examining the tables carefully, speculating on various patterns that might appear when the tables are filled in with collected data, and deciding how you might interpret them. If you do this systematically, you are more likely to collect information useful for your problem and less likely to overlook any revisions (especially on controls needed) that would improve your later possibilities for analysis.

Your plan for analysis should include your criteria for concluding both statistical and theoretical significance. Again, they should be as clear as you can make them, but even rough versions are worthwhile. Thus you need to decide how you will judge that the pattern of observations in your sample is not due to chance and so is statistically significant, or likely to exist in the parent class as well, *and* decide what outline and intensity of pattern must be present in the data for that pattern to matter, or have theoretical significance.

In the illustration given earlier, for instance, how often could some pattern of relationships between education and occupation have occurred by chance in every hundred samples picked in the same way before you would decide the frequency was high enough that you could *not* say the pattern was statistically significant? Once in every hundred times? Ten? Thirty? Somewhere in here you will find yourself thinking that the expected frequency would be low enough that the pattern could be accepted as likely to be present in the parent class, and somewhere you will conclude that the frequency would be too high to justify that inference. Similarly, what shape or general outline would the pattern have

to take and how intensely or pronouncedly shown before you would feel justified in saying it mattered theoretically? Would 90 percent of the units have to fit into the general outline and only 10 percent allowed to deviate from it? Or would 75 percent in the pattern be adequate? How about 55 percent? Again, somewhere in here you will feel the proportion would be high enough for the pattern to matter, and somewhere you will feel the proportion would be so low that the pattern was simply too fuzzy to merit generalization.

One final bit of advice to beginners on selecting a problem and developing an initial analysis plan: Think big when selecting your problem, but think small when settling on a narrowed problem to investigate. You should start out by trying to consider all you can think of that might relate to your topic. Here theoretical relevance is your prime guide. But when you settle on a specific narrowed problem, you need to worry about feasibility. For instance, you might be trying to account for leisure time usage, and so your dependent variables would have to do with this usage. As independent variables you might select from socioeconomic status, family structure, extent of geographic mobility, religious commitment, age, sex, or whatever, and look at some joint as well as separate effects. That is, your independent variables might be many and complex. Or, you might take just socioeconomic status as an independent variable and attempt to see its effects on several areas of life, such as political behavior, family organization, religious behavior, and the like. That is, your dependent variables might be many and complex. In general, a good strategy for a beginner is to have either the independent or the dependent variables, but *not both,* be complex.

4. Complete Plan for Investigation

So far you have achieved part of an empirical interpretation (or "operational-ization") for your theoretical problem. By now you have narrowed the problem that you want to investigate and that is related to a particular portion of the basic puzzle.

Through a series of interdependent steps, you should have settled on the level of your study, on the variables and relation-ships involved, including the categories for the variables and how the relationships will be examined, and on the general cri-teria you intend to employ in determining both the statistical and theoretical signifi-cance of your results. Now that your prob-lem has been narrowed this far, you need to complete its empirical interpretation by completing a plan for collecting concrete observations.

You need to decide on your basic strat-egy: cross-sectional or longitudinal. Then you need to decide on your design, or the details of your strategy. You need to be concerned with controls and sample selec-tion, as well as the source of your observa-tions and the form they will be in. To make the decisions needed in this phase of completing your plan for investigation, you need to be aware of (a) the usual op-tions available to you for each decision, (b) the general merits and demerits of each option, and (c) some typical practical diffi-culties likely to be encountered. Finally, you need to decide how you will allocate your resources for this project, that is, how you will apportion whatever time, money, personnel, and equipment you have avail-able for it. Then you will be ready to move on to the second portion of the research process.

As the poet Robert Burns reminded us some time ago, even the "best-laid schemes of mice and men gang aft agley." But if you try to be as clear as you can on what you want to do and on how you want to do it, then when you encounter occasional and largely unpredictable difficulties along the way to actually doing it — which seems to be a universal and possibly inevitable experience — your responses to them are less likely to resemble either random, rat-like movements or those of a cornered member of any species.

4.1 BASIC STRATEGY. A state description gives the state of affairs as of one period of time, while a process description de-scribes the process of change between at least two periods. Making a process de-scription typically requires more effort. For a process description you not only need at least two state descriptions but you also need a description of the change between them. To achieve a state description you use a cross-sectional strategy, while to achieve a process description you use a longitudinal strategy.

In order to decide which you want to make, you should be aware of the kinds and strength of possible generalizations based on cross-sectional versus longitudinal strategies in light of the basic puzzle of science: to explain why events occur and change as they do, with that explanation expressed in terms of necessary conditions, sufficient ones, or possibly both. So the task comes down to judging how well cross-sectional versus longitudinal observations can provide information on the *nature* of any associations found, that is, whether they represent necessary, sufficient, both, or neither relationships. Balancing this judgment against a judgment of the feasibility of doing whatever is needed to obtain one or the other kind of observations leads to your final choice. You need to know the options available to you and their limitations in order to make the first judgment, and you need to be aware of some typical practical difficulties associated with each option in order to make the second judgment.

Cross-sectional observations can be obtained according to several designs. The simplest situation consists of observations on a single case at one point in time.

Suppose you select a case of some type which interests you, say a rapidly growing city or an obviously successful industrial organization, or whatever. Let us call what interests you, and hence the reason you selected that case, an "effect" and symbolize it by E. You want to know what conditions are associated with E and what the nature of the association is. Using small letters of the alphabet to symbolize conditions, your observation of the single case might be shown as:

$$a, b, c, d \text{ ------} E$$

What kinds of generalizations can you make, using this observation to base them on? You can legitimately say that at some point in time a, b, c, and d were associated with E, but that's about all you can say. For none of the conditions can you legitimately say the association is *merely* accidental, i.e., neither necessary nor sufficient, or that it is *not* accidental. You can say an association exists, but you can say little about its nature for any of the conditions coexisting with the effect.

Now let us take another cross-sectional possibility, this time somewhat stronger as far as what you can say when you are through. Suppose this time you observe at least two cases, each having E present. Now symbolization might be:

$$a, b, c, d \text{ ------} E$$
$$b, f, g \quad \text{ ------} E$$

Two conclusions are possible, one much weaker than the other. The stronger conclusion is that none of the factors a, c, d, f, or g can be necessary for E. This conclusion is based on the first basic principle of elimination cited in Part I: No condition can be necessary for something if it is absent when that something is present.

For the first case above, the effect is present but f and g are not and so cannot be necessary for E. (There is still the possibility that one or both might be sufficient for E rather than just accidentally related, but at least from the information you have you can state definitely that they are not necessary.) Similarly, a, c, and d cannot be necessary, because the effect was present in the second case and they were absent.

All but one of the conditions have been shown not necessary for the effect. The one left, b, seems more promising now, since so far it has not been eliminated, but the legitimate conclusion possible is still weak: b and E occur together. But one cannot conclude much from knowing only that an association exists: The relationship *might* be a necessary one, *might* be a sufficient one, or *might* even be accidental. Further information is needed to decide anything about the nature of the association.

Before going on to the kinds of additional information needed to generalize about the nature of an association, let us first consider the kind of cross-sectional design needed to eliminate conditions as far as their being sufficient. Now the second principle of elimination is used: No condition can be sufficient for something if that something is absent when the condition is present.

Now you need to observe at least two cases of the same general type, but this time one case where the effect is present and another case where it is absent. In symbolic form:

$$m, n, o, p \text{ ------} E$$
$$\not{m}, n, o, p \text{ ------} \not{E}$$

(where the diagonal through a symbol means "is absent")

Two conclusions are again possible and again one is stronger, or can be stated in more definite terms, than the other. The weaker conclusion is the same as in the preceding situation except that m is substituted for b. The stronger conclusion is that none of the other conditions, n, o, or p, is sufficient for E, since they were present in the second case yet the effect did not occur. While it is now somewhat more probable that m is importantly and not merely accidentally related to E, any conclusion about m is still weak, statable only in might-be terms. Further information would be needed to decide the nature of the association between m and E.

The design conformed to in the first situation is known as Mill's Method of Agreement and that in the second as Mill's Method of Difference. The man whose name these carry is John Stuart Mill, a man of considerable and varied talents who lived in the Victorian era. Note that Agreement is most efficiently used when the cases *differ* except for one condition and Difference when the cases are the *same,* or matched, except for one condition.

Perhaps it has occurred to you that still stronger than using Agreement or Difference only would be to use the two in sequence. This procedure is known as Mill's Joint Method (of Agreement and Differ-

ence). Using the Method of Agreement may enable you to say some conditions are not necessary. They still might be sufficient or accidental. If you can then set up a Method of Difference to show they are not sufficient either, then they must be accidental and can be discarded from further consideration. Nonetheless, even with this more efficient procedure for elimination, any conclusion about associations between *none*liminated factors and the effect is still weak, in the sense already noted. Further information would be needed to decide on the nature of an association which, given only the knowledge that it exists, might be necessary, sufficient, or accidental.

Still on a cross-sectional basis, variations are possible. Instead of dealing with conditions or effects that can only be said to be present or absent, or "attributes," common possibilities are that the conditions or the effects or both can vary, or be present in differing amounts or intensity. (To cement the idea, for an individual being pregnant is an attribute: one is never "a little bit" pregnant. But for a community, the proportion of pregnant inhabitants is a variable: the proportion can vary between the theoretical limits of 0 and 100 percent.)

Two means of eliminating items can be used, depending on whether you have situations where the effect varies while the conditions remain constant or whether the conditions vary while the effect remains constant. (The procedures used are subsumed under the name, Mill's Method of Concomitant Variation.) In the first, you eliminate on the basis that something that varies cannot be accounted for by things that remain the same. In the second, you eliminate on the basis that something that stays the same cannot be accounted for by things that vary. More generally stated, a constant cannot account for or be accounted for by a variable.

Just as in the preceding cases involving attributes, the stronger conclusion has to do with those factors eliminated. The weaker conclusion has to do with any conditions exhibiting a *systematic* pattern of variation along with variation in the effect. A few examples of such patterns might be: as one increases so does the other (called "direct" correlation or covariation); as one increases the other decreases (called "inverse" correlation); as one increases the other increases for a while and then remains constant or else decreases. The conclusion is weak because it can only state that the association revealed by the systematic pattern *might* be in the nature of necessity or sufficiency but it also might be accidental.

As we have seen, generalizations from cross-sectional observations are weak as far as what they can legitimately say about the nature of any associations *not* eliminated on the basis of one or another principle of elimination. To say anything about the nature of the association requires further information, so let us see whether longitudinal observations can provide that information. It turns out that under certain conditions they can, and depending on those conditions, can more or less strongly support — although not prove — generalizations about the nature of an association.

Recall that in discussing applications of knowledge of necessary and sufficient conditions in Part I, I stated that if a condition is truly necessary, removing it must thereby *prevent* the effect from occurring. If a condition is truly sufficient, inserting it must *guarantee* the effect's occurrence.

Suppose you again observe two sets of cases but now you observe at more than one point in time, or use a longitudinal strategy. In particular, suppose that when you observe at the earlier point *both* sets show whatever effect you are interested in and the cases are the same, or homogeneous, as far as conditions present at that point. Further suppose that when you observe at a later point in time one set still shows the effect but the other does not, and for the set not now showing the effect one of the conditions present earlier is now absent. If nothing else relevant has happened in the meantime (an assumption essential for the logic involved, but often very difficult to actually meet) then the conclusion is fairly strong that the condition present for the first observations and absent for the second is a necessary condition for the effect. (Of course, if the condition is absent later and there is no change in the effect then the first principle of elimination applies and you can state definitely that the condition must *not* have been necessary.)

As far as sufficient conditions, suppose you again observe two sets of cases for at least two periods of time. In particular, suppose that when first observed the cases are homogeneous but *neither* shows the effect of interest. When observed later, one set now shows the effect while the other still does not and an additional factor is now present for those cases showing the effect and absent for the others. Again, if nothing else relevant has happened, the conclusion is fairly strong. This time the conclusion is that the added condition is sufficient for the effect.

Notice that for each of the above what we have is a longitudinal version of Mill's Method of Difference. The cases start out the same, one thing changes, and the cases end up different. This longitudinal version gives us more strongly based conclusions about the nature of associations than did the cross-sectional strategies.

If we call the set of cases to which something happens the "experimental" or manipulated group, the set left alone the "control" or comparison group, and the something done (whether adding or removing some condition) a "stimulus" then we can use the *same* diagram to symbolize either situation, as shown below.

	Stimulus	
	Before	After
Experimental group	a	b
Control group	c	d

(where a, b, c, d stand for observations made)

Keep in mind that whatever strategy is used, we aim at answering the question: Is some condition (or "stimulus") importantly related to some effect? This amounts to trying to answer two questions as accurately as we can:

1. Can the difference between the before and after observations (that is, $[b - a]$ minus $[d - c]$) be attributed to the stimulus or could some *alternative* interpretation be true, namely that the difference results from some other stimulus?
2. Does the difference reflect a difference actually present in the parent class or could some *alternative* interpretation be true, namely that the difference is due to chance and is not present in the parent class?

Answering the first question depends on the kind of *ds* description that can legitimately be made; answering the second depends on the kind of *du* description that can legitimately be made. Whether or not the answer to the first question contains

an adequate discounting of the alternative interpretation depends on a number of matters having to do with *controls*. Whether or not the answer to the second question contains an adequate discounting of the alternative interpretation depends largely on the *sampling* procedures used to select observations from the parent class. And in either case an adequate answer rests on having all four kinds of observations available: before and after for the experimental group; before and after for the control group.

One way of judging strategies, then, would be to check which of the four cells, if any, does not contain actual observations but instead must be filled in by using more or less imagination. But having all four cells contain actual observations is not enough for us to feel confident in a generalization that some stimulus is importantly related to some effect. Some other matters, having to do with sampling and controls, must be considered. We would like to be sure that the following are true:

a. An adequate sample of cases was obtained to begin with.
b. The full set of cases for the before observations is the same as the set for the after observations, so that we do not have a situation where we started out with a representative sample but ended with a biased one.
c. The experimental and control groups really are the "same" to begin with.
d. It is clear what the stimulus is, and it is clear that it was applied only to the experimental group.
e. Nothing else relevant happened to either group except the stimulus.

An ideal strategy, then, would be one for which all four cells in the basic design are filled in with actual observations and for which conditions *a* through *e* above were met. Keeping in mind this "ideal" strategy that we would like to achieve, let us now turn to a discussion of various kinds of cross-sectional and longitudinal strategies commonly used. Then we will turn to controls and sampling in more detail.

4.11 Cross-sectional. Various cross-sectional designs are employed in practice. They all have in common that no more than one set of observations is available on either the experimental or control group. The usual possibilities are illustrated below, and I have given labels to them to facilitate the discussion. Solid lines are used for the observations actually obtained and dashed lines for those that must be filled in with imagination.

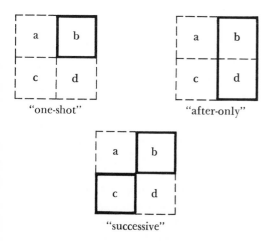

"one-shot"   "after-only"

"successive"

Let me begin with some examples and then draw some general conclusions. Suppose you drew the inference that all viable bureaucracies must show a certain pattern of division of labor, or form of organization of roles within the bureaucracy. You would be claiming that the particular pattern of division of labor is a necessary condition for a bureaucracy to continue to

operate at all and want to check whether your guess is correct.

You might try to use a one-shot design to do this checking. If the pattern is not present in the bureaucracies studied, you would either have to revise your guess somehow (perhaps that the pattern is not necessary, but is sufficient) or else replace it completely and look for something else to account for successfully functioning bureaucracies. But on the other hand, if your guess *is* consistent with the cross-sectional evidence, you are not really much further ahead than when you began your study. From cross-sectional results it might be that you are correct and the association is a necessary one. However, it might be that you are wrong and the association present is either one of sufficiency or else truly accidental.

Suppose you had been able to use an appropriate longitudinal design and observe what happened to the functioning of the bureaucracy when the pattern of division of labor was altered in some way. Then you may be better able to decide on the nature of the association shown. Potentially, you could either have negative evidence (which the cross-sectional study could give you too, if you are in fact wrong) or else you could have positive evidence that the nature of the association is as you say it is (which the cross-sectional study could *not* give you, if you are in fact right).

As an example of an after-only design, suppose you made a study of college seniors in a large metropolitan area and of young adults of comparable age in a small rural area who had not attended college. Suppose the results showed the college seniors to be more "liberal" (as measured by degree of concern with civil rights, problems of poverty, and the like) and you concluded that a college education produced the greater liberality. Possibly so, but possibly the two groups were inherently different to begin with and *neither* has shown any real change. It might well be urban versus rural culture, or the greater initiative and social awareness required to secure a college education (or ? ?) that is "responsible."

To stay with a college-related example, a successive design might be used to make observations of a sample of college freshmen four years ago and a different sample of college seniors now, concluding that any difference is solely the result of completing college. Possibly, but just possibly conditions occurring in the country at large and having no necessary relationship to getting a college education might account for any difference observed.

In general, when you decide to use a one-shot design, your best bet is to come as close as you can to a Mill's Method of Agreement. This means you want to observe more than just one case of whatever interests you and you would like the cases to be as heterogeneous, or unlike each other, as possible. Then when you examine them carefully you may be able to eliminate some factors as not being necessary. That way you can at least narrow the field of possibilities, even though any conclusions you might draw about factors not eliminated would be weak if you try to make claims about the nature of the associations left.

When you use an after-only design, your best bet is to try to approximate Mill's Method of Difference cross-sectionally. Again, you need more than one case, but this time you would like them to be as homogeneous, or like each other, as possible except that one shows the effect and the other does not. Then you may be able to eliminate some factors as not being

sufficient, although your conclusions about the nature of the associations not eliminated would be weak.

A successive design is an attempt to cross-sectionally approximate that kind of longitudinal design called a panel study (see next section). The before observations on the control group are used as proxy for what you hope the before observations for the experimental group were like. As with the other cross-sectional versions you are forced to use more or less imagination to fill in the missing cells.

All cross-sectional versions have a common limitation, then, that no matter how well-designed the other parts to the study might be certain cells are inherently missing, by the nature of the strategy picked. Therefore, it is risky to talk about any actual "differences," let alone to what particular stimulus they might be attributable. Reminding yourself to ask the question about whether the method used is appropriate to the problem should enable you to spot in the reports of others which cells are in fact missing and so must be filled in with imagination. Remembering to ask whether the researcher has changed the subject should help you spot how well he is aware of any limitations imposed because of the strategy he picked.

To summarize, using one or another of Mill's Methods cross-sectionally we may be able to eliminate some factors as far as their being necessary or sufficient, but any statements about the associations left are weak. All we can say is that there *is* an association, but we can say nothing legitimately about the kind of association it is. And this is the best that *any* cross-sectional design, no matter how ideally carried out otherwise, can do for us. We cannot conclude, at least with much strength to the argument, anything about the nature of the association unless we have an adequate longitudinal design. What we can say then depends on whether the stimulus was added or removed.

Cross-sectional designs, despite their obvious limitations, are very common. It is not certain whether this is because of questions of feasibility, real or imagined, or because researchers are not consciously enough aware of how much they *are* filling in with imagination when they make their later generalizations.

4.12 Longitudinal without control group. Again using solid lines for those cells containing actual observations and dashed lines for those filled in by using imagination, another alteration of the desired design can be shown as below.

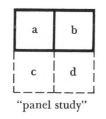

"panel study"

Designs involving repeated observations are often termed panel studies, but I would like to reserve the term for longitudinal observations of just one group, not both the experimental and control groups. You could take a single case and observe it through time, or you could take repeated interviews of the same group as a national election draws near, and so on.

Any kind of panel study (as the term is used here), no matter how well done it might otherwise be, shares the same limitation. While you do have more than one observation of the same group and so may be able to say a real change has occurred — you are not misled by possibly having ob-

served inherently different groups, as might be the case for some cross-sectional designs — you are not in a strong position to attribute the change to some presumed stimulus. Without observations on a control or comparison group, you cannot be sure that the change would not have occurred anyway, even if the stimulus you have focused on were absent. In other words, you may be able to say a change actually did occur, but not why.

Panel studies may be either prospective or retrospective. All prospective studies share certain practical difficulties, as do retrospective studies. Prospective studies begin at some point in time and move forward to collect information, while retrospective studies begin at some point in time and move backward. As far as limitations on any generalizations made, if the other conditions are met for a design to be of a particular type (such as a panel study or a comparative method version of longitudinal with control group), whether a version is prospective or retrospective makes little logical difference. Whatever basic limitations there are for the type will be present, prospectively or retrospectively. But there are some differences in the practical difficulties likely to be encountered in trying to fill in the cells with data.

Major prospective difficulties can be termed (1) losses and (2) possible alteration of behavior solely because of the details of the method used in investigation. In shorthand form, the latter problem is sometimes referred to as measurement effect.

Under losses are included any factors resulting in the full set of cases for the before observations not being the full set of cases for the after observations. For humans, this includes death, migration, and refusals as main sources of loss of cases.

You can hope that death is a random process affecting cases with equal likelihood, and can do some checking to see whether this seems to be true. Hopefully, its effect could then be discounted. If migration may be a problem you can try to build in ways to trace people, which is often difficult but not impossible. This leaves refusals.

It helps to have well-trained personnel, of course, because if people suspect that the researcher or his employees do not know what they are doing, then they may no longer cooperate as subjects or they may refuse to allow you access to information needed to complete your after observations. This is just another of the many reasons leading to the general guide that it is always good strategy to plan your study as well as you can.

But the best way to minimize losses from refusals is to have a good rationale for doing the study in the first place, and an adequate and understandable statement of that rationale. You should bear in mind that you are not likely to have a great deal to offer in tangible exchange for cooperation in your research. In return for imposing on people, primarily all you can offer is the satisfaction of knowing they are participating in a worthwhile contribution to knowledge, and it is your job to convince them that this is the case. If you cannot, then perhaps it is only just that you should encounter refusals along the way.

Under possible alteration of behavior is subsumed the problem that the very act of taking observations or measurements may alter the behavior you want to observe. Your task becomes one of trying to see if you can find out how much the measurement effect is, minimize it if you can, and if not adjust your generalizations accordingly.

To use a non–social science example, the act of inserting a thermometer into a liquid to take its temperature will either cool or warm the liquid by some amount, depending on the instrument's temperature relative to the liquid's. In medicine, it is not unknown for dramatic recovery to occur when the patient has been given a placebo (such as a sugar pill, or more likely a bitter-tasting one!) but thinks he has been given medicine. Chimpanzees are known to behave differently sometimes when they are aware they are being observed than when they are not so aware. People may be on their "best behavior" if they know they are being studied, and so on.

As far as retrospective versions of longitudinal designs are concerned, the main problem is adequacy of prior information. If you want data about past events, you must rely either on existing records or on people's memories about past events when asked questions about them.

We know that people remember selectively, not necessarily for nefarious reasons. Some aspect you are interested in, or even the entire event, may not have seemed important enough at the time to be remembered. If you are aware of this possibility, you may be able to design the way you ask questions to place the event in context or lead back to it in a manner to jog memory and aid recall. Or you may simply have to settle for less detail than you would like, and adjust your generalizations accordingly.

Analogously, records are maintained for various purposes and these earlier purposes may not have involved information collecting on events you care about. Not only may items be obviously missing, there is the related problem that definitions of what is included under some heading may change. To take one example, the United States Census has long collected data on urban places, but the definition of what is included under the rubric "urban" has changed on occasion, sometimes substantially. Watch for footnotes, and read them carefully!

I mention these several kinds of difficulties to illustrate that if you are aware of common problems you can try to plan to minimize them. If you cannot minimize them, then you have an obligation to allow for them when trying to discount possible alternative interpretations of your results.

4.13 Longitudinal with control group. For these designs, all four cells are filled in with observations. Since there are no missing cells, the diagram is like that shown for an "ideal" strategy in an earlier section. If you are able to find naturally occurring cases for the four cells, then the term "comparative method" can be given to the design. On the other hand, if you were able to form the cases and determine whether or not some factor would be added or removed, then the term "experiment" is used for the design. The difference hinges on whether the situations were deliberately manipulated by the researcher or whether any addition or removal of conditions occurred outside the researcher's control. In either case, the reasoning involved is the same.

For example, it is unlikely you could deliberately run a freeway through some but not the rest of a set of matched communities and then observe the differences that result. In other words, it is unlikely that you could do an experiment here.

But if you were able to find communities with the same population size and industrial base (or whatever else you thought communities should be matched on), and learned that a freeway was planned for construction through the centers of some of the communities and not through the others you might try to set up a prospective comparative method design. You could try

to observe now some aspect of community organization in all the communities and observe again after the freeway has gone through some of them. If nothing else important happened, such as some industry deciding to locate major branch plants in the communities scheduled to be bisected by a freeway — or in the other communities, for that matter — then you could fairly strongly conclude that differences in organization at the later point could be accounted for by the freeway.

Comparative method designs can be either prospective or retrospective, while experiments can only be prospective. This characteristic of comparative method can be of great advantage, since many of the phenomena of interest to science have already occurred, or at least their "before" state has.

In comparative method designs, you *find* your cases as they occur naturally, while in experiments you *form* your cases into manipulated and comparison groups, either by setting up cases initially matched according to one or another selected control or by randomly assigning some to the experimental and some to the control group, and then doing something to the experimental group only. If the various matters of sampling and adequate controls can be solved for either version of the longitudinal with control group strategy, the generalizations should be founded on quite acceptable evidence. There should be no limitations because of missing cells, as in the cross-sectional and longitudinal without control group designs. Hence there are not problems because you might be observing inherently different groups and so could not say any real change occurred, or because control group observations are missing and so you would be limited as far as saying why any change occurred.

On the practical level, this may turn out

to be a big if. For comparative method versions, the main problem seems to be not to run out of cases that occur naturally and can be satisfactorily matched for the before observations. Further, depending on whether a prospective or retrospective comparative method is used, different ones of the practical difficulties discussed in the preceding section have to be faced: losses, measurement effect, adequacy of prior information. Experiments are always prospective, so only the first two of these are likely to cause difficulty. However, experiments have certain practical difficulties of their own.

Experiments can be roughly subdivided into laboratory and field types. In either type, you should be able to form cases into experimental and control groups and should have control over the insertion or removal of factors serving as the stimulus.

Especially in the social sciences, laboratory experiments are sometimes criticized as being artificial. Artificiality in two ways is meant. On the one hand operationalization of variables and relationships may have unusually limited theoretical relevance and so be "artificial" and on the other hand the setting may be considered artificial.

By the time a concept such as conformity or delinquency has been empirically interpreted in a form that can be handled in the laboratory, theoretical relevance may not be as close as one would wish. Nor do human groups exist in isolation. They always have some kind of social as well as physical environment, and the kinds of other groups with which a group is normally in interaction may affect its behavior. Yet in most laboratory situations the units are frequently treated as though they do exist in isolation. These problems of artificiality may be minimized somewhat if the researcher is aware of them, and so I would

class them as difficulties rather than out-and-out limitations on the generalizations that can be made.

Field experiments are typically able to overcome these artificiality problems, but they have difficulties of their own. Seldom is one allowed to assign human beings arbitrarily to one or another group and then do something to one but not the other. Thus, most field experiments tend to be done with groups that are in some sense captive populations. They may be persons who have forfeited some of the normal civil rights, such as delinquents or persons in one or another medical or correctional institution for treatment. Or else the "powers that be" — government, employers, instructors, or whatever — have decided that those over whom they have some control will participate. If the groups are not captive in these ways, then considerable persuasion may have to be used to obtain enough cases (such as the field trials of the Salk polio vaccine), and the usual researcher may find this beyond his resources to achieve.

Where accomplished, however, such as some of the experiments with delinquents where the researchers could exercise control over which of the delinquents would be assigned some treatment and what it would be, or some of the learning experiments with students, the field version does manage to overcome the artificiality cited for the laboratory version. For example, the operationalization of delinquent would have close theoretical relevance — persons societally accused and "convicted" of delinquency — as it has not been given an empirical interpretation which alters the concept almost beyond recognition.

Experiments are always prospective, of course. The cases are formed by the researcher and he controls the kind and extent of the stimulus to be applied following the before observations. A number of versions of basic experimental design (which is seldom used in the simple four-celled version because other experimental designs are so much more efficient) have been developed, and some are intended to help solve the problem of how to discount measurement effect.

I will describe only two, to illustrate what might be done if you are aware of this possible difficulty: two-control-group design; double-blind design. If you go on to become a producer of scientific knowledge you will need to become familiar with a variety of useful techniques, such as refinements of basic designs, in much more depth than I can provide on this introductory level. If you remain solely a consumer of scientific knowledge, as is likely true of many of you, then I think these two brief illustrations will suffice to stress that you should be aware not only that measurement effect may be a problem, but that it is not necessarily insurmountable and so you should look for and evaluate the ways in which a researcher states he has tried to overcome it.

One way of deciding how much is measurement effect and how much is stimulus effect is to begin with three similar groups, one to serve as experimental group and two as controls. Take before measurements on only two of these, the experimental group and control group I. Apply the stimulus. Then take after measurements, but this time on all three groups. The rationale is that the difference in the after measurements for control groups I and II can be attributed to measurement alone and subtracted from the difference between the before and after measurements for control group I. Then this result is compared with the difference between the before and after measurements for the experimental group and the remainder attributed to the

stimulus. The accompanying diagram may help.

	Before	*After*
Experimental	a	b
Control I	c	d
Control II	—	f

(where a, b, c, d, f are observations)

Based on the diagram,

$(d - f) =$ measurement effect

$(d - c) - (d - f) =$ change in control group that is not due to measurement effect, and let us call the result Y

$(b - a) =$ change in experimental group, and let us call the result X

$(X - Y) =$ stimulus effect

A double-blind design is a way of trying to minimize some common difficulties under the broad heading of measurement effect, and can be used with a two-control-group or some other version of experimental design. In a double-blind design, often used in medical tests of the effect of some treatment, neither the person making the immediate observations nor the subjects know which receive the stimulus and which do not.

The rationale here is that not only may the subjects behave differently if they know they have been given, say, a placebo rather than a drug, but the observer may consciously or unconsciously have certain expectations of behavior alteration because of the drug and so his observations may not be as impartial as they should be. This latter problem, incidentally, is one of the reasons why scientists try to substitute nonhuman measuring instruments whenever possible (and to calibrate carefully and do periodic quality checks on those instruments). An electrocardiogram, for example, is simply likely to give more reliable results — let alone be more sensitive to small differences in heart action — than the average doctor, with or without a stethoscope.

Any way in which the act of taking observations might alter the observed behavior can be put under the heading "measurement effect." Thus, these problems may exist for any study, not just those employing some version of experimental design. Recall, for instance, the rationale for why it was important for you to be unobtrusive when collecting your observations for Exercise I-2. Research workers using experiments were among the first, however, to try to develop specific ways to discount the difficulty rather than pretend it was not there or hope it was not important. Some of the logic used by them to adjust to the problem might profitably be adapted, I think, by workers using other designs.

4.2 CONTROLS AND SAMPLE SELECTION. Broadly speaking, controls include all procedures used to try to produce accurate descriptions of patterns in your sample (*ds* descriptions), in the sense that both the arguments employed to justify your interpretation and those employed to eliminate alternative interpretations to yours are as strong and sound as possible. Sampling procedures are chosen in accord with trying to produce *du* descriptions, in the same sense of the term "accuracy" as just given for *ds* descriptions.

An accurate *ds* description would mean for an exploratory or reconnoitering level study that the associations you say are present at all, are, and their nature is as you say it is; for a surveying or reconnaissance level study, that the pervasiveness of the association and the variation in its patterns under varying circumstances are as you say they are; for a testing level study, that whether the test indicates that the initial explanation is confirmed and that the extent and nature of that confirmation are thus-and-so, *or* that revisions are needed in the initial explanation and the nature and extent of the revisions are thus-and-so, is as you say it is.

The logic underlying the four-celled basic design and the conditions we would like to be able to meet in addition to having all four cells filled in, discussed in an earlier section, is more or less explicitly used in the reasoning involved in claims for a study made at any level. Whenever you say you have examined one or more units of a certain type and found a certain kind of association to be present, you are making three interrelated subclaims:

1. What you have studied is in fact an instance of that certain type and so is both homogeneous with other units of the type and distinct from units of other types.
2. The association is as you have described it and not of some other kind, nor is it present in *all types* of units (otherwise your generalization would border on being empty).
3. Something is accounting for the presence of the observed association, although your speculation about what the something is and how it accounts for the association may be more or less vague and tentative.

In terms of the basic strategy desired, 3 has to do with identifying the stimulus, 2 with the effect, and 1 with the separation of units into experimental and comparison groups. Reconnoitering level studies tend to emphasize part 1 of the general claim more heavily, reconnaissance level studies tend to emphasize detailing part 2, and testing level studies tend to emphasize part 3, but all three parts are contained   to some degree in the *ds* descriptions always present in a study on any level. And controls are needed to justify each part.

For instance, suppose from an exploratory study you conclude that a particular pattern of child rearing is present in a family you studied, which was of matriarchal type. The kind of generalization at least implicit in your conclusion is that the pattern of child rearing is not present in all types of families and that something connected with the matriarchal form of the family is responsible for this pattern. You have isolated an association. The "something" may be common to families with characteristics other than matriarchy and the pattern of child rearing may vary in detail according to economic status or other conditions. Also, you may or may not be able to say much about whether this something is necessary or sufficient for the pattern. But these are matters which following studies on other levels can clarify more than you were able to in your exploratory one.

If we carefully examine your conclusion, we can see that for it to be justified, controls or certain kinds of procedures were needed. First, you are concluding that you did manage to pick a family for study, which means you needed rules or procedures for selecting families, or selecting units which were the "same" to begin with. Second, you are concluding that you were able to determine that the family was a matriarchal one, which means you needed procedures for determining which families among all families are matriarchal and perhaps even procedures for determining the amount of matriarchy. In other words, you needed procedures for determining the kind and extent of the stimulus ("matriarchy"). Third, you needed procedures to ensure that the pattern of child rearing is present as you say it is, or procedures to

ensure an accurate measurement of the effect.

Thus for your conclusion to be justified, you needed controls or procedures for ensuring that the experimental and control groups were the same to begin with, or homogeneous in all relevant aspects, for determining what the stimulus was, and for ensuring that nothing else relevant except the stimulus occurred in the meantime so that you could decide the effect *is* attributable to the stimulus.

Let us take one other example, this time for a testing level study. Suppose you try some new treatment for a disease and the recovery rate seems to be quite high. Before deciding the treatment should be immediately tried on everyone with the disease you should be concerned about controls. If the treatment is to be considered truly effective, then you want to be sure it is the treatment and not something else that is responsible for recovery.

You would want answers to questions such as the following. What percentage would have recovered when treated by the usual method or left alone? Were the patients mainly young adults, or did most of them have just mild cases of the disease, or was the disease present only in early stages, or were there any other characteristics of the patients that might influence the recovery rate? Was the treatment the same for all patients or did it differ on such items as the dosage of any drugs given or the length of time the treatment was applied or the presence of any other ameliorative measures besides the treatment of interest?

Age could be controlled by looking at recovery rates within each of the categories used to group people of similar ages. Severity of the disease could be controlled analogously, and you would likely decide that a joint classification, or controlling on both age and severity simultaneously, would be even better.

Note that you could apply these controls in advance by selecting your groups appropriately. Or, if you had data on enough patients covering the necessary ranges of characteristics, you could apply the controls later, by manipulating your information to divide patients into the appropriate categories and examine the results.

To aid in isolating how much of the effect is attributable to a particular stimulus, you need to decide how to pick one or more groups to serve as comparisons and decide in what sense they do not receive the stimulus and nothing else relevant happens. For the example, your control group will be patients with similar initial characteristics to the treated ones. But should they be left alone or should they be given the usual method of treatment or should they be given some lower dosage or shorter version of the treatment you are investigating or should all these and perhaps even other "comparison groups" be used? That is, in what sense is the comparison group(s) to be "left alone" and the stimulus given only to the experimental group(s)? Note that depending on how you set up your analysis plans, you could use a series of groups, each serving as "experimental" group in turn, with the remainder as controls. Obviously, this would usually be much more efficient than just the simple four-celled situation given in the basic diagram. The logic is still the same, however, as that given in the discussion of the basic diagram.

All attempts to ensure the accuracy of *ds* descriptions of observations made are attempts to achieve as adequate controls as possible. In a broader sense, the accuracy of the descriptions includes both reliability and validity. Reliability means that repe-

titions in comparable circumstances give comparable results, while validity means that the empirical results do correspond to whatever is of interest theoretically.

The conclusion that an observational procedure is reliable is a prerequisite for the conclusion that an observational procedure leads to valid results. In terms that should be amply familiar by now, reliability is a necessary but not a sufficient condition for validity.

Although in itself often not easy, finding evidence that satisfactorily (i.e., strongly and soundly) justifies conclusions about reliability is usually far and away easier than to do so for conclusions about validity. Each kind of conclusion is justified, if at all, through other observations.

Repeating entire projects or particular measurement procedures (using measurement in a very broad sense), then observing and describing the results, is used to check reliability. For instance, independent observers should get comparable results when they use the same set of rules for assigning units to one or another category. Making predictions about situations and consequences not yet examined, whether they occur in the future or the past, examining them and describing the results, is used to try to check validity. That is, the results from an observational procedure should vary in an *orderly* way with related observations.

For example, the "scratch test" is one way to determine the hardness of materials: If one material can scratch the other but not vice versa, then the first is the harder. This procedure gives reliable results, in that independent observers customarily agree. But unless the results could also be related in an orderly way to other kinds of information, such as measures of the rate of erosion of one or another material, it would be questionable whether the scratch test procedure was valid as well, and not just reliable.

So far in this section we have been concerned with adequate controls, in order to ensure that *ds* descriptions made will be as justified as possible. Now we turn to adequate sample selection, to help ensure making justified *du* descriptions.

Only a portion, or sample, of all relevant observations of the same type, or universe or parent class, can ever really be observed. Yet it is the appropriate universe we want to generalize to and describe. It is these *du* descriptions that comprise what is to be accounted for in our explanations. The task, with *du* as with *ds* descriptions, is to ensure accuracy in the sense noted before. The arguments used to justify your interpretation, or *du* description, and the related arguments used to justify eliminating alternative interpretations should be as strong and as sound as possible. Here you particularly want to discount the interpretation that your *du* description is not warranted because you had an inadequate sample of observations.

Some sampling design is involved in any study at any level, although it may be more or less implicitly stated in a published report and perhaps even in the mind of the researcher who prepared the report. Of course, the more consciously used a sampling design is, the more likely a researcher is to be aware of the implications of the procedures he actually employed and to adjust his generalizations. Otherwise, he is likely to be guilty of some changes of subject, and his report correspondingly devalued.

Several sampling options are possible. As always, your choice between options should be influenced both by theoretical considerations, or what you would like to achieve, and by feasibility considerations, or how close to this it is practical for you

to come. Sample designs are judged according to the likelihood that the *procedures* used in selecting items yield samples that are likely to reflect adequately the parent class from which they come, in the sense that whatever pattern is present in the parent class appears in undistorted form in the sample as well.

You would like to be able to state how far off you are likely to be if you use as an estimate for the universe your sample estimate — whatever it may be, such as the amount of correlation between A and B, or the percentage with some characteristic y. That is, you would like to feel justified in making such statements as, If I set a range of 6 percent around my sample estimate, or an interval ranging from 3 percent below the estimate to 3 percent above it, then the chances are 95 out of 100 that the universe, or "true" value, will be present somewhere in this range.

Two things have to be specified in statements like that: some particular range, called a confidence interval in statistical terminology, around the sample estimate (your *ds* descriptions); some probability that the universe value lies somewhere within the range. In order to do this, you need some procedures for selecting samples that can legitimately support the following claim: If you were to (a) use this procedure to draw many, many samples of the same kind, and (b) make the same kind of estimate for each of the samples, and (c) set up an interval around each sample estimate in the same way, *then* you could state the chances that in some specifiable proportion of the samples the interval placed around the sample estimate would contain the universe value somewhere within the interval.

It turns out that for some procedures for drawing samples the claim is legitimately supported, namely, for random (or probability) sampling procedures, those in which each sample (or *set* of units) of the same kind drawn from the same universe has a chance of selection that is independent of and equal to the chance of selection for any other such sample. Further, for some specific probability designs and some kinds of estimates, mathematical formulas have already been worked out for making the specifications needed, i.e., interval around the kind of estimate and proportion of the samples for which the interval contains the correct, or universe, value.

The formulas vary somewhat, depending on the details of the probability design used. But if you have used one of these designs your problem of justifiably estimating how far off you are likely to be solely because you took a sample, or looked at just a portion, is solvable. You can learn enough statistics to locate the appropriate formula, plug in the needed data, and grind out the required algebraic computations. (For some typically used designs, this does not amount to much statistics or to anything but simple calculations. And, even for complex calculations the calculating gets mechanically easier all the time, as standard computer programs for the needed calculations become widely available.) Or, you can locate a statistician, describe in detail the particular probability design used, pay him to locate the appropriate formula for you, and *then* plug in the data and perform the calculations.

What if you have not used probability sampling procedures? Then you have no *legitimate* basis for making the kind of claim desired. You can guess how far off you are, but that is all.

If you have a choice, then, probability designs represent the wiser option, and there are several simple kinds for which the needed formulas are available. This does not mean that nonprobability designs

can never be used with profit. After all, you may not have a choice. And, even though less desirable, because of the underlying objectives for various levels of studies some nonprobability designs may be acceptable. It is for surveying or reconnaissance level studies that the employment of probability sampling procedures is likely to be critical if useful information is to be obtained, while some version of grab-bag or expert choice sampling may be acceptable for some exploratory and testing level studies. Both grab-bag and expert choice are nonprobability sampling types and are the most commonly used *non-probability* designs in the social sciences.

Sampling designs can be classified into two major types with two principal subtypes under each. This is illustrated in Figure II.2. In the following subsections I will discuss these in order from left to right across the diagram.

4.21 Nonprobability sampling. In the grab-bag type you take what you are lucky enough to get, hence these are also called fortuitous designs. Examples can range from those stars you can observe with existing telescopes, the first *n* cases of a particular kind of cancer that appear at a clinic, those artifacts your archaeological spade turns up, those chunks of radioactive substances you happen to use in analysis, to those particular rats sent over when you request some for an experiment, and so on.

As can be seen from the examples, sometimes a grab-bag sample is used because you have no choice. You have no choice but to make do with whatever the existing technology in telescopes happens to be, for instance.

Sometimes this type of sampling procedure is used because you have reason to feel that the units are homogeneous, or uniform, enough that the particular batch

Fig. II. 2.

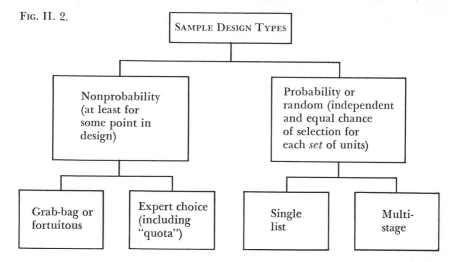

you pick will not seriously affect the results. A piece of radium can be considered chemically homogeneous to any other piece without serious error, and within limits one batch of rats may be considered like any other batch. This is a little shakier, however, and is one reason why rat suppliers for laboratory purposes emphasize in their advertisements their attempts at producing uniformity in the rats they sell.

The conditions under which grab-bag sampling procedures can be considered likely to yield samples that are accurate reflections of their universes are very limited (only if those universes are uniform). Those who use grab-bag samples because they have no other choice are forced to spend some effort to try to determine the actual extent of uniformity and its effects on their results. If a universe is truly uniform then a grab-bag sample is perfectly acceptable and in fact a very small sample size — one — is enough to give you the information you want about that universe. Either one unit or one situation will do. If each unit is exactly the same a sample of one unit is enough and if the distribution within any situation of the same type is the same as the distribution in all other situations of the same type, a sample of one situation will suffice.

The social sciences, particularly, are seldom in a position where an assumption of uniformity seems warranted. Seldom indeed are we willing to assume that, say, one family with delinquent children is the same in all relevant respects as every other such family.

Generalizing from a grab-bag sample, such as a single case study or those students willing to be stopped in the cafeteria to answer questions for an interview, is hazardous. Feasibility considerations may dictate that you must use a grab-bag sample, but when you do you should be aware of the price you will be paying as far as being able to make the kinds of generalizations you would like to make.

Grab-bag samples are typically used, then, either if we feel justified in assuming uniformity in the sample's universe (recall discussion about picking the sample for Exercise I-2) or if we have no other choice. Usually we do have some other choice, though, if we are willing to make the effort to implement it.

If you are not willing to grant the assumption of uniformity and you do not merely have to take what you can get, then you need to consider what other options are available. The other main kind of nonprobability sampling can be called expert choice.

You may not be willing to assume that the universe you are interested in is uniformly distributed. Perhaps you have reason to think it is skewed somehow or perhaps you have no basis for expecting a particular kind of distribution, except that you do not think it is a uniform one, or constant, and so you do not want to take a grab-bag sample if you can avoid it.

Suppose you know someone you think is expert enough that you could leave it to his discretion to pick a sample that will reflect its universe, whatever it may be like. You could ask him to pick your sample and we would say you are using an "expert choice" design. Of course, you may serve as the expert yourself.

If the expert can and does in fact pick a sample that appropriately reflects its universe, then any generalizations you make from that sample should be satisfactory. The difficulty is that if he has *not* picked such a sample you are in trouble as far as the usefulness of the generalizations you make, and you seldom have any way of knowing whether he has, or you have, truly picked an appropriate sample.

Grab-bag and expert choice samples may sometimes be useful in exploring and testing level studies. If you state that something is present for all members of a class of objects, then it certainly should be present for any particular members of that class and a grab-bag sample may suffice to test the statement's truth. However, we are usually in the position of having to make such statements as X exists in most, or some percentage, of the members of the class. If you take a grab-bag sample and X

is not present, you have no way of knowing whether you are wrong and X does not exist at all or whether you just happened to "grab" some cases from that percentage in which X would not be expected.

If you have very little idea what to anticipate in the way of possible associations between factors you think might be relevant, a grab-bag sample will give you some exploratory information. But, if you have some flexibility a kind of expert choice sample would probably be a better selection, in particular, an expert choice of cases at the extremes for exploration.

For instance, to return to an illustration given earlier, suppose you have some reason to suspect child-rearing differs in matriarchal families compared to other types but you have very little idea what differences to expect, if any exist. Rather than exploring with a grab-bag sample of one or two families, your exploring will likely be more profitable if you deliberately choose at least two families, at opposite extremes of matriarchy, to explore. And, of course, if you could choose three cases, one as pronouncedly matriarchal as you can find, one as little matriarchal, and one in the middle, this expert choice sample would be even better, and certainly better than just a grab-bag one.

Choosing extreme cases may be useful in exploratory work for another reason, having to do with measurement accuracy. When you explore you may be in *terra incognito* not only as far as associations are concerned but also as far as ways of finding out. Your measurement techniques, using measurement in a very broad sense, are likely to be rather crude when you know little about an area of investigation. If measurement errors are large, an effect would have to be marked for you to pick it up at all. Then, as you learn more about the area, your ways of finding out may be improved enough to pick up an effect in less noticeable form as well.

If you wish to test a proposition, you may be able to use an *a fortiori* argument, as discussed earlier, and using an expert choice design to pick some extreme case would be acceptable if your argument is adequate. Or, if you are not using *a fortiori* reasoning, picking cases at both extremes, and preferably also somewhere in the middle, is likely to provide a much more adequate test than a grab-bag sample could.

Note, however, that in all these exploring and testing possibilities a uniformity assumption is implicit at some point. That is, you are assuming that every extreme case is like every other extreme case. Even stronger, then, would be to pick a small-sized probability sample of extreme cases to explore or test. Then you could feel more confident that you have a sample that represents what the parent classes for extreme cases are like, and so feel more justified in whatever generalizations you might make.

One version of nonprobability sampling widely used and employing "expert choice" at one or another stage is called quota sampling. This kind is intended to provide a closer approximation of the representativeness given by probability samples than either grab-bag or other expert choice designs typically can.

Quite possibly you may know enough to expect certain proportions in the universe of interest (say, people with college educations or living in cities of a certain size or a certain region of the country) and neither want a grab-bag sample nor to leave sample selection *completely* up to an expert's discretion. If you decide your sample should contain the same propor-

tions (or "quotas") you think exist in the universe, you can select your sample so that it does. Be sure to select so that you have, say, 10 percent in cities of one size and 20 percent in cities of another size, and so on.

But how will you select the particular units to comprise that 10 or 20 percent? If the units in the 10 percent group are homogeneous, even though differing from the units in the 20 percent one, then you could justifiably use a grab-bag selection. Usually we are not willing to assume this. In the customary versions of quota sampling, it is left to the discretion of the interviewers to pick units within each quota that are supposed to be representative of it. Because of this customary element of discretion I have classed quota sampling as one kind of expert choice. If the interviewer *is* expert enough, then the resulting sample will reflect its universe, and you have a closer approximation to probability sampling than either grab-bag or other expert choice kinds can provide, but not close enough to use the available formulas justifiably. If the interviewer is not expert enough, then you are faced with the same difficulties as with any other version of expert choice sampling, and unfortunately you have no way, usually, of knowing how expert the interviewer was in practice.

There is some evidence for the suspicion that interviewers do not normally possess the necessary expertise. We know that all people seem to talk most comfortably and easily with others who are similar to themselves. In practice, many interviewers are middle-class housewives who work part-time doing interviewing. To take possibilities for which we have some data that they occur, if an interviewer is expected to select respondents according to some quotas for high, medium, and low income, she tends to select from the low end of the high group and the high end of the low group. In other words, she tends to select respondents who are most like her own middle-income status, and so does not achieve a sample representative of the entire range. In addition, not everyone takes kindly to being asked to answer questions by strangers. Given the discretion the interviewer has, she tends to select people who are pleasant to strangers and willing to be interviewed. As is no surprise, these people are not always representative of the entire populace.

4.22 Probability sampling. The available formulas for estimating sampling variation all presume the use of random, or probability, methods for obtaining the sample. Each sample (or *set* of units) in the appropriate universe must have an independent chance of being picked and so probability sampling design comes down to the task of devising procedures to ensure this. Many probability sampling designs are straightforward and easy to understand.

Let us first consider the situation where there is a single complete and up-to-date list available of all units in the desired universe. Suppose, for example, you wanted to select a sample of students at some college and then interview them about their participation in extra-curricular college activities, such as student government, attendance at sports events or college-wide dances, or membership in special interest clubs. Somewhere there will be a complete list of all students in attendance at the college. Let us assume you can solve the practical problem of obtaining access to this list and work on the theoretical problem of obtaining a probability sample of students from it.

To keep the arithmetic simple, let us

suppose there are exactly 10,000 students and you have resources enough to obtain interviews with 200 of them. If you pick 200 names from the list *in a random fashion,* then each student could have a chance of 1 in 50, or 200 divided by 10,000, of being selected.

There are several ways of ensuring that the selection is done "in a random fashion." One way is to use a table of random numbers, select 200 random numbers from it, number the list of students, and pick into the sample those students whose numbers correspond to the random numbers you chose. In this case, you would use five columns of digits in the table (such a table can consist of many, many pages) and select 200 numbers between 00,001 and 10,000. This kind of sample design is called unrestricted simple random sampling. If, as would likely be true for most social science problems, you would not want to pick the same unit into the sample more than once, then you eliminate duplicate random numbers selected and pick additional ones in the same way until you have 200 distinct random numbers. This design is called simple random sampling without replacement. I mention the names because the needed formulas for estimating sampling variation, or judging how far off you are likely to be just because you looked only at a portion of the universe, differ, as was mentioned earlier, and you would want to be sure to pick the appropriate formula.

Tables of random numbers are widely available. Virtually any good introductory statistics book will have a portion of such a table in its appendix and at least some of these books should be available in any library. Tables of random numbers consist of columns of digits, with each digit from 0 to 9 and each combination of digits equally likely to appear throughout the table, whether you form combinations of digits by grouping along the columns, along the rows, along either diagonal, along the columns and then the rows, and so on.

If you feel there is no periodicity present (such as every 50th student being president of some campus club, or every 5th being a freshman, or whatever) in your complete and up-to-date list of students, that might affect your interpretation in an illusory way, there is a less tedious method of picking the sample. This is called systematic sampling.

Let us assume you still want just 200 students. This number is one-fiftieth of the total of 10,000. You could give yourself a random start for your first selection, which would be somewhere between the number 1 and the number 50, and then take every 50th student after that. Tables of random digits could be used to get a random start. Place your finger anywhere on the page without looking and then run your finger down two columns at a time until you come to the first number between 01 and 50. Suppose your starting number turns out to be 37. Then, since your sampling interval (or skip interval, or k, as it is also called) is 50, your first selection is 37, your second is 87, or 37 plus 50, the third is 137 and so on through the list of 10,000 students.

If you do not have a table of random numbers handy, you can always flip a coin to obtain a random number to use as a starting point, by using the following procedure. Recall that if you flip a coin twice, 4 permutations are possible and are equally likely to occur. The 4 are shown below on the left. If you assign the digit 1 to a head and 0 to a tail, then each of the four sequences or permutations can be read as a binary number. (Nowadays, by the time you complete junior high school, most of you will be exposed to numbers in other

bases than the familiar 10 and so will recall that binary numbers use the base 2. Even if you have not studied binary numbers in a formal way, the system is easy to understand.) The binary equivalents are shown on the right below. Since each number's appearance is independent of the others and equally likely to occur, each can be thought of as *generated by a random process,* or in other words, as being a "random number."

tail, tail	00
tail, head	01
head, tail	10
head, head	11

All you have to do is toss a coin enough times to be sure you have covered the skip interval. In the illustration using students you need a skip interval of 50 and so you want a random number between 1 and 50 as your starting point. Since head and tail are equally likely (assuming a fair coin), tossing twice gives 2^2 permutations, as shown above; tossing 3 times gives two to the third ($2 \times 2 \times 2$) or 8 permutations; 4 times gives 2^4 or 16; 5 times gives 2^5 or 32; and 6 times gives 2^6 or 64. That is enough tosses because 64 is larger than the skip interval, 50. To get your random start between 1 and 50, you would toss a coin 6 times, note the order of heads and tails, assign 1 for a head and 0 for a tail, translate the particular one of the 64 possible binary numbers (corresponding to the 64 possible permutations) that did occur into its ordinary decimal equivalent, and use the first binary number that shows up between 1 and 50 as your start.

For example, suppose you toss a coin 6 times and get the following sequence of heads and tails and the corresponding binary number:

tail, tail, head, head, tail, head----001101

Reading the number from *right* to *left*, this says there is one in the ones place, none in the twos place, one in the fours place, one in the eights place, none in the sixteens place and none in the thirty-twos place. This is the number 13 in the ordinary decimal system and so your random start would be 13. (As you go left from a decimal point, the *base* — ten in the decimal system and two in the binary system — is raised to the next higher power, or exponent. In the decimal system you have the ones, tens, hundreds, thousands, and so on places. Similarly, in a binary system you have the ones, twos, fours, eights, and so on places.) If you toss 6 times and get either the binary equivalent of zero (all tails, or 000000) or a number larger than 50 (such as head, head, head, tail, head, tail, or the binary number 111010 and 58 as the decimal equivalent), you toss 6 times again until you get a random number between 1 and 50. This number would then be used as your starting point for picking a systematic sample with 50 as the skip interval.

As you can see, using systematic sampling need hardly be a complicated probability sampling design. And, as long as there is no relevant periodicity in your list it is perfectly acceptable. It is certainly a much less tedious procedure than selecting random numbers, either from a table or doing something like the coin-tossing described above, and rearranging them in numerical order to be sure there are no duplicates. If there is known or suspected periodicity, then the more tedious procedure is safer than systematic sampling and should be used. Note that in either case each student of the 10,000 has an equal chance of selection into a particular sample, one in fifty.

But it is not necessary that each unit have an equal chance of selection into the sample. Perhaps you feel that full-time students are more likely than part-time ones to participate in extra-curricular activities. Perhaps you have reason to believe part-time students are more likely to be employed and hence other activities would be curtailed. Whatever your rationale, you might decide you would like more detailed information for full-time students while you can get by with minimum detail for the others, and so you decide to obtain 150 full-time and 50 part-time students for the 200 you can afford to interview. Again for arithmetic purposes, let us assume there are exactly 6,000 full-time and 4,000 part-time students.

Divide your original list into two parts, so that you have one sublist for full-time and one for part-time students. Randomly select from each list, 150 from the full-time and 50 from the part-time. Within each of the two groups, or strata, each student on the sublist has an equal chance of selection, but overall each student does not have the same chance of being picked. Each of the 6,000 full-time students has a chance of 150 in 6,000, or 1 in 40, of being picked and each of the 4,000 part-time students has a chance of 50 in 4,000, or 1 in 80, of being selected. Each of the 10,000 *students* has a calculable, though not necessarily an equal chance of being brought into the sample. But, each *set* of 200 students where three-fourths of the set are full-time and one-fourth are part-time has a chance of selection that is independent of and equal to the chance for any other such set, or sample. This design is called stratified sampling, and of course any number of strata and not just two could be used.

I do not wish to make further remarks here about the mechanics of other kinds of random sampling designs from a single list. The basic types discussed (simple random sampling with and without replacement, systematic sampling, and stratified sampling) should be ample for most problems you will encounter, especially for small-scale studies.

I would stress, though, that adequate lists may often be available, or available lists can be made adequate without undue difficulty by updating them where necessary. Their use in drawing a probability sample rather than using grab-bag or expert choice designs should make any generalizations based on the selected sample much better grounded.

Examples of lists likely to be useful for social scientists and readily available are: all high schools in a state; all metropolitan areas in the United States as of various dates and of all cities of certain sizes as well; all counties; all social welfare or industrial organizations in the nation or a state or a community; all elected officials; all United States civil servants above a given rank; Standard and Poor's directory of business executives; city directories; directories of the members of one or another professional association, etc. and yet etc. Such lists are often not merely that but contain data about each unit on the list and those data may be sufficient for a study without additional observations or questioning.

But what if a single adequate list is not and cannot be made available, or at least making it available is not practical? One way to proceed is by what is called a multistage design. You proceed in stages, make yourself an appropriate list at each *stage* and sample from *these* lists rather than some single one. A common version is called multistage area probability sampling, which may sound complicated but usually is not.

Suppose you want a sample of units and these units can be assigned to one and only one geographic location at a given point in time (the reason for the term "area" in the name). Dwelling units or households, for instance, are units of this kind. Each household in the United States can be assigned to some specific geographic location, but no adequate listing of these locations is available and it would not be practical to make such a single list. How, then, might you proceed to select a probability sample of all households as of, say, this year? One way would be roughly as follows.

First divide the United States into geographic areas for which an adequate list is or can be made available. The list of counties found in the Census volumes and elsewhere will do, although in practice you might want to divide some of the unusually large counties and list the pieces separately. Take some kind of probability sample (for example, a systematic sample) of counties. Then divide each of the selected counties into smaller geographic areas, such as the size of a city block. Using the available lists of city blocks, again found in Census publications and elsewhere, will cover most of the populated area in each picked county and you can mark off "block-equivalent" (as they are usually called) units in suburban and rural areas as necessary and add these to the list of city blocks. Now you have made for yourself an adequate list of "blocks" within each county selected. Pick a probability sample of blocks.

So far you have been able to sit in your office or the library and use maps and perhaps a table of random numbers to select the first two stages of the sample. For the next stage you will have to "get into the field" and do at least some block-listing. This means that for the sample of blocks selected, especially in areas where there has been a lot of new construction or demolition and perhaps for all the blocks, you prepare a list of *all* the separate dwelling units, or households, on each selected block, being sure not to overlook converted apartments tucked away in odd corners. Very likely you can use recent city directories or other sources for up-to-date lists of households in most of the stable blocks and just block-list for the rest, although you might feel safer if you block-listed all. Now you have prepared for yourself an adequate list of households in the selected blocks in the selected counties. Pick a probability sample of households for each block.

The chance that any particular household in the United States will be selected in the sample is contingent, or conditional, on its block and its county being selected in prior stages. Conditional probabilities are multiplied, so a household's chance of selection is equal to the probability that its county was selected, times the probability that its block was selected, times its probability of being selected from the households on its block.

Suppose, purely to make things a little more concrete, that there are exactly 3,000 counties and 100 of them are picked; that each of the counties is divided into exactly 500 blocks and 150 of these are picked; that each block has exactly 20 households and 2 of these are picked. The chance that any specific household will be picked is equal to $100/3000 \times 150/500 \times 2/20$, or $1/1000$ (one in a thousand). What has just been calculated can be stated as being the chance of selection for any household in the United States in the year ———, using a three-stage area probability sampling design. This statement might be used to impress uninitiated friends with, but as we have seen, while the procedures may get a little tedious, they and the logic that underlies them can hardly be said to be complicated or mysterious.

Some sampling designs used in practice *can* get complicated in details. This is not usually because the underlying logic becomes more complex, but because operating survey organizations live in the real world, which is the usual euphemism for saying costs are important to them.

If you want a very high probability, say 999 chances out of 1000, that a 2 percent range for any estimate you make contains the universe value, then the sample will cost more than if you can tolerate a lower probability and a wider range. For example, if you want to estimate the proportion of Democrats among all registered voters, it will cost more to obtain a sample for which the chances are 95 out of 100 that plus and minus 1 percent of the sample estimate includes the correct, or universe, proportion than it will if you are willing to settle for a chance of 75 out of 100 and a range of plus and minus 5 percent. If it is satisfactory to be moderately sure that Democrats are between 45 and 55 percent of the registered voters, a quite inexpensive sample may do. But if the need is to predict who will win the next election if all registered voters vote, this would not be good enough and a more expensive sample would be necessary. How you specify your objectives will set bounds to the kind of sample you need to attain them.

Costs also enter into the design because the cost of obtaining *information* about the units in the sample, which includes such "field" costs as interviewers' salaries, transportation, and the like, can represent a large fraction of the total budget available. It is often wiser, i.e., cheaper for the same accuracy or more accurate for the same cost, to devise a more complex way of selecting units if you can then cut down on field costs by doing so. Paying for one highly skilled sampling statistician to spend some time sitting at his desk devising the sampling design and developing an appropriate sampling variation formula may mean you can cut down on field costs and so may be a wiser choice than to use a simpler design but one for which field costs are higher. [Getting the cheapest possible sample design to provide the accuracy you want, or conversely getting the most accurate sample design for the money you have to spend, can lead to a number of refinements in sample design that we certainly are not going to get into here.]

No matter what the particulars of the probability design used, the underlying logic is to achieve an independent chance of selection for each sample, or *set* of units, so that you can legitimately use the formulas to estimate, within specified limits that you can set as narrow as you please and can afford, how far off you are likely to be in your generalizations solely because you observed a sample and not the total. As you may have noted, in probability sampling there is no "discretion" as to which particular units will be picked and so the problems of expert choice designs are avoided; nor must any restrictive and probably unwarranted assumption of uniformity be made. The sample itself can be used to tell you, within limits, what its universe is like.

One last point on sampling before leaving the topic. Sometimes a researcher may feel his universe is fairly small and so he will look at all the units in it and need not be troubled about sampling considerations. As examples, he might take all fraternities on a college campus, or all industrial organizations with at least a certain dollar level of assets, or all the two hundred or so SMSAs (Standard Metropolitan Statistical Areas) in the United States as of this year. Whether it is "all right" not to worry about any sampling variation component

to his generalizations hinges on the level of abstraction he wants to be on when making those generalizations.

If he truly does not want to generalize beyond, say, the SMSAs in the United States as of this year, fine. But if, as is likely to be the case although not necessarily consciously so, he intends his statements to apply to other times in the United States and perhaps to similar units in other countries, then he is right back to sampling questions and cannot avoid concern with how adequate his sample of "all" SMSAs is for *these* parent classes.

And so we are led back to objectives: (*a*) What does the researcher want to know? (*b*) With what degree of accuracy? (*c*) About which population, or parent class? As far as stages in developing an empirical interpretation to attain those objectives, problem specifying decisions are most directly concerned with (*a*), control decisions with (*b*), and sample selection decisions with (*c*), although by now it is undoubtedly evident that each kind must be concerned with all three to some extent.

4.3 SOURCE AND FORM OF OBSERVATIONS. Now you need to decide whether you will generate situations and information about them for your particular study or whether you will use situations for which information has been, or will be, generated by someone else. Along with this you need to decide whether your observations will be in the form of direct observations, answers to questions, or records — which will ultimately consist of one or both of the other two. In practice, of course, you will no doubt have considered different possibilities for the source(s) and form(s) of your observations while making decisions about your analysis plan and procedures for controls and sampling.

As usual, your decision is affected both

by theoretical and practical considerations, or both by what you want to do and how feasible it is for you to do it. The basic task is to select observations in such a manner that when you are through there will be as few as possible legitimate alternative interpretations of the same data. How well you can ensure this rests on how adequate the sample of and controls on those observations are.

One of the alternative interpretations you always want to try to eliminate is that what you say is the pattern you observe is actually an illusion, due solely to chance. Your ability to eliminate this interpretation is based on the kind of sample you were able to obtain. You also want to eliminate alternative interpretations that amount to saying that your conclusions about the kinds of associations you say you see are not justified, because you did not employ adequate enough controls to say legitimately that *this* pattern rather than some other pattern is the one present. Deciding whether to generate your own information or to use information available in some form depends, then, on which source can give you the most satisfactory sample and controls, in light of your specific problem.

Superficially, it might seem that generating your own information would always ensure better sampling and controls. And so it might, if everything else were equal. But everything else is never equal and here is where feasibility considerations particularly enter in.

Trying to generate your own data may be foolhardy for many of the problems of interest to social scientists, at least if you want to have any hope of having satisfactory controls and a satisfactory sample. A brief selection of such problems might include the following:

1. What conditions are present in cities that have riots and absent in those that do not?
2. What effect will legislative reapportionment have on governmental responsiveness to urban problems in various parts of the United States?
3. Is there a common explanation for those situations where fluoridation has been voted down even though widely recommended by appropriate professional groups, such as dentists, and if so to what extent is this explanation applicable to situations where regional government or transportation plans or educational bond issues have been widely recommended yet voted down?
4. What is common in the organization and operation of all large bureaucratic groups, whether they be political, economic, religious, penal, ameliorative, or whatever, in type?
5. What and why are the differences and similarities in the pattern of social welfare services in nations at a comparable level of economic development?
6. Which stages are essential and which may be omitted with impunity in the process of modernization of currently underdeveloped areas?

For even quite narrowed versions of these and many other questions, most researchers, especially but not exclusively if working with limited financial support, simply would not have the resources to generate information based on adequate samples and controls. But data that are already available or will become available might be used.

Especially in what are termed the economically advanced countries, a vast quantity of information is routinely collected. Much of it is published in repository form. For example, several dozen substantial social science projects dealing with the United States could be carried out using just the summary kinds of information available in the *Statistical Abstract* or the *County and City Data Book*. Each is periodically updated as information becomes routinely available or is collected for the first time; each is present even in quite small libraries and so can be used at no cost to the researcher, or he may purchase a copy of either for well under ten dollars. Also, much information is not published but listings exist which tell what information is available and the (typically low) cost of purchasing a copy of some part of it.

In addition to various official or governmental "data banks," other data banks are increasing in number. Basic data on a series of items for a range of different societies, or data from a variety of large-scale questionnaire surveys may be included, or the bank may contain data on a particular field of interest, such as politcal behavior. The cost of obtaining a copy of some of the available data in the bank is deliberately kept low to increase its accessibility to potential users.

Published reports, themselves containing an analysis of information, can be re-analyzed. A report often includes much more detailed information in an appendix section than appears in the text. A series of studies related to the same topic could be collected, even including case studies or anthropological monographs, and the data available on some point analyzed in a comparative fashion.

Of course it may turn out that what you need is simply not available and you have no choice but to try and generate it. Or

some before observations may be available and you can then generate the after ones. But before deciding that you must generate your own information, you would be wise to explore the possibility that usable information may already exist or could be made available. You may have to do considerable combining and rearranging, or other kinds of manipulating, to get it in the form you want for analysis purposes. But the payoff in the quality and coverage of the information compared to the cost to you in money and effort to obtain it may be substantial.

Whether generated or gathered from other sources, data come in some typical forms. Ultimately, they consist of reports about something directly observed, or of answers to questions asked of those who did make direct observations, or of some kind of index, or substitute observations.

One major caution to be noted here is that you not change the subject about the kind of observation used. Particularly in the social sciences, be sure that you do not mix up the answers to questions about behavior with direct observations of behavior when making generalizations. When you ask questions what you observe directly is verbal behavior, which may be interesting in its own right but is not necessarily equatable to direct observations of other behavior.

Indexes are often used when it is not feasible, or when it is much less feasible, to make direct observations. Those indexes or substitute observations known as barometric readings are familiar to everyone and electrocardiogram tracings are almost as familiar.

A promising kind of index just beginning to be widely used in many sciences is computer models or simulations. The computer's ability to make routine and tedious calculations rapidly was recognized and applied early, although with some lag in the social sciences. Its potential for studying complex situations by simulating them and for separating the implications if one or more factor is altered in some way, is only now being realized. These simulations are particularly promising as far as the number of controls that can be employed. The human mind, although it has its advantages, is much more limited than a computer in its ability to juggle many variables simultaneously.

Also, several standard parlor games and games invented deliberately (some of which cannot be played at all unless a computer is accessible) can be used for simulation-like purposes. For instance, games such as that parental-sanity-preserver while traveling with children, Twenty Questions, can be repeatedly used with a group of strangers to explore the development of more and less efficient search strategies, and the emergence of patterns of interaction and norms from amorphous and incipient stages to developed ones.

Besides index or substitute observations, data come in the form of more direct observations and of answers to questions. Records, of course, consist of one or more of these basic types.

Accurately reporting what you yourself have seen is not as easy as it might appear. Some people find this hard to believe, thinking that because they participated in an event or at least were present and saw it occur with their own eyes, their reports must be accurate and complete.

Many ways can be used to demonstrate that this is not necessarily so. A dramatic device to illustrate this is often employed in introductory psychology classes. At some point while the instructor is lecturing an assistant may come in, outlandishly attired and shouting something, stay briefly and leave. Students are asked to describe what they observed, which can lead to some lively arguments about the details of what actually happened.

Even in less hectic situations, people observe selectively unless they are well prepared with observational categories and procedures in advance. No matter what your intentions, you cannot observe everything. The purpose of trying to decide in advance what you will look for and how you will more or less *systematically* observe, keeping careful records, in order to see it if it is there, is to try and ensure that you overlook as little as possible that in your considered and reflective judgment is relevant to your problem.

You also want your observations to be as reliable as possible, both with respect to intraobserver and interobserver reliability (recall discussion in Exercise I-2). This is the purpose of deciding what categories you will use and what procedures will be employed to decide when an observation fits in one category rather than another. Science in general seems to have progressed as standardized measuring instruments and ways of using them are developed and agreed on. This is especially important in surveying and testing level studies, and is as applicable to the use of questioning or other indirect kinds of observations as it is for more directly made ones.

Before making some comments on questioning, though, I want to say a little about participant observation. This is a technique often used with what was referred to earlier as a panel strategy and is frequently enough used in the social sciences to warrant a little elaboration. I would divide participant observation into two subtypes, pure and field. When researchers talk about themselves using this technique they sometimes distinguish between the two kinds and sometimes not. I think th distinction is worth preserving here, because the sorts of difficulties typically encountered can differ.

In the pure form the observer becomes an actual participant, a functioning member, in the group he is also observing. In the field form the observer remains with the group as an outsider long enough that he is presumed to "become part of the furniture" and the group is presumed to behave as it would were he not present. Some practical difficulties are involved in the pure form that are less pronounced in the field form. To mention some of the more important, one may be termed the entry problem and another the limited viewpoint problem.

To take the first, if an observer is really to become a member of a group he must be able to occupy some role, some "legitimate niche," and this may be easier said than done. If you consider for a moment the difficulties involved in becoming a participant observer in some family other than your own, the matter becomes clear. The only legitimate ways of entering a family in our society are by being born in, adopted in, or marrying in. This certainly limits the sample of family groups that can be observed by any one researcher using this technique. To take less extreme examples, consider the practical problems in securing entry into a group of prostitutes, prison convicts, or the board of directors of AT&T or General Motors, and the like.

Sometimes when publishing their generalizations, researchers using participant observation who have been able to solve the entry problem satisfactorily sound as though this thereby guarantees the accuracy of their descriptions. This often implicit assumption may be too facilely made. Solving the entry problem does not necessarily guarantee accurate descriptions. This

is because of the other difficulty cited, limited viewpoint.

Another problem usually more troublesome in the pure than the applied form is the matter of limited viewpoint provided by this technique. If you do manage to occupy a legitimate niche, then as with any role some kinds of behavior will be required, some prohibited, and some optional. If you enter a community, for instance, you must do so at some socioeconomic status level and may find it quite difficult to observe accurately those in the community occupying different — especially much higher or much lower — status levels. You may find it just is not done for someone at your status level to try to enter others, even if you do try to pass it off as "slumming" or "social climbing." This does not begin to touch such problems as what dialect you will use in conversing with various community members. All of us are aware that there are idiomatic phrases used by legitimate group members of a foreign culture that are difficult for strangers to use appropriately. Sometimes we forget just how foreign the language used by members of other socioeconomic statuses or particular occupations or particular age groups really is. These problems are much less pronounced in the field form. A number of *faux pas* are tolerated from a recognized outsider, not only of language but of other kinds of behavior as well, since he just is not expected to know all the rules.

Both pure and field forms share some common difficulties, since the observer will be with the group for a more or less long period of time. If the observer draws conclusions too soon, he may not do so any better than a short-term stranger might and so lose much of the advantage of observing off-guard behavior. If he waits too long he may begin to think with all the rationalizations the group members use and lose the advantages of having an outsider's view. It is just very difficult to be both inside and outside and observe from both vantage points.

Despite the problems, the technique is well worth the attention of social scientists, if too much is not expected of it. We are all concerned with one or another aspect of human behavior. We all exist in some society and we all occupy roles in many, many groups, fully legitimately, and it seems to me we ought to take advantage of this. With training in one or another of the social sciences, we know better what we could be looking for and how to interpret it when seen. Both as a source of leads for possibly relevant associations, which might have to be confirmed with some other techniques and designs, and perhaps as a source of test cases for some of our generalizations in naturally occurring groups without some of the artificiality problems described for experiments, it seems to me that using the groups we already belong to and functioning as participant observers once in a while can be invaluable.

As is true for other forms of observing, questioning can vary from little more than the use of a guide, perhaps even an implicit one, blocking out major areas to be noted, to highly systematic procedures, with precisely defined categories and rules for placement of items in them. Two basic types of questions are used. Closed questions are those for which the respondent selects from a fixed set of alternative responses. Open questions permit the respondent to answer as he chooses, and his response is recorded as fully as possible. The two may be used in sequence, and then typically the open question appears first, with the related closed question later. Various combination versions, such as a mainly closed question but with one open

alternative as well, are also used. As simple examples, here are a possible closed question and an open one, both dealing with age.

Closed question:

In which age category would you place yourself?
_____under 21
_____21 to 34
_____35 to 49
_____50 and over

Open question:

What is your birth date?_____

In a sense, closed questions are preclassified (or "coded") since you have set up the categories in which you will place the responses in advance, while responses to open questions must be categorized later. Typically, this is done by taking a sample of the questionnaires, noting the kinds of responses and the frequency of each kind, and later trying to set up categories to cover them. It is partly a matter, then, of when you choose to do your thinking about categorization, before or after gathering data. It is also partly a matter of how sure you are that you think you know what to expect.

But even when making up open kinds of questions it is a good idea to think of the *kinds* of responses you would like to have, or in other words to do some thinking about categories, so that your question is designed to get at the dimension of interest. Otherwise, you may have one dimension in mind and yet the question may be ambiguous enough that some answer according to the dimension you wanted and others answer according to another dimension. If so, you may face an awkward problem in deciding the utility of the information given in the answers. Consider this possible open question:

What do you think are the major problems facing the United States today?

You may have had domestic problems in mind, but some respondents may well answer according to an international dimension. If you mean domestic problems, you should phrase the question to get that information. On the other hand, if your interest lies in finding out whether domestic or international problems seem to be uppermost in people's minds, then the question is fine as it stands. As with just about everything else in the research process, what you should do rests on what your objectives are.

With many open questions and some closed ones it is often a good idea to follow the question with some kind of neutral probe question, to be surer what you are getting. Examples of neutral-type probes are:

How do you mean that?
Could you give me an example of that?
Anything else?

In other words, the probe is designed to get an amplification from the respondent; it should imply neither approval nor disapproval of his response.

It is distressingly easy to ask questions that beg the question, or tell the respondent how you would like him to answer. As an extreme example: You don't drink, do you? Less extreme examples are far from rare, and most people have such ingrained habits of courtesy that if they can oblige the interviewer they may well try to do so, regardless of what they really think, or how they really behave.

Not only the form of the question but other cues — verbal and nonverbal — from the interviewer may tell the respondent what is wanted, and is just one reason why interviewer training is important. The point can be readily brought home by recalling the children's game in which you take any question at all and repeat it over and over, each time emphasizing a different word in the question, to see the often amusing differences in meaning that result.

It takes training to learn both to ask questions in an interested but neutral fashion *and* to receive the answers in an equally interested but neutral fashion. This kind of neutrality goes against our training and experience in everyday social intercourse. But the interviewer is a recording instrument, and as with any instrument, consistency from one situation to another is desirable.

If you are using a personal interviewer to ask the questions you can rely on him (or more likely in actual practice, her), with proper training, to do several things for you. He should be able to establish enough rapport at the beginning to gain entry to start the interview. He should be able to spot fatigue on the part of the respondent and perhaps be able to rouse interest again, or at least make a note to aid your interpretation. Notes on fatigue or other factors that might affect the quality of responses can be very helpful for interpreting the results, such as a noisy TV the respondent could not be persuaded to turn off, or inquisitive neighbors who could not be persuaded to leave for the duration of the interview.

Further, he should be well enough trained in the objectives for each question that he can spot when the respondent has misunderstood the question or in some other fashion is not providing a responsive answer. If so, he may be able to use neutral probes, or tactfully ask the question again (*not* rephrase it!) and hope that this time the answer is responsive. He can spot inconsistencies, if any exist, between responses made to one question and responses made to others. He can be sure no question is overlooked and hence not answered.

If the questionnaire is self-administered, such as a mail-back questionnaire, then if you are aware of the kinds of things a well-trained interviewer can do for you, you can try to build into the questionnaire itself, including its introductory statement used to gain rapport, ways to cope with at least some of these. Neutral-type probes can be used in print, as well as in speech, for instance.

But whether self- or personal-interviewer-administered, the easiest way to gain entry and maintain rapport and interest is to have a good reason for doing the study and so seeking to impose on the respondent's time and to prepare a good description (not necessarily detailed, but easily understandable) of the reason; and to have well-designed questions. Check your questions, preferably on a few people who might have been picked into your sample but were not, to see that they are nonambiguous and noninsulting. It is surprisingly easy to write questions which you consider unambiguous and not even vaguely insulting, only to discover — hopefully on your pretesting trials and not when the study is under way — that they do not seem so to others.

In general, it is better to begin with a broader question and work down to more specific ones, for each main topic asked about. If you have unusually sensitive questions, they might better come later than earlier, after rapport has been established. That way, should the respondent decide to break off the interview at that point, you may be able to salvage most of the questionnaire for that respondent, rather than have to discard it as a refusal.

As far as the quality of the information you can expect to obtain by asking questions, a good rule-of-thumb to follow is: Is this information the respondent could reasonably be expected to have, and were the conditions surrounding obtaining his answers such that he could be expected to give it? Here is an extreme example of the kind of question likely to be answered somehow but with the quality of the information likely to be poor:

> How did you feel about the way your mother disciplined you when you were three years old?

Also, you may often have contingent questions, to be asked only of those giving a certain response to prior questions, such as some to be asked only of those who said they had preschool children. Try to have your basic interview no longer than about forty-five minutes and the full interview, including any contingent questions, no longer than an hour. If your interview is much longer than this, you run the risk that the fatigue level will be so high that the quality of the answers to later questions would be questionable.

Finally, remember to ask yourself whether you have changed the subject, if you are making generalizations based on verbal behavior, as well as asking some version of this when reading reports by others. Obtaining data on what people say they think and do and then generalizing as though you had data on what people actually think and do is a far too prevalent change of subject in the social sciences. This is a sticky problem, indeed, but just because it is sticky is no justification for pretending the problem is not there.

Records consist of one or more of the basic types of observations, therefore the comments made about them are applicable. For this reason, my remarks here will be brief.

Especially when dealing with informally prepared reports, such as diaries, letters, accounts by travelers, and the like, it is much safer to try to get reports of the same event from independent observers and check the agreement between them. This is true for more formally prepared reports as well. For instance, figures on the number of young men living at home or on assets available to families might vary widely, depending on whether the information was obtained for tax assessment purposes, or to provide estimates of the pool of military manpower, or for the assessment of relief payments to be made by the government. Independently made estimates, if they are available, can be invaluable to you, but in each case check the auspices under which they were given and the reason for initially obtaining the information.

Remember to ask yourself whether the preparer of the record could be expected to have the information in his possession or whether more or less guesswork was involved. For instance, in some questionnaire surveys we have learned that people may give strongly held opinions about certain international figures or detailed comments about some governmental program, yet when asked questions to ascertain their knowledge about these figures or the details of the existing program their statements reflect a lack of factual knowledge.

And do not let yourself be lulled into thinking that because reports exist, even reports by participants in the event, they must therefore be complete and accurate. Particularly assess the likelihood that a "limited viewpoint" problem is present in reports by participants, especially by those who were decidedly emotionally involved. Getting reports from different observers, and preferably those "on opposite sides," can help you in sifting out what probably occurred.

I would summarize here, then, by merely stressing the two major rules-of-thumb already cited: Do independent observers agree? Is the reported information such as the reporter could reasonably be expected to have and were the conditions surrounding obtaining his report such that his report could reasonably be expected to be full and accurate?

5. Concluding Remarks

By selecting a problem and giving it a full empirical interpretation, you have developed a research proposal, in more or less explicit and documented form. The proposal should contain both the general kinds of choices and the specific operational decisions finally made, as well as justifications for them.

Preparing a research proposal involves making the set of decisions that will be presented in final and summary form in any report prepared later on the entire project, under the first two headings of the Topical Outline for preparing and evaluating reports: Problem and Method. Both the broad problem of interest and the narrowed problem investigated, along with justification for the way the problem was specifically narrowed, should appear under the first heading. Both the strategy for obtaining data and the strategy for analyzing it, along with appropriate justifications for your choices, should appear under the second heading.

When a proposal for an investigation is highly detailed throughout it is sometimes termed a research protocol document. These detailed documents also include such ancillary items as how you will physically store and manipulate your data, a statement on how you will allocate the resources available to you during the various stages of carrying out the project, and specimen copies of any forms to be used — a questionnaire, or interviewer instructions, or a code manual, or the guide to be followed in recording field or laboratory notes, and the like.

The protocol document is designed to be *used* by the researcher in carrying through his project, so the more detailed it is the more useful it is likely to be to him. A shorter version of this is the kind of proposal that would usually be submitted if you were requesting approval or financial support of some kind.

For instance, you might be trying to secure the approval of your boss to divert your time and effort from your usual activities in order to carry out the project and perhaps even be assigned other personnel to aid you. Or you might be requesting funds in the form of a grant from a foundation such as the National Science Foundation or the Ford Foundation, or from an agency such as the Department of Health, Education and Welfare. Or you might be trying to secure your instructor's approval of a proposed project as part of the course requirements, or for use as a Master's or Ph.D. thesis.

In practice, the value of the kind of thinking-in-advance needed to prepare a research protocol document, in order to improve the chances of making a worthwhile addition to knowledge, is increasingly being recognized. More and more frequently, then, a preliminary review of the literature and narrowing of the topic of interest is immediately followed by a request for time, money, and personnel to do the kind of detailed thinking, planning, and preparing of data collection tools and techniques needed in advance of the conduct of a large study.

These planning grants, as they are usually called, allow for the time and personnel needed to prepare a detailed estimate of the cost of carrying out the project proposed. Then after a final assessment is made of whether the probable utility of the information sufficiently outweighs the cost of obtaining it, those who could release the funds, personnel, and equipment needed decide whether or not to do so.

Especially for a large project, a consultant may be used in the planning stages. The consultant's job is to diagnose planning problems and to measure planning progress, unlike those reviewers who assess utility against cost in deciding whether a project should be carried out or those reviewers concerned with evaluating a published report of a completed project. The consultant is not much concerned, typically, with whether you *should* want to go where you do, but with whether you can get there at all with the way you are heading, and with whether there might be a better route to take.

To diagnose planning problems, under each topic in the protocol he notes whether (*a*) what is there is obscure, (*b*) what is there is clear but not adequate, or (*c*) if what is there is adequate, there is an even better way he can suggest. To measure planning progress, he notes which items are inadequately or improperly handled and will require more work (and tries to point out whether a little or a lot more) before you are ready to collect useful data.

The advance thinking needed to prepare a research protocol document can be invaluable for quite small projects as well. It is always a good idea to serve as your own consultant in the planning stage, whether or not anyone else is used as well, and it is an equally good idea to serve as your own reviewer before making a final decision about whether or not you should carry out your proposed project.

Periodic brief summaries have appeared throughout Part II so far. Below, as an overall summary in a form I thought might be most helpful to you for reminder and reference, is a suggested outline for you to follow in preparing a detailed research proposal, or protocol document. I have arranged the items in the order in which you would be likely to summarize the points in the Problem and Method sections of your final report.

This "presentation order" is not identical with the logical order that might be followed in trying to justify your choices for your empirical interpretation. Nor is it identical with the order I tried to follow roughly in the preceding sections, namely, the order in which matters requiring a decision would likely arise in practice. But the decisions involved, requiring as they do a choice among available options based on an evaluation of the merits and demerits of each option in light of your objectives, are so interdependent that they are only analytically separable anyway.

Outline for detailed research proposal

(*Note:* (1) Implicit in the listing of the items below is the understanding that justifications should appear throughout the document, therefore a justification item in separate form rarely appears. (2) Items are given in the order in which they are likely to be summarized in the Problem and Method sections of a final report, and this order is similar but not identical to either the logical or the temporal order involved in making these interrelated decisions.)

1. Problem
    1.1 The broad problem
    1.2 The narrowed problem
        1.21 Perspective on problem
            1.211 Where it fits in with what is already known
                (including literature review, or evaluation and major documentation of what is known now)
            1.212 Underlying objectives
                (including the level of the study)
            1.213 Specific objectives
                (including variables and relationships to be covered)
        1.22 Justification for narrowing problem as you did
            (including relative role of theoretical and feasibility considerations involved in the narrowing)

2. Method
    2.1 Plan for obtaining data
        2.11 Source and form of observations
        2.12 Design: specific version of basic four-celled strategy
            (including justification for particular version used, especially if certain cells will be missing)
        2.13 Sample: specific version of probability or nonprobability
    2.2 Plan for analysis
        2.21 Which variables will be cross-classified, according to what categories, what joint classifications will be used, what relationships will be examined and how
            (preferably including dummy appendix-type tables, as precise as you can manage to make them, and accompanied by a discussion of controls used; tables may be in appendix and just referred to here)
        2.22 Tentative criteria for concluding statistical and theoretical significance of results

3. Appendix
    3.1 Allocation of resources for stages in carrying out project
        (allocation of time, money, personnel, and equipment for any further planning and for collection, analysis, and report writing; be sure to allow enough time for revisions of report after first draft)
    3.2 Physical storage and handling of data
        (such as use of $3'' \times 5''$ cards, IBM punch cards, notebooks for recording field observations; hand tallies, computer runs, etc.)
    3.3 Selected specimen forms
        (such as detailed dummy analysis or appendix-type tables, questionnaire and code manual, interviewer instructions, guide to be followed for field notes, guide for recording laboratory observations, and so on)

Exercise Set II

II-1. Some Desirable Skills: Locating and Evaluating What Is Known

This exercise is in two main parts, with subparts for each. Part A deals with the location of, and Part B with the evaluation of, available information. Section A-1 is a library tour, covering some general background information needed to locate specific items; section A-2 requires you to locate selected pieces of information. Under Part B, you will be given two articles to read and evaluate, following the guides in Part II of the text. The article in section B-1 is about a research project and is a fairly obviously discipline-generated report; the article in section B-2 is a summary-critique of some existing work and is a fairly obviously application-generated report.

Part A: Location

A-1: Library tour   Your instructor will decide whether to arrange a special library tour for the class, to have you take whatever standard tour is given, or to assign you to scout around on your own. Whatever turns out to be the case, there are certain pieces of background knowledge you should acquire.

1. In what section of your library are books for your field located? (Preferably, also find out where books for closely related fields may be found.)
2. Where are the general reference volumes located? In particular, try to find these volumes: *Encyclopedia of the Social Sciences; Book Review Digest; Reader's Guide to Periodical Literature; Social Sciences and Humanities Index.*
3. Are government documents in a separate section(s)? Locate at least these hard-cover volumes: *Historical Statistics of the United States;* the latest decennial census volumes for the United States as a whole and for your state of current residence; *Statistical Abstract; County and City Data Book.* As far as government documents not in hard-cover form, at least find out where the periodic reports from the Current Population Survey are stored.

4. Does your discipline have a journal consisting solely of abstracts of recently published articles, and if so, where in your library may issues of this journal be found?

5. Where are the issues of the "official" journal(s), that is, those coming with payment of dues to the appropriate professional association, for your discipline stored? It is highly desirable for any social scientist to be aware of the principal journals in disciplines closely related to his as well. Therefore, here is a list of the major journals to which a subscription is included in the annual membership dues for various social science disciplines. The association involved is given in parentheses beside the name of its principal "official" journal. Later on, when you engage in a serious review of the literature, if you note the references given in articles in these principal journals, you will soon learn what the other major journals are for a particular discipline.

American Anthropologist (American Anthropological Association)
American Economic Review (American Economic Association)
American Political Science Review (American Political Science Association)
American Psychologist (American Psychological Association)
American Sociological Review (American Sociological Association)
Annals of the Association of American Geographers (Association of American Geographers)
Demography (Population Association of America)

6. What special audio-visual facilities does your library have? For instance, does it have facilities for viewing microfilms and for listening to tape recordings? (Many Master's and Ph.D. theses are available on microfilm and may be borrowed for viewing. Also, sessions of the annual meetings of the American Association for the Advancement of Science are recorded on tapes that may be purchased at nominal cost.)

A-2: Location of selected pieces of information   Below is a series of items you are to locate. When you have completed the series, turn your answers in to your instructor.

1. What is the *name(s)* of the journal(s) for your discipline that is routinely monitored for the *Book Review Digest?*

2. What is the *date* of the *latest* issue of the *Statistical Abstract* available in your library?

3. What is the *date* of the *latest* issue of the *County and City Data Book* available in your library?

4. Using the most recent United States Census of Population information available in your library:

(a) Find the *percentage* of all *employed males* in the United States in the following major *occupational categories:*

professional, technical and kindred workers
farmers and farm managers
managers, officials, and proprietors, except farm
clerical and kindred workers
sales workers
craftsmen, foremen, and kindred workers
operatives and kindred workers
private household workers
service workers, except private household
farm laborers and farm foremen
laborers, except farm and mine
(*Hint:* if you hunt around a little, you will no doubt be able to find a table with the percentages already computed for you)

(b) The percentage distribution found for (a) will not add to 100 percent. To make it add to 100 percent, you need to know the percentage of employed males classified as "occupation not reported." What is this percentage?

5. Find the *percentage change* over the last two Census decades (depending on which is the most recent Census in your library, this will be either between 1940 and 1960 or between 1950 and 1970) for all employed United States males in the following *selected* occupations:

engineers, technical
mechanics and repairmen
laborers in manufacturing

6. Using *one* of the following three items available from the United States Census — median family income; median years of school completed for persons aged at least twenty-five years old; percentage of the labor force in white-collar occupations:

(a) Find the value of the item for:

the United States as a whole
the Northeast Region
the East South Central Division
your current state of residence

(b) For the item picked:

which of the four regions had the *highest* value?
which of the regions had the *lowest* value?
which of the nine divisions had the *highest* value?
which of the divisions had the *lowest* value?

7. Use cumulative indexes for journals. As an illustration, I am using the latest cumulative index to the *American Journal of Sociology,* which as of this writing covers volumes 1–70, or years 1895–1965.

   (*a*) What are the names given to the major subdivisions, or sections, in the index?

   (*b*) By opening the index to page 11, the following entry can be found:

   > Bernard, Jessie. Some Current Conceptualizations in the Field of Conflict (70:442–54). T: Reviews various theories of games and conflict.

   What does the entry in parentheses mean?
   What does the symbol "T" stand for, and on what page of the index did you find this information?

8. Select *two* broad topics (from the list of three below or using other broad topics that occur to you), and for *each* topic picked you are to locate *one* applicable article.

   Relation between change in population size of a group and aspects of its internal organization or operation
   Relation between external pressures on a group and its internal cohesion
   Relation between the distribution of power within a group and its ability to solve problems

   Here are some comments to help you get started. Often the hardest part in trying to get started locating articles for a broad topic is to develop some sort of interpretation of the topic that will aid you in your search. For instance, interpretations of the first topic could include: the impact of rapid metropolitan growth on the interrelations between local governments in the entire metropolitan area; effect of having their children grow up and leave the family on the harmoniousness of relationships between husbands and wives. The first interpretation involves large and formally organized groups and focuses on size increase; the second involves small and informally organized groups and focuses on size decrease. Sometimes when you have difficulty getting started, it helps to pick either an extreme case or one with which you are very familiar and try to use the case to generalize from and so develop some interpretation to aid your search of the literature. For instance, for the second topic what about a nation such as Israel or Rhodesia as cases in point? Or, a class you are in and for which you feel the work is being piled on in increasingly unreasonable amounts? What happens to "togetherness" amongst you and your fellow sufferers in the class? Is there increased cooperation and helpfulness or do you tend to withdraw in your misery and ignore each other? Depending on what you decide, can you state your conclusions in more generally applicable form and so develop an interpretation for the second broad topic listed? One final hint: For part of this, what about using the broad topic you picked for your own project and the interpretation made of it for your narrowed problem, using one of the articles you selected as appropriate for your list of twenty items on your bibliography (see Exercise I-3)?

To summarize, for *each* of the two broad topics picked:

(*a*) State the topic, your interpretation of it, and why you feel your interpretation is a justifiable one.

(*b*) Provide a complete reference for the article picked and state why you feel the article is an applicable one for the interpretation developed above for (*a*).

PART B:
EVALUATION

Two reprinted reports follow, one in section B-1, evaluating a research report, and one in section B-2, evaluating a summary-critique report. Each is to be read and evaluated, following the general guide in **Part II** of the text. You will need both to summarize according to the topic headings given in the guide and to provide answers to the "suggested questions" to ask.

When you have completed this task, exchange your evaluations for someone else's. Hopefully, there will be little disagreement on the summarizing portions of your evaluations, although there may be for the rest. Try to reconcile any major differences between your evaluation and someone else's for the same article. Note points of disagreement and give what you think are the reasons for the disagreement. For instance, was something overlooked, or weighted more heavily by one of you compared to the other?

Several criteria guided my choices for items to reprint. I wanted examples of both primarily discipline-generated problems and primarily application-generated problems. Further, I wanted each report to be relatively brief, and understandable by persons with little background in statistical techniques. Most important, I wanted each to be of high quality. Finally, I tried to select reports on topics I thought might be of interest to *several* social science disciplines: some aspects of the concept of power in the social sphere; and a critique of various proposals for dealing with the current "population explosion."

As noted in the text, authors will not necessarily completely follow the listed order of topic headings. Here are some general suggestions for you to consider as aids to completing any evaluation of an article.

First read the article with an eye to summarizing it. As you take notes, in parentheses beside each note indicate the main topic heading and subheading for which you think it is relevant. For example (II-1) would refer to the first subheading under Method. Then mentally or actually group your notes so they follow the order of headings and subheadings given in the guide, being especially careful to note whether any items that should be covered are missing.

Now reread the paper more critically, this time with an eye to obtaining answers to the suggested questions to be asked. As you take notes on what the author says or make comments of your own, indicate in parentheses the relevant question, e.g. (Q C).

Finally, summarize your entire evaluation of the article (completeness as well as other aspects of quality) according to the particular content included under the various headings and your judgment of that content. Eventually, you should be able to do this kind of summary (which you would probably file as permanent notes) on one or perhaps both sides of a single sheet of paper, for most articles. If you find you are writing substantially more than this for your final evaluation, look over your statements and phrases to see if your remarks can be digested into a more concise form.

Especially as you become more practiced, you may find the evaluation mechanically easier if you begin by putting the reference to the article at the top of a sheet of paper and then place the various topic headings on the left side. Leave space below each heading for you to fill in with notes as you read the article, and leave space on the right side of the paper to write the answers you obtained to the various suggested questions. If you follow these mechanics you will not have to rearrange your notes later. Even so, until you become practiced in the use of the guide, I would urge you to read the article *twice,* the first time to yield a summary of the content and the second to yield a critique of that content.

B-1: Evaluating
a research report

Community Power and Urban Renewal Success [1]
AMOS H. HAWLEY

Abstract

Starting from the position that power is an attribute of a social system rather than of an individual, this study examines the relationship of the extent of power concentration to urban renewal success. The ratio of managers, proprietors, and officials to the employed labor force measures the concentration of power, and success in urban renewal is represented by arrival of cities at the execution stage in that program. The relationship is found to be statistically significant and remains so under a series of controlled observations. Thus it appears that the conception of power employed offers a promising procedure for comparative studies.

Power, in most sociological studies, is conceived as the ability to exercise influence in a decision-making process. It is viewed as a personal attribute that distinguishes leaders from followers. Working with that conception investigators normally proceed by inquiring into the reputations of members of a community, establishing juries to winnow the great from the small, constructing socio-

Amos H. Hawley, "Community Power and Urban Renewal Success," reprinted from the *American Journal of Sociology,* January 1963, pp. 422–31, by permission of The University of Chicago Press and the author. Copyright 1963 by The University of Chicago.

grams to determine who interacts with whom, and so on. No matter what the methodological apparatus, investigators are uniformly led to the discovery that managerial and proprietary personnel, with occasional exceptions, constitute the power figures.[2] Some of the more sophisticated start with the assumption that managers and proprietors are the principal power figures and use their sociometric tools to discover how members of an elite are grouped about various kinds of issues to form power centers. Both procedures, as Wolfinger has recently pointed out, often rest on certain unspoken and unwarranted assumptions.[3] They appear to assume, for example, that lines of influence are clearly perceptible to respondents. They also assume a static distribution of power among certain personalities. But the chief difficulty with the usual approach is that it is only applicable in a case study; it offers no facility for quantitative and comparative studies of the phenomenon. And that, it seems to me, is a disability inherent in a social-psychological approach to the study of community structure.

Before turning to an alternative way of treating the matter, a prefatory comment on the nature of that which is in question seems to be appropriate. It should be obvious that power in the social sphere, as with energy in the physical world, is ubiquitous. It is like energy, too, in that it appears in many forms. Every social act is an exercise of power, every social relationship is a power equation, and every social group or system is an organization of power. Accordingly, it is possible to transpose any system of social relationships into terms of potential or active power. Perhaps such a transposition is nothing more than the substitution of one terminology for another. At the very least, however, it focuses attention on the instruments of control and causes a social system to be viewed as a control mechanism.

The community, for example, may be conceived as an energy system. That is, as a system of relationships among functionally differentiated units the community constitutes a mobilization of power — the capacity to produce results — for dealing with the environment, whether physical or social. Each unit or subsystem — family, church, store, industry — is also an organization of power for the conduct of a function. Both the system and its subsystems tend to approximate a single organization model. Moreover, since the performance of its function by any one part affects in greater or lesser degree the conditions under which other parts carry out their functions, the parent system and each subsystem is an arena in which a more or less continuous interplay of influence occurs. Power, then, is expressed in two ways: (1) as functional power — that required to execute a function; and (2) as derivative power — that which spills over into external relationships and regulates the interaction between parts. The two modes of manifestation are necessarily connected. The type of function performed determines the kind of derivative influence transmitted to other parts or subsystems. There might also be a quantitative association, though the magnitude of the derivative influence is a consequence not only of the scale to which a function has developed but also of its position in the system. Those subsystems that are most instrumental in relating the system to the environment doubtlessly exert a greater derivative effect than do subsystems one or more steps removed from the key position. Space does not permit a full exposition of a system conception of power. Perhaps enough has been said to indicate that power is a product of a system having developed, that it is lodged only in a system, and that it is most appropriately treated, therefore, as a system property.[4] Whatever power an individual might appear to possess is in effect attached to the office he occupies in a system. He acquires power by attaining to an office and he loses it when he is separated from the office. But the acquiring and losing of power is illusory; the property belongs rather with the office or, better still, to the system in which the office is a specialized function.[5]

In the conduct of its routine activities the system exercises its power through established and well-worn channels; the interplay of influence is institutionalized. But the structure of relationships through which power is communicated may leave various areas of interest or activity unattended, for example, private charity, religious digression and reform, the supervision of adolescents. When crises occur in such matters or when non-routine issues affecting the whole system arise, the existing structure is put to a test. It may or may not be effective in dealing with the exceptional circumstance. Whether it is effective would appear to be contingent on the way in which derivative power is distributed in the system. Where it is highly concentrated the community should be able to act as a unit in almost any emergency. On the other hand, where power is widely distributed a community may be able to act coherently only with great difficulty, if at all, when confronted with a novel problem.

This suggests a way of dealing with the variable quantitatively. A frustrating feature of studies of power has been the understandable failure to find a way to measure its amount. If, however, we can assume that an enduring system has sufficient force to regularly perform its normal functions, we can conclude that all systems of the same kind generate equivalent amounts of power. There remains a variable, namely, the way in which power is distributed. Any given amount may be in some instances concentrated in a small sector of the system or in other instances distributed more or less uniformly over all sectors or subsystems. The measurement of distribution appears to present fewer difficulties than does the measurement of the amount of power.

Now let me propose that the greater the concentration of power in a community the greater the probability of success in any collective action affecting the welfare of the whole. This follows, if it be granted that (1) success in a collective action requires the ability to mobilize the personnel and resources of the community and (2) that ability is greatest where power is most highly concentrated. The proposition does not say that a concentration of power assures success in any community venture. Various factors might intervene to defeat a collective project. Moreover, a concentration of power might be used to block a course of action. Power concentration, however, is not needed to defeat an action on the part of a community. That might occur as a result of power being so diffusely held that mobilization of the community cannot be accomplished.

Proceeding from the notion that system power resides in the subsystems or functional units of a community, we can infer that it must be exercised through the managerial functions of the subsystems. For it is those functions that coordinate the several other functions in their respective subsystems and articulate the latter with the larger system. In the absence of data on the number of managerial functions, I shall use the number of managerial personnel, that is, the number of people who reported occupations as manager, proprietor, or official in the Population Census, to measure concentration of power. Personnel, it should be stressed, is used only as a substitute for, and as an index of, functions.[6] Since the significance of the number of functions varies with the number of all other functions (i.e., the size of the employed labor force), it should be expressed as a ratio to the latter. Hence the lower the ratio of managers, proprietors, and officials [7] to the employed labor force the greater is the concentration of power. (This measure will hereafter be called the MPO ratio.)

As the dependent variable, that is, an example of collective action, I shall use success in urban renewal. Urban renewal, programed and administered by the Housing and Home Finance Agency, has the advantage of involving a standard procedure to which all participating communities must submit in like manner. Participation in the program by a municipality involves passage through a series of stages, differentiated by the extent to which the planning and other local arrangements required for federal financial support have been fulfilled. The stages are *planning, execution,* and *completion.* Arrival at the completion stage is unquestionably the best measure of success. Unfortunately only eighteen cities in the continental United States had by the end of 1959 advanced so far — hardly enough for statistical purposes. The next best indication of success in urban renewal is arrival at the execution stage. At that stage a city has completed its planning and has satisfied all administrative requirements for the receipt of a capital grant from the Housing and Home Finance Agency. The city is then either at the point of, or has embarked upon, the acquisition of land, the relocation of current occupants, and clearing and improving the land. At the end of 1959, ninety-five cities with population of 50,000 or more (in 1950) had advanced to the execution stage.[8]

For control purposes data on two other classes of cities of 50,000 or more population are employed. One class includes cities that entered the urban renewal program but for one reason or another abandoned their efforts sometime between 1950 and 1960. The thirty-eight cities that had that experience are called "dropouts." The second control class is made up of all cities, in states where urban renewal is legally permissible, that have not attempted urban renewal at any time. There are sixty-one such cities. All the members of this class, it is to be noted, are eligible for urban renewal assistance from the federal agency. There remains a sizable group of cities that are still in the planning stage. Eventually they will either pass into the execution stage or terminate their efforts; but at present their status is indeterminate. For that reason they are not included in the present study.

Whether urban renewal is a form of collective action that would call into operation the organization of the entire community may be debatable. The general scale of urban renewal projects is clearly relevant to the question. The average acreage involved in urban renewal projects in the 253 cities that were in the program in mid-1959 was 78.6 per city, or about one-eighth of a square mile. But one-fourth of all urban renewal acreage was contained in five cities; half the total was in nineteen cities. In the remaining cities the average acreage per city was 42.5, or a little over one-sixteenth of a square mile. That urban renewal, in the light of these magnitudes, represents a significant challenge to a community must be left as an unanswered question for the present. If it is regarded as a major undertaking in a community, it should certainly involve the local power structure. If it is considered to be a rather insignificant form of collective action, then as a dependent variable it provides a fairly severe test of the hypothesis.[9]

It seems advisable to restate the hypothesis in the operational terms set forth. The hypothesis is: MPO ratios are lowest in urban renewal cities that have reached the execution stage and highest in cities that have never attempted urban renewal. Dropout cities are expected to occupy an intermediate position between the polar classes.

The hypothesis is to be examined with reference to cities of 50,000 population or more. The abundance of data available for cities in that size range offers considerable latitude for refining the measure of power concentration and for the development of controls. In the following, however, the analysis of power concentration as an independent variable is confined primarily to ratios for the entire class of MPO's. Differentials within that class will be investigated in a later report.

As a preliminary test of the representativeness of cities of 50,000 population or more, their MPO ratios, for each urban renewal status class, are compared with those for all cities of 15,000–50,000 population, in Table 1. Observe that the two series of ratios are very similar. Thus it seems possible that findings for large cities might apply to all cities regardless of size. Further, though somewhat tangential, support of that conclusion is found in the fact that the number of years spent in the planning stage before reaching the execution stage is unrelated to size of city. No further attempt to ascertain the representativeness of large cities has been made.

It is also to be noted in Table 1 that the ratios conform to the hypothesis. Power is most highly concentrated in the execution-stage cities and most diffusely distributed in the never-in-program cities. That the concentration of power, as represented by the ratio of all MPO's to the employed labor force, is significantly greater in cities that have reached the execution stage in urban renewal than in the other classes of cities is apparent in Table 2. The probability that the association shown there is due to chance is less than 1 in a 100.

The quintile distribution of cities shown in Table 2 displays a considerable spread over the ratio range in each urban renewal status class. That raises a question of how some cities manage to get to the execution stage without a

TABLE 1. NUMBER AND RATIOS, CITIES BY SIZE CLASS AND BY URBAN RENEWAL STATUS

Urban renewal status	All cities of 15,000 population and over		Cities of 50,000 population and over		Cities of 15,000–50,000 population	
	No.	MPO ratio	No.	MPO ratio	No.	MPO ratio
Execution stage	136	9.0	95	9.0	41	9.1
Dropout	79	10.0	38	10.1	41	9.8
Never in program	402	11.0	61	10.8	341	11.1
Total	617	10.4	194	9.5	423	10.7

TABLE 2. QUINTILE DISTRIBUTION OF CITIES (MPO RATIOS), BY URBAN RENEWAL STATUS [a]

Urban renewal status	1st (under 7.7)	2d (7.8– 8.9)	3d (9.0– 9.9)	4th (10.0– 11.7)	5th (11.8 and over)
Execution stage	27	22	21	17	9
Dropout	3	9	8	8	7
Never in program	9	9	8	13	22

[a] $\chi^2 = 23.516$, $C = .330$, $P < .01$.

concentration of power. The complementary question of how other cities with marked concentrations of power escape urban renewal may be given a tentative a priori answer: that is, they are susceptible and may yet enter the program. In any event, it is doubtlessly true that factors other than the distribution of power operate on urban renewal experience or the lack of it.

For example, the probability that urban renewal might recommend itself to a community as a course of action should be somewhat contingent on the state of its physical equipment. If the equipment, in this instance its buildings, is fairly new and in good condition, urban renewal would make little sense. But where buildings are old or dilapidated a proposal to renew or rehabilitate would appear to be appropriate. Two measures of the condition of buildings are used here: (1) the percentage of all residential units constructed before 1920, and (2) the percentage of all residential units reported as dilapidated. Cities are classified relative to the median for each characteristic, providing two dichotomies. "Young" cities have less than 65 percent of their houses built before 1920, and "old" cities 65 percent or more of their houses built prior to that date. Cities with less than 4.7 percent of their houses dilapidated are described as "low" on that variable while those with 4.7 percent and over are classified as "high."

It is conceivable, too, that some cities might have anticipated the problems that invite urban renewal by having established a well-financed and strongly supported planning agency. Cities that have done so might not have to seek federal assistance for improvements. A contrary argument can also be advanced. Perhaps cities with substantial commitments to planning are more prepared to enter into a renewal project than are cities in which planning has not been developed to any appreciable extent. Notwithstanding my inability to resolve this question, the size of the planning budget might prove to be a factor of some consequence. For the purpose of control, planning expenditures are expressed as a ratio to total government operating costs in 1955. Ratios of less than .4 are below the median and thus identify their respective cities as "low" with respect to planning budgets, while ratios of .4 and over indicate cities with "high" planning budgets.

There is a strong likelihood, too, that central cities of metropolitan areas might be more favorably disposed toward urban renewal than suburban cities. That should follow from the fact that central cities are generally older than are suburbs. But it should also derive from the deconcentration trend through which central cities have been losing population and industry to outlying areas. Many large suburban cities have also begun to experience declining growth rates, though in only a few cases has the trend reached a critical stage. Where substantial losses, real or threatened, have been encountered urban renewal might appear to offer a means by which to reverse the trend. There is a second factor that calls attention to the central city–suburb distinction. That is the peculiar residential distribution of managers, proprietors, and officials. Since members of those groups tend to live in suburbs while working in central cities their numbers as reported in the Census fail to reflect accurately the number of such positions in each place. The only practicable solution to this difficulty is to control for metropolitan status, that is, central city and suburb.

My operationalization of the concentration of power represents but one facet of a complex phenomenon. Other dimensions of that phenomenon should at least be admitted as control variables. For example, power may lie mainly in either the manufacturing or in the local service sector of a community's economy, whichever is most important. Relative importance is here measured by the ratio of manufacturing payroll to the combined payrolls in retailing, wholesaling, and service enterprises. Service cities have ratios of 1.5 or less and manufacturing cities have ratios of over 1.5.

The average size of manufacturing plant is another possible dimension of the distribution of power, especially if it may be construed as an indicator of the general scale of functional activities in the community. Size of plant is measured by the average number of employees per plant. Small-plant cities have averages of less than 70 employees; large-plant cities have over 70 employees per plant.

Still another expression of power distribution is found in the type of city government. In cities having a commission form of government, administrative responsibility is spread over a large number of non-elective officials. Such cities probably are unable to mobilize for action unless there is a fairly high concentration of power of the kind under study here. Administrative authority is more centralized where a mayor-council government exists. And in a city manager government administrative authority reaches its highest degree of centralization and articulation. Hence, contrary to the findings of another study that type of city government is not important in determining urban renewal success,[10] I shall employ it as a control.

Two other controls having to do with the socioeconomic level of the resident population are used. Both assume that where the socioeconomic level is high the community may be prepared to act in a matter such as urban renewal independently of a concentration of power. The first, education, is represented by the proportion of the population with four or more years of college completed. The second, income, is measured by median income. Cities are dichotomized on the median for each variable. Cities with less than 6.0 percent of their residents with four years or more of college education are "low," and those with over that proportion are "high." The median position for the median income array falls at $3,450; cities below and above that figure are "low" and "high," respectively.

Finally, region is included among the controls. To some extent regional differences combine differences in age of cities, dilapidation, income, education, and possibly other of the control variables discussed above. Thus it is reasonable to expect that the association of power distribution with urban renewal success might vary by region. Four regions are recognized for control purposes; northeast, north central, south, and west.[11]

MPO ratios for each urban renewal status class and with each of the ten controls applied successively are shown in Table 3. In no instance does the introduction of a control vitiate the association of power concentration with urban renewal success, though in a number of instances the dropout cities fail to hold an intermediate position between execution stage and never-in-program cities. Although the averages for dropout cities are affected by small numbers of cities in many cases, it is also possible that power concentration has been employed to defeat urban renewal in those cities. It is worth noting that even where the concentration of power is relatively great, as in old cities, mayor-council cities, manufacturing cities, large-plant cities, low-education cities, and cities in the northeast, the concentration varies with urban renewal success. There is no indication, in short, that the importance attached to the concentration of power is peculiar to any one type or class of city. Despite the fact

TABLE 3. MEAN MPO RATIOS IN CITIES, BY URBAN RENEWAL STATUS, WITH SELECTED VARIABLES CONTROLLED

Control variable	Urban renewal status		
	Execution stage	Dropout	Never in program
Age of housing:			
Young	10.1	10.7	12.2
Old	8.2	9.5	9.5
Extent of dilapidation:			
Low	9.1	9.2	11.0
High	9.1	10.9	10.2
Planning budget:			
Small	8.8	9.3a	11.0
Large	9.6	11.3	11.6
Metropolitan status:			
Central city	9.0	10.8	10.1
Suburban city	8.9	8.5	11.9
Government:			
Manager	9.5	9.7	12.3
Mayor-council	8.8	9.4	9.7
Commission	8.7	12.1	10.2b
Industry:			
Service	10.0	10.9	12.6
Manufacturing	8.1	9.2	9.7
Size of manufacturing plant:			
Small	9.5	11.0	12.0
Large	8.1	8.8	9.5
Median income:			
Low	8.8	10.7	9.6
High	9.2	9.7	11.4
Education:			
Low	8.2	9.8	8.6
High	9.8	10.5	12.4
Region:			
Northeast	8.5	8.1	9.8
North central	8.5	10.6	10.4
South	9.4	11.0	12.2b
West	11.9b	12.8a	12.6

a N is 5 or less.
b N is less than 10.

that suburban cities are the preferred places of residence for a large proportion of the holders of administrative positions, urban renewal success seems to require as great a concentration of power in suburbs as it does in central cities. Also of interest is the evidence that manager cities appear to be able to achieve urban renewal with less power concentration than do cities of other government classes.

To better assess the closeness of the association of power concentration with urban renewal success I have employed rank correlation analysis, using Kendall's tau–*c*. For this purpose the three urban renewal status classes are assumed to constitute a scale. Evidence that such an assumption is reasonable is present in Tables 1 and 3. The independent variable is treated in a quintile distribution of cities by MPO ratios, as in Table 2. The results are shown in Table 4, for which data a one-tailed test of significance was used.

It is clear from the findings in Table 4 that the concentration of power is

TABLE 4. MEASURES OF ASSOCIATION OF MPO RATIOS WITH URBAN RENEWAL STATUS, WITH SELECTED VARIABLES CONTROLLED

Control variable	*Tau*	x/σ	*P*
All cities	.267	4.112	.00003
Age of housing:			
Young	.239	2.568	.00510
Old	.236	2.689	.00360
Extent of dilapidation:			
Low	.258	2.801	.00260
High	.267	2.951	.00160
Planning budget:			
Small	.243	2.159	.01540
Large	.305	2.430	.00750
Metropolitan status:			
Central city	.214	2.874	.00200
Suburban city	.402	3.337	.00048
Government:			
Manager	.429	3.711	.00011
Mayor-council	.134	1.387	.08230
Commission	.302	3.337	.00048
Industry:			
Service	.169	.998	.15870
Manufacturing	.220	3.175	.00068
Size of manufacturing plant:			
Small	.301	3.292	.00048
Large	.186	2.065	.01960
Median income:			
Low	.219	2.533	.00570
High	.266	2.833	.00230
Education:			
Low	.122	1.382	.08380
High	.363	3.995	.00003
Region:			
Northeast	.108	1.096	.13350
North central	.233	2.062	.01970
South	.388	2.805	.00260
West	.105	.649	.25780

positively and significantly associated with urban renewal success under virtually all conditions of control. Several exceptions occur, however. The relationship is not dependable for cities with mayor-council governments, with a predominance of service industry, with small proportions of college graduates among their residents, and with locations in the northeast and the west. Some of these exceptions appear to be contrary to the positive findings involving variables known to be closely associated with them (education and income, northeastern location, and manufacturing industry). Had it been possible to refine the controls, some of the inconsistencies doubtlessly would have disappeared.

The category of all managers, proprietors, and officials is quite heterogeneous; it embraces the full range of both size and type of unit in which such positions occur. Thus it is not unlikely that one or another subclass or industry group of managers, proprietors, and officials might be primarily responsible for the observed association. But the measures reported in Table 5 indicate that that is not the case. The correlation is statistically significant for every industrial class of managers, proprietors, and officials but one. The one, public administration, not only falls short of significance, it is negative. Why the prospects for urban renewal success should tend to increase with increases in the relative numbers of managers and officials in public administration poses an interesting problem. But that is not a question that can be pursued here. Nor is it possible to press the analysis of industry class of managers, proprietors, and officials further at present, though the fact that the relationship for each industry class taken separately responds differently to the application of controls clearly points to a need for a more intensive investigation.

While the findings reported in this paper should be regarded as exploratory, they clearly support the hypothesis that the lower the MPO ratio the greater the chance of success in an action program such as urban renewal. They also demonstrate the facility and the economy in research of a conception of power as a system property. Much remains to be done, however, to develop knowledge about that property. A factor of some importance is the composition of managerial positions in a city. The relative numbers in the key industry should prove decisive, if my initial argument is correct. What constitutes a key industry, of course, is contingent upon the function the city performs for the regional and national society. The pursuit of that question will doubtlessly suggest further lines of investigation.

TABLE 5. MEASURES OF ASSOCIATION OF MPO RATIOS WITH URBAN RENEWAL STATUS, BY CLASS OF INDUSTRY, WITH SELECTED VARIABLES CONTROLLED

Industry class	Tau	x/σ	P
All industries	.267	4.112	.00003
Manufacturing:			
Salaried MPO's	.170	2.622	.00440
Self-employed MPO's	.209	3.229	.00137
Retail and wholesale trade	.214	3.300	.00097
Banking and finance	.209	3.229	.00137
Public administration	−.105	−1.612	.10740

Notes

[1] I am indebted to Professors Albert J. Reiss, Jr., and Robert Somers for helpful advice in the preparation of this paper.

[2] Representative studies include Floyd Hunter, *Community Power Structure* (Chapel Hill: University of North Carolina Press, 1953); Robert O. Schultz and Leonard U. Blumberg, "The Determinants of Local Power Elites," *American Journal of Sociology*, LXIII (1957), 290–96; Delbert C. Miller, "Decision-making Cliques in Community Power Structure," *American Journal of Sociology*, LXIV (1958), 299–309; Paul Miller, "The Process of Decision-making within the Context of Community Organization," *Rural Sociology*, XVII (1952), 153–61.

[3] Raymond E. Wolfinger, "The Study of Community Power," *American Sociological Review*, XXV (1960), 636–44.

[4] This position has been stated recently by Richard M. Emerson, though he objects to the assumption of generalized power that is adopted, at least for present purposes, in this study ("Power-Dependence Relations," *American Sociological Review*, XXVII [1962], 31–32).

[5] The conception of power developed here is interchangeable with the ecological concept of dominance. Ecologists, however, have been content to treat dominance as an attribute of location or type of place, though the concept has always carried overtones of organizational properties. They have neglected to exploit the concept as an entree into the general problem of organization.

[6] A similar notion appears in the introductory remarks of C. Wright Mills in his book on *The Power Elite* (New York: Oxford University Press, 1956). Nevertheless it soon becomes apparent that Mills is mainly concerned with the personal characteristics of the occupants of such positions.

[7] For present purposes only managers, proprietors, and officials "not elsewhere classified" are used, thus eliminating technical positions that have no management or policy-determining functions. The category, it should be noted, is not limited to management positions in pecuniary establishments. It includes managers of art galleries, libraries, community funds, welfare agencies, and others.

[8] Data on cities that have had urban renewal experience have been obtained from the *Annual Report of the Housing and Home Finance Agency*, 1951 through 1960 (Washington, D.C.).

[9] *Urban Renewal Project Characteristics* (Washington, D.C.: Housing and Home Finance Agency, Urban Renewal Administration, June 30, 1959).

[10] George S. Duggar, "The Relation of Local Government Structure to Urban Renewal," *Law and Contemporary Problems*, XXVI (1961), 49–69.

[11] Two other controls were used with similar results: population size and income as represented by the proportion of families with incomes of $10,000 or more per year.

B-2: Evaluating a summary-critique report

Beyond Family Planning

BERNARD BERELSON

This paper rests on these propositions: (1) among the great problems on the world agenda is the population problem; (2) that problem is most urgent in the developing countries where rapid population growth retards social and economic development; (3) there is a time penalty on the problem in the sense that, other things equal, anything not done sooner may be harder to do later, due to increased numbers; and accordingly (4) everything that can properly be done to lower population growth rates should be done, now. As has been asked on other occasions, the question is: what is to be done? There is a certain agreement on the general objective (i.e., on the desirability of lowering birth rates, though not on how far how fast), but there is disagreement as to means.

Reprinted by permission of the author and The Population Council from *Studies in Family Planning*, no. 38 (February, 1969), pp. 1–16. © 1969 The Population Council.

The 1960's have witnessed a substantial increase of awareness and concern with population matters throughout the world [1] and of efforts to do something about the problem, particularly in the developing countries. That something typically turns out to be the establishment of national family planning programs, or rough equivalents thereof. There are now 20 to 25 countries with efforts along this line, on all three developing continents, all of them either set up or revitalized in this decade. Thus, the first response to too high growth rates deriving from too high birth rates is to introduce voluntary contraception on a mass basis, or try to.

Why is family planning the first step taken on the road to population control? Probably because from a broad political standpoint it is the most acceptable one: since closely tied to maternal and child care it can be perceived as a health measure beyond dispute; and since voluntary it can be justified as a contribution to the effective personal freedom of individual couples. On both scores, the practice ties into accepted values and thus achieves political viability. In some situations, it is an oblique approach, seen as the politically acceptable way to start toward "population control" on the national level by promoting fertility control and smaller family size among individual couples. Moreover, it is a gradual effort and an inexpensive one, both of which contribute to its political acceptability. Though the introduction of family planning as a response to a country's population problem may be calculated to minimize opposition, even that policy has been attacked in several countries by politicians who are unconvinced and/or see an electoral advantage in the issue.

How effective have family planning programs been as a means toward population control? There is currently some controversy among qualified observers as to their efficacy,[2] and this is not the place to review that issue. But there is sufficient agreement on the magnitude and consequence of the problem that additional efforts are needed to reach a "solution," however that is responsibly defined.

For the purpose of this paper, then, let us assume that today's national family planning programs, mainly via voluntary contraception, are not "enough" — where "enough" is defined not necessarily as achieving zero growth in some extended present but simply as lowering birth rates quickly and substantially. "Enough" begs the question of the ultimate goal and only asks that a faster decline in population growth rates be brought about than is presently in process or in prospect — and, within the range of the possible, the faster the better.[3] Just to indicate the rough order of magnitude, let us say that the proximate goal is the halving of the birth rate in the developing countries in the next decade or two — from, say, over 40 births per thousand per year to 20–25.[4] For obvious reasons, both emigration and increased death rates are ruled out of consideration.

What is to be done to bring that about, beyond present programs of voluntary family planning?[5] I address that question in two ways: first, by listing the programs or policies more or less responsibly suggested to this end in recent years; and second, by reviewing the issues raised by the suggested approaches.

PROPOSALS: BEYOND FAMILY PLANNING

Here is a listing of the several proposals, arranged in descriptive categories. (There may be a semantic question involved in some cases: when is a proposal a proposal? Are "suggestions" or "offers for consideration" or lists of alternatives to be considered as proposals? In general, I have included all those cases presented in a context in which they were readily perceived as providing a supplementary or alternative approach to present efforts. The list may include both proposals for consideration and proposals for action.)

A. *Extension of Voluntary Fertility Control*
1. Institutionalization of maternal care in rural areas of developing countries: a feasibility study of what would be required in order to bring some degree of modern medical or paramedical attention to every pregnant woman in the rural areas of five developing countries with professional back-up for difficult cases and with family planning education and services a central component of the program aimed particularly at women of low parity (Taylor & Berelson [6]).
2. Liberalization of induced abortion (Davis,[7] Ehrlich,[8] Chandrasekhar [9]).

B. *Establishment of Involuntary Fertility Control*
1. Mass use of "fertility control agent" by government to regulate births at acceptable level: the "fertility control agent" designed to lower fertility in the society by 5 percent to 75 percent less than the present birth rate, as needed; substance now unknown but believed to be available for field testing after 5–15 years of research work; to be included in water supply in urban areas and by "other methods" elsewhere (Ketchel [10]); "addition of temporary sterilants to water supplies or staple food" (Ehrlich [11]).
2. "Marketable licenses to have children," given to women and perhaps men in "whatever number would ensure a reproduction rate of one," say 2.2 children per couple: for example, "the unit certificate might be the 'deci-child,' and accumulation of ten of these units by purchase, inheritance or gift, would permit a woman in maturity to have one legal child" (Boulding [12]).
3. Temporary sterilization of all girls via time-capsule contraceptives, and again after each delivery, with reversibility allowed only upon governmental approval; certificates of approval distributed according to popular vote on desired population growth for a country, and saleable on open market (Shockley [13]).
4. Compulsory sterilization of men with three or more living children (Chandrasekhar [14]); requirement of induced abortion for all illegitimate pregnancies (Davis [15]).

C. *Intensified Educational Campaigns*
1. Inclusion of population materials in primary and secondary schools systems (Davis,[16] Wayland,[17] Visaria [18]): materials on demographic and physiological aspects, perhaps family planning and sex education as well; introduced at the secondary level in order to reach next waves of public school teachers throughout the country.
2. Promotion of national satellite television systems for direct informational effect on population and family planning as well as for indirect effect on modernization in general: satellite broadcasting probably through ground relays with village receivers (Ehrlich,[19] Meier & Meier,[20] UNESCO,[21] Schramm & Nelson [22]).

D. *Incentive Programs:* This term requires clarification. As used here, it refers to payments, or their equivalent, made directly to contracepting couples and/or to couples not bearing children for specified periods. It does *not* refer to payments to field workers, medical personnel, volunteers, et al., for securing acceptance of contraceptive practice; that type of payment, now utilized in many programs, is better called a fee or a stipend in order to differentiate it from an incentive as used here. Beyond that distinction, however, the term is fuzzy at the edges: is the provision of free contraceptive consultation and supplies to be considered an incentive? or free milk to the infant along with family planning information to the mother? or free transport to the family planning service, which then provides general health care? or a generous payment in lieu of time off from work for a vasectomy operation? or even a financial burden imposed for undesirable fertility behavior? In the usage here, I try to limit the term to direct payment of money (or goods or services) to members of the target population in return for the desired practice. This usage is sometimes referred to as a "positive" incentive in distinction to the "negative" incentive inherent in tax or welfare penalties for "too many" children (E below).

1. Payment for the initiation or the effective practice of contraception: payment or equivalent (e.g., transistor radio) for sterilization (Chandrasekhar,[23] Pohlman,[24] Samuel,[25] Davis [26]) or for contraception (Simon,[27] Enke,[28] Samuel [29]).

2. Payment for periods of non-pregnancy or non-birth: a bonus for child spacing or non-pregnancy (Young,[30] Bhatia,[31] Enke,[32] Spengler,[33] Leasure [34]); a savings certificate plan for twelve-month periods of non-birth (Balfour [35]); a lottery scheme for preventing illegitimate births among teenagers in a small country (Mauldin [36]); "responsibility prizes" for each five years of childless marriage or for vasectomy before the third child, and special lotteries with tickets available to the childless (Ehrlich [37]).

E. *Tax and Welfare Benefits and Penalties:* i.e., an anti-natalist system of social services in place of the present pro-natalist tendencies.

1. Withdrawal of maternity benefits, perhaps after N (3?) children (Bhatia,[38] Samuel,[39] Davis [40]) or unless certain limiting conditions have been met, like sufficient child spacing, knowledge of family planning, or level of income (Titmuss & Abel-Smith [41]).

2. Withdrawal of children or family allowances, perhaps after N children (Bhatia,[42] Titmuss & Abel-Smith,[43] Davis [44]).

3. Tax on births after the Nth (Bhatia,[45] Samuel,[46] Spengler [47]).

4. Limitation of governmentally provided medical treatment, housing, scholarships, loans and subsidies, etc., to families with fewer than N children (Bhatia,[48] Davis [49]).

5. Reversal of tax benefits, to favor the unmarried and the parents of fewer rather than more children (Bhatia,[50] Titmuss & Abel-Smith,[51] Samuel,[52] Davis,[53] Ehrlich,[54] David [55]).

6. Provision by the state of N years of free schooling at all levels to each nuclear family, to be allocated by the family among the children as desired (Fawcett [56]).

7. Pensions for poor parents with fewer than N children as social security for their old age (Samuel,[57] Ohlin,[58] Davison [59]).

F. *Shifts in Social and Economic Institutions:* i.e., broad changes in fundamental institutional arrangements that could have the effect of lowering
fertility.

1. Increase in minimum age of marriage: through legislation or through substantial fee for marriage licenses (David,[60] Davis [61]); or through direct
bonuses for delayed marriage (Young [62]); or through payment of marriage
benefits only to parents of brides over 21 years of age (Titmuss & Abel-
Smith [63]); or through a program of government loans for wedding ceremonies
when the bride is of a sufficient age, or with the interest rate inversely related to the bride's age (Davis [64]); or through a "governmental 'first marriage grant' . . . awarded each couple in which the age of both [*sic*] partners
was 25 or more" (Ehrlich [65]); or through establishment of a domestic "national service" program for all men for the appropriate two-year period in
order to develop social services, inculcate modern attitudes including family
planning and population control, and at the same time delay age of marriage
(Berelson, Etzioni [66]).

2. Promotion or requirement of female participation in labor force (outside
the home) to provide roles and interests for women alternative or supplementary to marriage (Hauser,[67] Davis,[68] David [69]).

3. "Direct manipulation of family structure itself — planned efforts at deflecting
the family's socializing function, reducing the noneconomic utilities of offspring, or introducing nonfamilial distractions and opportunity costs into
people's lives"; specifically, through employment of women outside the home
(Blake [70]); "selective restructuring of the family in relation to the rest of
society" (Davis [71]).

4. Promotion of "two types of marriage, one of them childless and readily
dissolved, and the other licensed for children and designed to be stable";
the former needs to be from 20–40 percent of the total in order to allow the
remainder to choose family size freely (Meier & Meier [72]).

5. Encouragement of long-range social trends leading toward lower fertility,
e.g., "improved and universal general education, or new roads facilitating
communication, or improved agricultural methods, or a new industry
that would increase productivity, or other types of innovation that may
break the 'cake of custom' and produce social foment" (Hauser [73]); and improved status of women (U.N./ECOSOC [74]).

6. Efforts to lower death rates even further, particularly infant and child
death rates, on the inference that birth rates will follow them down
(Revelle,[75] Heer & Smith [76]).

G. *Approaches via Political Channels and Organizations*

1. U.S. insistence on "population control as the price of food aid," with highly
selective assistance based thereon, and exertion of political pressures on
governments or religious groups impeding "solution" of the population
problem, including shifts in sovereignty (Ehrlich [77]).

2. Re-organization of national and international agencies to deal with the
population problem: within the United States, "coordination by a powerful
governmental agency, a Federal Department of Population and Environment (DPE) . . . with the power to take whatever steps are necessary to
establish a reasonable population size" (Ehrlich [78]); within India, creation of

"a separate Ministry of Population Control" (Chandrasekhar [79]); development of an "international specialized agency larger than WHO to operate programs for extending family limitation techniques to the world . . . charged with the responsibility of effecting the transfer to population equilibrium" (Meier & Meier [80]).

3. Promotion of zero growth in population, as the ultimate goal needed to be accepted now in order to place intermediate goals of lowered fertility in proper context (Davis [81]).

H. *Augmented Research Efforts*

1. More research on social means for achieving necessary fertility goals (Davis [82]).
2. Focused research on practical methods of sex determination (Polgar [83]).
3. Increased research toward an improved contraceptive technology (NAS [84]).

PROPOSALS: REVIEW OF THE ISSUES

Here are 29 proposals beyond family planning for dealing with the problem of undue population growth in the developing world. I naturally cannot claim that these are all the proposals made more or less responsibly toward that end, but my guess is that there are not many more and that these proposals are a reasonably good sample of the total list. In any case, these are perhaps the most visible at the present time and the following analysis is limited to them.

Since several of the proposals tend in the same direction, it seems appropriate to review them illustratively against the criteria that any such proposals might be required to meet. What are such criteria? There are at least six: (1) scientific/medical/technological readiness, (2) political viability, (3) administrative feasibility, (4) economic capability, (5) moral/ethical/philosophical acceptability, and (6) presumed effectiveness. In other words, the key questions are: is the scientific/medical/technological base available or likely? will governments approve? can the proposal be administered? can the society afford the proposal? is it morally acceptable? and finally, will it work?

Such criteria and questions have to be considered against some time scale. As indicated at the outset of this paper, I suggest the next decade or two on the double grounds that the future is dim enough at that point let alone beyond and that in any case it is difficult to develop plans and programs now for a more remote future. National economic plans, for example, are typically limited to five years and then a new one made in accord with the conditions existing at that time. In any case, long-run social goals are normally approached through successive short-run efforts.

Since the population problem in the developing world is particularly serious in its implications for human welfare, such proposals deserve serious consideration indeed. What do the proposals come to, viewed against the indicated criteria? (I use India throughout as the major illustrative case since it is the key example of the problem; disregarding Mainland China, India has a much larger population than all the other countries with population programs combined.)

SCIENTIFIC/MEDICAL/TECHNOLOGICAL READINESS

Two questions are involved: (1) is the needed technology available? and (2) are the needed medical or para-medical personnel available or readily trainable to assure medical administration and safety?

With regard to temporary contraception, sterilization, and abortion, the needed technology is not only available now but is being steadily improved and expanded. The IUD (intrauterine device) and the oral pill have been major contraceptive developments of the past decade, and several promising leads are now being followed up [85] — though it cannot be said with much confidence that any of them will eventuate for mass use within the next few years.[86] Improved technologies for sterilization, both male and female, are being worked on; and there has been a recent development in abortion technique, the so-called suction device now being utilized in Eastern Europe and the U.S.S.R.[87]

However, neither Ehrlich's "temporary sterilants" nor Ketchel's "fertility control agent" (B-1) is now available or on the technological horizon — though that does not mean that the research task ought not to be pursued against a subsequent need, especially since such substances could be administered voluntarily and individually as well as involuntarily and collectively. In the latter case, if administered through the water supply or a similar source, the substance would need to be medically safe and free of side effects for men and women, young and old, well and ill, physiologically normal and physiologically marginal, as well as for animals and perhaps plants. As some people have remarked, such an involuntary addition to a water supply would face far greater difficulties of acceptance simply on medical grounds than the far milder proposals with regard to fluoridation to prevent tooth decay.

Though a substantial technology in fertility control does exist, that does not mean that it can be automatically applied where most needed, partly because of limitations of trained personnel. In general, the more the technology requires the services of medical or para-medical personnel (or, what is much the same, is perceived as requiring them), the more difficult it is to administer in the developing countries. For example, such traditional contraceptives as condoms or foams can be distributed freely through a variety of non-medical channels, including commercial ones, though that network is not without limitations in the poorer countries. Oral contraceptive pills *are* now distributed in large numbers without substantial medical intervention in a number of countries — sold by pharmacies without prescription — but not with medical sanction; and most qualified medical specialists here and abroad believe that the pills should be given only after proper medical examination and with proper medical follow-up. IUD's were first inserted only by obstetricians, then by medical doctors, and now, in a few situations where female medical personnel are unavailable in sufficient numbers, by specially trained para-medical personnel (notably, on a large scale, in Pakistan).

In the case of sterilization and abortion, the medical requirement becomes more severe. For example, when the policy of compulsory vasectomy of men with three or more children was first being considered in India (see footnote 14), an estimate was made that the policy would affect about 40 million males: "one thousand surgeons or para-surgeons each averaging 20 operations a day for five days a week would take eight years to cope with the existing candidates, and during this time of course a constant supply of new candidates would be coming along" [88] — at present birth rates, probably of the order of 3.5 million a year. Large-scale abortion practice, assuming legality and acceptability, might additionally require hospital beds, which are in particularly short supply in most developing countries. Just as an indication of order of magnitude, in India, for example, there are approximately 22 million births annually; to abort five million would require the equivalent of about 800 physicians, each doing 25 a day five days a week fifty weeks a year, which is approximately 10 percent of the obstetrical/gynecological specialists in India, or perhaps 25 percent of the female specialists; and about 10 million bed days, which is over half the estimated number of maternity bed days in the country at present.[89] However, the newer abortion technique might not require hospitalization — theoretically, the abortion "camp" may be feasible, as was the vasectomy "camp," except perhaps for the greater sensitivities attaching to the status of women, though it is not medically desirable — and para-medical personnel may be acceptable as well. Reportedly, the newer technique does not involve hospitalization in some parts of Eastern Europe and Mainland China.

In short, the technology is available for some but not all current proposals, and the same may be the case for properly trained personnel.

POLITICAL VIABILITY

As mentioned earlier, the "population problem" has been increasingly recognized by national governments and international agencies over the past decade, and favorable policies have been increasingly adopted: national family planning programs in some 20–25 countries, positive resolutions and actions within the United Nations family, large programs of support by such developed countries as United States and Sweden, the so-called World Leaders' Statement. There is no reason to think that that positive trend has run its course.

At the same time, the political picture is by no means unblemished. Some favorable policies are not strong enough to support a vigorous program even where limited to family planning on health grounds; in national politics "population control" can become a handy issue for a determined opposition; internal ethnic balances are sometimes delicately involved, with political ramifications; national size is often equated with national power, from the standpoint of international relations and regional military balances; the motives behind the support and encouragement of population control by the developed countries are sometimes perceived as politically expedient if not neo-colonialist or neo-imperialist; and on the international front, as represented by the United Nations, there is still considerable reluctance based on both religio-moral and political considerations. In short, elite ambivalence and perceived political liability are not absent even in the favoring countries. That state of affairs may not be surprising looked at historically and given the sensitive religious, military, and political issues involved, but it does not provide maximum support for energetic measures directed at the "necessary" degree of population control.

The question of political acceptability of such proposals becomes in effect two questions: what is presumably acceptable within the present situation? and what might be done to enlarge the sphere of acceptability (as for example, in proposals G-1 and G-2)?

In the nature of the political case, population measures are not taken in isolation — which is to say, they are not given overriding claim upon the nation's attention and resources even though they have been given special authority in a few countries. They must thus compete in the political arena with other claims and values, and that kind of competition accords with the political bases of an open society.

Any social policy adopted by government rests on some minimum consensus upon goals and means. They need not be the ultimate goals or the final means; as noted above, the socio-economic plans of developing countries are typically five-year plans, not 20- or 40- or 100-year plans. Indeed, an ultimate goal of population policy — that is, zero growth — need not be agreed upon or even considered by officials who can agree upon the immediate goal of lowering growth by a specified amount or by "as much as possible" within a period of years. And since there are always goals beyond goals, one does not even need to know what the ultimate goal is, only the direction in which it will be found (which is usually more likely of agreement). Would the insistence *now* on the acknowledgment of an *ultimate* goal of zero growth advance the effort or change its direction?

The means to such ends need not be final either. Indeed, at least at the outset of a somewhat controversial program, the means probably must fit within the framework of existing values, elite or mass, and preferably both — for example, a family planning program for maternal and child health and for preventing unwanted births even though the resultant growth rate may still remain "too high" by ultimate standards.

Specifically, against this background, how politically acceptable do some of the proposals appear to be?

To start with, the proposals of involuntary controls in India in 1967 (B-4) precipitated "a storm of questions in Parliament," [90] was withdrawn, and resulted in a high-level personnel shift within the family planning organization. No other country has seriously entertained the idea. Leaving aside other considerations, political instability in many countries would make implementation virtually impossible.

Social measures designed to affect the birth rate indirectly — e.g., tax benefits, social security arrangements, etc. — have been proposed from time to time. In India, there have been several such proposals: for example, by the United Nations mission,[91] by the Small Family Norm Committee,[92] by the Central Family Planning Council (e.g., with regard to age of marriage, the education and employment of women, and various social welfare benefits),[93] and in almost every issue of such publications as *Family Planning News, Centre Calling,* and *Planned Parenthood* (illustrative recent headings: "Tax to Reduce Family Size," "Relief for Bachelors Urged," "Scholarships for Children, Family Planning for Parents"). As Samuel reports, with accompanying documentation, "the desirability of imposing a tax on births of fourth or higher order has been afloat for some time. However, time and again, the suggestion has been rejected by the Government of India." [94] In some cases, action has been taken by either the Central Government (e.g., income tax "deductions for dependent children are given for the first and second child only" [95]) or certain states (e.g., "Maharashtra and Uttar Pradesh have decided to grant educational concessions and benefits only to those children whose parents restrict the size of their families . . ." [96] and the former state is reportedly beginning to penalize families with more than three children by withholding maternity leave, educational benefits, and housing privileges, though in the nature of the case only a small proportion of the state's population is affected by these disincentives [97]). As an indication of political sensitivity, an order withdrawing maternity leave for non-industrial women employees with three or more living children — at best a tiny number of educated women — was revoked before it really went into effect.[98] There is a special political problem in many countries, in that economic constraints on fertility often turn out in practice to be selective on class, racial, or ethnic grounds, and thus exacerbate political tensions.

As another example, promoting female participation in the labor force runs up against the political problem that such employment would be competitive with men in situations of already high male un- and under-employment. One inquiry concludes: "The prospective quantitative effect of moves in this direction seems very questionable. The number of unemployed in India has been rising by approximately 50 percent every five years, and this is a well-known and very hot political issue. The government can hardly be blamed for being reluctant to promote female employment at the expense of male employment, which the great bulk of female employment almost surely would be." [99]

Given the present and likely political climate both within and between countries, whether programs for lowering population growth and birth rates are politically acceptable or not appears to depend largely upon whether they are perceived as positive or negative: where "positive" means that they are seen as promoting other social values as well as population limitation and where "negative" means that they are seen as limited per se. For example, family planning programs, as noted above, are often rationalized as contributing both to maternal and child health and to the effective freedom of the individual family; a large-scale television network would contribute to other informational goals (though it is also politically suspect as providing too much power to the government in office); promotion of female participation in the labor force would add to economic productivity at the same time that it subtracted from the birth rate; extension of MCH services to rural areas is clearly desirable in itself, with or without family planning attached; incorporation of population material in school systems can be justified on educational grounds as well as population ones; a pension for the elderly would have social welfare benefits as well as indirect impact upon the large family as a social security system; contraceptive programs in Latin America are promoted by the medical community as a medical and humanitarian answer not to the population problem but to the extensive illegal and dangerous practice of abortion. On the other hand, imposing tax liabilities or withdrawing benefits after the Nth child, not to mention involuntary measures, can be attacked as a punitive means whose only purpose is that of population limitation.

It would thus require great political courage joined to very firm demographic convictions for a national leader to move toward an unpopular and severe prescription designed to cure his country's population ills. Indeed, it is difficult to envisage such a political move in an open society where a political opposition could present a counter view and perhaps prevail. Witness the views of two strong advocates of additional measures beyond family planning:

> A realistic proposal for a government policy of lowering the birth rate reads like a catalogue of horrors. . . . No government will institute such hardship simply for the purpose of controlling population growth.[100]

> If a perfected control agent were available now, I am certain that it would not be utilized in any democratic country, for no population would be likely to vote to have such agents used on itself. This means that the effects of overpopulation are not yet acute enough for people to accept an unpleasant alternative.[101]

The political problem of population control, like many political matters of consequence, is a matter of timing: in the 1950's nothing much could be done but in the 1960's a number of countries and international agencies moved at least as far as family planning programs. Political accommodation is typically a matter of several small steps with an occasional large one; and in this case it rests upon the seriousness with which the population problem is viewed. That is growing, hence political acceptability of added measures may also grow. Regardless of what the future may bring in this regard, several social measures like those in the list of proposals have been made from time to time and have encountered political obstacles. At least for the time being, such obstacles are real and must be taken into account in any realistic proposal.

The governmental decisions about measures taken to deal with undue population growth must be taken mainly by the countries directly involved: after all, it is their people and their nation whose prospects are most centrally affected. But in an interconnected world, with peace and human welfare at issue, others are properly concerned from both self-interested and humanitarian standpoints — other governments from the developed world, the international community, private groups. What of the political considerations in this connection?

A recommendation (G-1) that the United States exert strong political pressures to effect population control in developing countries seems more likely to generate political opposition abroad than acceptance. It is conceivable that such measures might be adopted by the Congress, though if so certainly against the advice of the executive agencies, but it is hardly conceivable that they would be agreed to by the proposed recipients. Such a policy is probably more likely to boomerang against a population effort than to advance the effort.

The proposal to create an international super-agency (G-2) seems more likely of success, but not without difficulty. WHO, UNICEF, and UNESCO have moved some distance toward family planning, if not population control, but only slowly and against considerable political restraint on the international front.[102] A new international agency would find the road easier only if restricted to the convinced countries. Certainly the present international organizations at interest would not be expected to abdicate in its favor. If it could be brought into being and given a strong charter for action, then almost by definition the international political climate would be such as to favor action by the present agencies, and then efficiency and not political acceptability would be the issue.

ADMINISTRATIVE FEASIBILITY

Given technical availability and political acceptability, what can actually be done in the field? This is where several "good ideas" run into difficulties in the developing world, in the translation of a theoretical probability into a practical program.

One of the underdeveloped elements of an underdeveloped country is administration: in most such countries there is not only a limited medical infrastructure but also a limited administrative apparatus to be applied to any program. Policies that look good on paper are difficult to put into practice — and that has been true in the case of family planning efforts themselves, where the simple organizational and logistic problems of delivering service and supplies have by no means been solved in several large countries after some years of trying. Again, this is one of the realities that must be dealt with in any proposals for action.

It is difficult to estimate the administrative feasibility of several of the proposals listed above, if for no other reason simply because the proponents do not put forward the necessary organizational plans or details. How are "fertility control agents" or "sterilants" to be administered on an involuntary mass basis in the absence of a central water supply or a food processing system? How are men with three or more children to be reliably identified in a peasant society and impelled to undergo sterilization against their will; and what is to be done if they decline, or if the fourth child is born? What is to be done with parents who evade the compulsory programs, or with the children born in consequence? How can an incentive system be honestly run in the absence of an organized network of offices positioned and staffed to carry out the regulatory activity? How can a system of social benefits and penalties, including marriage disincentives, be made to work under similar conditions?

Such questions are meant only to suggest the kinds of considerations that must be taken into account if proposals are to be translated into programs. They are difficult but perhaps not insurmountable: somewhat similar problems have been addressed in the development of family planning programs themselves, as with the availability of medical and para-medical personnel. But it would seem desirable that every responsible proposal address itself to such administrative problems in the attempt to convert a proposal into a workable plan.

Some proposals do move in that direction. The plan to institutionalize maternal care in rural areas with family planning attached (A-1) is currently under study in several developing countries with regard to feasibility in administration, personnel, and costs. The plans for a national television system for informational purposes (C-2) have worked out some of the administrative problems, though the basic question of how to keep a television set working in a non-electrified area of a non-mechanical rural culture is not addressed and is not easy (as in the parallel case of keeping vehicles in working order under such conditions). The plan to build population into the school curriculum (C-1) has been carried forward to the preparation of materials and in a few cases beyond that.[103] The plans for incentive programs sometimes come down to only the theoretical propositions that people will do things for money, in this case refrain from having children; but in some cases the permissible payment is proposed on the basis of an economic analysis, and in a few cases an administrative means is also proposed.[104] The plan for wedding loans tied to the bride's age appreciates that a birth registration system might be needed in order to control against misreporting of age.[105]

Thus the *why* of population control is easy, the *what* is not very hard, but the *how* is difficult. We may know that the extension of popular education or the increase of women in the labor force or a later age of marriage would all contribute to population control in a significant way. But there remains the administrative question of how to bring those developments about. For example, the proposal (F-1) to organize the young men of India into a social service program, directed toward later age at marriage and general modernization of attitudes, is extremely difficult from an administrative standpoint even if it were acceptable politically and financially: consider the administrative, supervisory, and instructional problems in the United States of handling nine to ten million young men (the number affected in India), many of them unwilling participants easily "hidden" by their families and associates in a series of camps away from home.[106] As has been observed, if a country could administer such a program it could more easily administer a family planning program, or perhaps not need one.

In short, several proposals assume administrable workability of a complicated scheme in a country that cannot now collect its own vital statistics in a reliable manner. Moreover, there is a near limit to how much administrative burden can be carried by the typical developing country at need: it cannot carry very many large-scale developmental efforts at the same time, either within the population field or overall. For population is not the only effort: agriculture, industry, education, health, communications, the military — all are important claimants. And within the field of population, a country that finds it difficult to organize and run a family planning program will find it still harder to add other programs along with that one. So difficult administrative choices must be made.

ECONOMIC CAPABILITY

From the standpoint of economic capability there are two questions: is the program worthwhile when measured against the criterion of economic return? and can it be afforded from present budgets even if worthwhile?

Most of the proposals probably pass the second screen: if scientifically available and politically and administratively acceptable, an involuntary fertility control agent would probably not be prohibitive economically; incorporation of population materials into the school curriculum is not unduly expensive, particularly when viewed as a long-term investment in population limitation; imposition of taxes or withdrawal of benefits or increased fees for marriage licenses might even return a net gain after administrative cost.

But a few proposals are costly in absolute if not relative terms. For example, the institutionalization of maternal care (A-1) might cost the order of $500,000,000 for construction and $200,000,000 for annual operation in India, or respectively $25,000,000 and $10,000,000 in a country of 25 million population [107] (although later estimates are substantially lower). The plan for a "youth corps" in India would cost upwards of $450,000,000 a year if the participants were paid only $50 annually. The plan for pensions to elderly fathers without sons could cost from $400 million to $1 billion a year, plus administrative costs.[108] The satellite television system for India would cost $50,000,000 for capital costs only on a restricted project,[109] with at least another $200,000,000 needed for receiving sets, broadcast terminals, and programming costs if national coverage is to be secured (depending largely on distribution of sets); or, by another estimate, $30–$35,000,000 a year over 20 years (or $700 million — $440 million in capital outlay and $250 million in operating costs) in order to cover 84 percent of the population by means of nearly 500,000 receiving sets.[110] All of these proposals are intended to have beneficial consequences beyond population and hence can be justified on multiple grounds, but they are still expensive in absolute amounts.

The broad social programs of popular education, rationalization of agriculture, and increased industrialization (F-4) already absorb even larger sums though they could no doubt utilize even more. Here, however, the better question is a different one. Presently less than one percent of the total funds devoted to economic development in such countries as India, Pakistan, South Korea, and Turkey are allocated to family planning programs — in most cases, much less. Would that tiny proportion make a greater contribution to population control, over some specified period, if given over to education or industrialization or road-building, for their indirect effect, rather than utilized directly for family planning purposes? [111] From what we now know, the answer is certainly No.

Still other proposals, particularly those concerned with incentives and benefits, are more problematic, and unfortunately no clear directions are apparent. For comparative purposes, let us start with the generally accepted proposition that in the typical developing country today, one prevented birth is worth one to two times the per capita income, on economic grounds alone. In that case, the typical family planning program as currently operated is economically warranted in some substantial degree.[112] The per caput annual income of the developing countries under consideration range, say, from $75 to $500. In similar order of magnitude, the typical family planning program operates annually at about six cents per caput, and in Taiwan and South Korea, where the programs are more effective, "each initial acceptor costs about $5; each acceptor continuing effective contraception for a year costs about $7–$10; each prevented birth costs, say, $20–$30 (at three years of protection per averted birth); and each point off the birth rate at its present level costs . . . about $25,000 per million population." [113]

This order of cost is not certified in all other situations, so even the economic value of family planning programs is not yet altogether clear [114] although most indications to date are that it is strongly positive.[115] Beyond family planning, the situation is still less clear. Assuming that some level of incentive or benefit would have a demographic impact, what would the level have to be to cut the birth rate by, say, 20 percent? We simply do not know: the necessary experiments on either administration or effectiveness have not been carried out. There is, of course, the possibility that what would be needed could not be afforded and that what could be afforded would not be effective.

For guidance, let us review what has been proposed with respect to incentives. Again we take the Indian case; and for comparative purposes, the present budget of the Indian family planning program is about $60,000,000 a year, far higher than in the recent past (only about $11,000,000 in the 1961–1966 Plan) and not yet fully spent.

On the ground that incentives for vasectomy are better than incentives for contraception — easier to administer and check on a one-time basis and likely to be more effective in preventing births [116] — Pohlman proposes for India a range of money benefits depending upon parity and group acceptance: from $7 to a father of four or more children if half the villagers in that category enter the program, up to $40 to a father of three children if 75 percent accept. If the 50 percent criterion were met in both categories throughout India, the current plan would cost on the order of $260,000,000 in incentives alone, omitting administrative costs (based on these figures: 90 million couples, of whom about 40 percent are parity four and above, and 15 percent are parity three; or about 36.0 and 13.5 million respectively; half of each times $7 and $20 respectively). The decline in the birth rate would be slightly over one-fourth, perhaps a third, or of the order of $35–$40 a prevented birth by a rough estimate.[117]

Simon proposes an incentive of half the per capita income "each year to each fertile woman who does not get pregnant." [118] Here a special problem arises. In a typical developing population of 1000, about 25–30 percent of the married women of reproductive age (MWRA) give birth each year: 1000 population means from 145–165 MWRA, with a birth rate of, say, 40. Thus, incentives could be paid to about three-fourths of the women with no effect on the birth rate — since they would not be having a child that year under normal circumstances — so that the cost could be three to four times larger than "needed" for any desired result. Even if the incentive were fully effective, and each one really did prevent a birth, a cut of ten points in the Indian birth rate would cost of the order of $250,000,000 (or 5,000,000 prevented births at $50 each) — and substantially larger if the anyway non-pregnant, including the non- or semi-fecund, could not be screened out efficiently. (Compare this level of incentive with Spengler's suggestion of "rewards to those who prevent births — say $5–$10 per married couple of reproductive age each year they avoid having offspring." [119] In the typical case, the couple could collect for three years and then, as before, have the child in the fourth year; or, if an incentive of this size were effective, the cost would be four times the indicated level.)

Enke addresses himself to this problem by suggesting a system of blocked accounts for Indian women who would have to remain non-pregnant for three to four years with examinations thrice yearly.[120] Here again the cost could be high: about $100 for three to four years of non-pregnancy at his proposed rates, or perhaps $500,000,000 a year to effect a similar cut in the birth rate (i.e., over 20,000,000 prevented births over four years at $100 each). And on the administrative side, the plan requires not only a substantial organization for management and record-keeping, but also the dubious assumption that the Indian peasant is sufficiently future-oriented and trustful of governmental bureaucracy.

Finally, Balfour has suggested an ingenious scheme for providing national saving certificates to married women in the reproductive ages who remain non-pregnant for three, four, five, or more years at the rate of about $3–$4 a year.[121] He estimates that this plan in action would cost about $200 per year per thousand population, which comes to about $100,000,000 for all India.

But these are only speculations: to date we simply do not know whether incentives will lower a birth rate or rather, how large they would have to be in order to do so. These illustrations show only that an incentive program could be expensive. In any case, incentive systems would require a good amount of supervision and record-keeping; and, presumably the higher the incentive (and hence the greater the chance of impact), the greater the risk of false reporting and the greater need of supervision — which is not only expensive but difficult administratively.

MORAL/ETHICAL/PHILOSOPHICAL ACCEPTABILITY

Beyond political acceptability, is the proposal considered right and proper — by the target population, government officials, professional or intellectual elites, the outside agencies committed to assistance?

"One reason the policy of seeking to make voluntary fertility universal is appealing — whether adequate or not — is that it is a natural extension of traditional democratic values: of providing each individual with the information he needs to make wise choices, and allowing the greatest freedom for each to work out his own destiny. The underlying rationale is that if every individual knowledgeably pursues his self-interest, the social interest will best be served." [122] But what if "stressing the right of parents to have the number of children they want . . . evades the basic question of population policy, which is how to give societies the number of children they need?" [123] Thus the issue rests at the center of political philosophy: how best to reconcile individual and collective interests.

Today, most observers would acknowledge that having a child is theoretically a free choice of the individual couple — but only theoretical in that the freedom is principled and legal. For many couples, particularly among the poor of the world, it is not effectively free in the sense that the individual couple does not have the information, services, and supplies to implement a free wish in this regard. Such couples are restrained by ignorance, not only of contraceptive practice but of the consequences of high fertility for themselves, their children, and their country; they are restrained by religious doctrine, even though they may not accept the doctrine; they are restrained legally, as with people who would abort a pregnancy if that action were open to them; they are restrained culturally, as with women subject to the subordination that reserves for them only the child-bearing and child-rearing role. Hence effective freedom in child-bearing is by no means realized in the world today, as recent policy statements have remarked.[124]

Where does effective freedom lie? With the free provision of information and services for voluntary fertility limitation? With that plus a heavy propaganda campaign to limit births in the national interest? With that plus an incentive system of small payments? large payments? finders fees? With that plus a program of social benefits and penalties geared to the desired result? Presumably it lies somewhere short of compulsory birth limitation enforced by the state.

One's answer may depend not only on his own ethical philosophy but also upon the seriousness with which he views the population problem: the worse the problem, the more one is willing to "give up" in ethical position in order to attain "a solution." As usual, the important and hard ethical questions are those involving a conflict of values. In some countries, for example, people who are willing to provide temporary contraception as a means for population control under present circumstances are reluctant to extend the practice to sterilization and firmly opposed to abortion [125] — though again the wheel of history seems to be moving the world across that range under the pressure of population growth. But in some groups, notably religious groups, morality in this connection is absolute and no compromise with social need is to be tolerated, as for example in the case of Pope Paul's encyclical of July 1968.

How much in ethical values should a society be willing to forego for the solution of a great social problem? Suppose a program for population control resulted in many more abortions in a society where abortion is not only morally repugnant but also widely unavailable by acceptable medical standards: how much fertility decline would be "worth" the result? What of infanticide under the same conditions? How many innocent or unknowing men may be vasectomized for a fee (for themselves or the finders) before the practice calls for a moral restraint? How large an increase in the regulatory bureaucracy, or in systematic corruption through incentives, or in differential effect by social class to the disadvantage of the poor,[126] is worth how much decrease in the birth rate? How much association of child-bearing with monetary incentive is warranted before "bribing people not to have children" becomes contaminating, with adverse long-run effects on parental responsibility? [127] How much "immorality," locally defined as extramarital sex, is worth importing along with how much contraceptive practice (assuming the association)? How much withholding of food aid is ethical, judged against how much performance in fertility decline? If it were possible to legislate a later age of marriage, would it be right to do so in a society in which young women have nothing else to do, and against their will? In countries, like our own, where urbanization is a serious population problem, is it right to tell people *where* to live, or to impose heavy economic constraints that in effect "force" the desired migration? Is it right to withdraw educational benefits from the children in "too large" families? — which is not only repressive from the standpoint of free education but in the long run would be unfortunate from the standpoint of fertility control. In the balance — and this is a question of great but neglected importance — what weight should be given to the opportunities of the next generations as against the ignorance, the prejudices, or the preferences of the present one?

These are not light questions, nor easy ones to answer. And they have not been seriously analyzed and ventilated, beyond the traditional religious concern about the acceptability of contraception and abortion. Most official doctrine in the emerging population programs is conservative — as is only to be expected at the outset of a great social experiment of this character.

Guidance on such ethical questions is needed. As an offer toward further consideration, these propositions are put forward: (1) "an ideal policy would permit a maximum of individual freedom and diversity. It would not prescribe a precise number of children for each category of married couple, nor lay down a universal norm to which all couples should conform"; [128] correlatively, it would move toward compulsion only very reluctantly and as the absolutely last resort; (2) "an ideal program designed to affect the number of children people want would help promote other goals that are worth supporting on their own merits, or at least not conflict with such goals"; [129] correlatively, it would not indirectly encourage undesirable outcomes, e.g., bureaucratic corruption; (3) an ideal program would not burden the innocent in an attempt to penalize the guilty — e.g., would not burden the Nth child by denying him a free education simply because he was the Nth child of irresponsible parents; (4) an ideal program would not weigh heavily upon the already disadvantaged — e.g., by withdrawing maternal or medical benefits or free education from large families, which would tend to further deprive the poor; (5) an ideal program would be comprehensible to those directly affected — i.e., it should be capable of being understood by those involved and hence subject to their response; (6) an ideal program would respect present values in family and children, which many people may not be willing to bargain away for other values in a cost-benefit analysis; and (7) an ideal program would not rest upon the designation of population control as the final value justifying all other; "preoccupation with population growth should not serve to justify measures more dangerous or of higher social cost than population growth itself." [130]

PRESUMED EFFECTIVENESS

If proposals are scientifically ready, politically and morally acceptable, and administratively and financially feasible, to what extent will they actually work in bringing population growth under control? That is the final question.

Again we do not know the answer. We are not even sure in the case of family planning programs, with which we now have some amount of experience. But as order of magnitude and as a kind of measuring rod for other proposals, the impact of family planning programs, when conducted with some energy at the rate of investment indicated above, ranges roughly as follows: in situations like Singapore, South Korea, and Taiwan, they have recruited 20–33 percent of the married women of reproductive age as contraceptive acceptors within 3–4 years, and in difficult situations like India and Pakistan, from 5–14 percent of the target population.[131] In other settings, like Malaysia or Ceylon or Turkey or Kenya or Tunisia or Morocco, either it is too early to tell or the program has been conducted under political or other restraints so that it is difficult to say what an energetic program could have achieved; as it is, family planning is being introduced into such situations at a pace politically acceptable and administratively feasible. Overall, it appears that a vigorous program *can* extend contraceptive practices by an economically worthwhile amount wherever conducted.[132]

What of the proposals beyond family planning? How well might they do, given administrative implementation?

To begin with, the compulsory measures would probably be quite effective in lowering fertility. Inevitably in such schemes, strongly motivated people are ingenious enough to find ways "to beat the system"; if they were numerous enough the system could not be enforced except under severe political repression.[133] Otherwise, if workable, compulsion could have its effect.

What about the proposals for the extension of voluntary contraception? Institutionalizing maternal care in the rural areas with family planning attached does promise to be effective over, say, five to ten years, particularly in its potential for reaching the younger and lower parity women. The International Postpartum Program did have that effect in the urban areas,[134] and presumably the impact would extend to the rural areas though probably not to the same degree because of the somewhat greater sophistication and modernization of the cities. The importance of the particular target is suggested in this observation: "The objective in India is to reach not the 500,000,000 people or the 200,000,000 people in the reproductive ages or the 90,000,000 married couples or even the 20–25,000,000 who had a child this year — but the 5,000,000 women who gave birth to their first child. And this may be the only institutionalized means for reaching them." [135] The total program is costly, but if it could establish family planning early in the reproductive period in a country like India, and thus encourage the spacing of children and not just stopping, it could have great demographic value in addition to the medical and humanitarian contribution.

A liberalized abortion system, again if workable, could also be effective in preventing unwanted birth, but it would probably have to be associated with a contraceptive effort: otherwise there might be too many abortions for the system as well as for the individual woman (who might need three a year to remain without issue; in Mainland China, where abortion on demand is available, it is reported that a woman may have only one a year [136]). Free abortion for contraceptive failures would probably make for a fertility decline, but how large a one would depend upon the quality of the contraceptive program. With modern contraception (the IUD and the pill) the failure rates are quite small, but women who only marginally tolerate either method, or both, would be available for abortion. Free abortion on demand has certainly lowered fertility in Japan and certain Eastern European countries,[137] and where medically feasible would do so elsewhere as well; as a colleague observes, in this field one should not underestimate the attraction of a certainty as compared to a probability. Abortion for illegitimate pregnancies, whether voluntary (A-2) or required (B-4), would not have a large impact on the birth rate in most developing countries since known illegitimacy is small (assuming that the children of the numerous consensual unions and other arrangements in Latin America are not considered "illegitimate").

The educational program, whether in the school system or in the mass media, would almost certainly have an effect over the years though it will be difficult for technical reasons to determine the precise or even approximate degree of impact. Anything that can be done to "bring home" the consequences of undue population growth to family and nation will help reach the goal of fertility decline, but in the nature of the case education alone will have a limited effect if life circumstances remain stable.

The large question of the effect of the various incentive and benefit/liability plans (D and E) simply cannot be answered: we have too little experience to know much about the conditions under which financial factors will affect childbearing to any substantial degree. Perhaps everyone has his price for everything; if so, we do not know what would have to be paid, directly or indirectly, to bring people not to bear children.

Such as it is, the evidence from the *pro*-natalist side is not encouraging. All the countries of Europe have family allowance programs of one kind or another,[138] most of them legislated in the 1930's and 1940's to raise the birth rate; collectively they have the lowest birth rate of any continent. The consensus among demographers appears to be that such programs cannot be shown to have effected an upward trend in the birth rate where tried. A recent review of the effect of children's allowances upon fertility concludes:

> It would be helpful to be able to state categorically that children's allowances do or do not increase the number of births among families that receive them. Unfortunately, there is no conclusive evidence one way or the other. . . To argue that the level of births in the United States or anywhere else depends upon the existence, coverage, and adequacy of a set of family allowances is certainly simplistic. Such a conclusion can and ought to be rejected not only on logical grounds but also on the basis of the demonstrated complexity of the factors producing specific birthrates. . . . Recent fertility statistics show no relation between the existence or character of a family allowance program and the level of the birthrate. In specific low-income agricultural countries with such programs, fertility is high. In specific high-income modernized nations with such programs, fertility is low. . . . Whether the less developed countries have any form of family or children's allowances appears wholly unrelated to the level of fertility.[139]

As in the case of abortion for illegitimate pregnancies, several of the benefit/liability proposals would affect only a trivial fraction of people in much of the developing world: for example, again in India, programs for governmental employees who make up perhaps 5 percent of the labor force, tax or social security systems where the rural masses are not regularly covered, maternity benefits since so few women are covered, fees for marriage licenses, control of public housing which is insignificant, denial of education benefits to married students who are trivially few and not now covered in any case. Such measures are probably more relevant to the developed than the developing countries. However, because the impact of incentive and benefit/liability plans is uncertain and may become important, the field needs to become better informed on the possibilities and limitations, which information can only come from experimentation under realistic circumstances and at realistic levels of payment.

A higher age of marriage and a greater participation of women in the labor force are generally credited with effecting fertility declines. In India, average female age at marriage has risen from about 13 to about 16 in this century, or about half a year a decade, although the age of marital consumation has remained rather steady at 17 years (since most of the rise is due to the decrease in child marriages). In a recent Indian conference on raising age at marriage, the specialists seemed to differ only on the magnitude of the fertility decline that would result: a decline of 30 percent in the birth rate in a generation of 28 years if the minimum female age of marriage were raised to 20 [140] or a decline of not more than 15 percent in 10 years [141] — "seemed to" since these figures are not necessarily incompatible. In either case, the decline is a valuable one. But the effectiveness of increased age of marriage rests in the first instance on its being realized; here are the perhaps not unrepresentative views of knowledgeable and committed observers:

> . . . In the absence of prolonged education and training, postponing the age of marriage becomes a formidable problem. (Chandrasekhar [142])

> . . . Legislation regarding marriage can rarely be used as a measure of fertility control in democratic countries. The marital pattern will mostly be determined by social circumstances and philosophies of life and any measure by government clashing with them will be regarded as a restriction on freedom rather than a population policy. (Dandekar [143])

Similarly, an increase in the proportion of working women — working for payment outside the home — might have its demographic effect,[144] but could probably come about only in conjunction with other broad social trends like education and industrialization, which themselves would powerfully affect fertility (just as a fertility decline would assist importantly in bringing them about).[145] Both compulsory education and restrictions on child labor would lower the economic value of children and hence tend toward fertility decline: The question is, how are they to be brought about?

Finally, whether research would affect fertility trends depends of course upon its nature and outcome, aside from the general proposition that "more research" as a principle can hardly be argued against. Most observers believe that under the typical conditions of the developing society, any improvement in the contraceptive technology would make an important difference to the realization of present fertility goals and might make an important contribution to turning the spiral down. Indeed, several believe that this is the single most important desideratum over the short run. Easy means for sex determination should have some effect upon the "need for sons" and thus cut completed family size to some extent. Research on the social-economic side would probably have to take effect through the kinds of programs discussed above.

The picture is not particularly encouraging. The measures that would work to sharply cut fertility are politically and morally unacceptable to the societies at issue, as with coercion, and in any case unavailable; or they are difficult of attainment in any visible future, as with the broad social trends or shift in age of marriage. The measures that might possibly be tried in some settings, like some version of incentives or benefit/liability plans, are uncertain of result at the probable level of operation. Legalization of abortion, where medically available, would almost certainly have a measurable effect, but acceptability is problematic.

CONCLUSION

Where does this review leave us with regard to proposals beyond family planning? Here is my own summary of the situation.

1. There is no easy way to population control. If this review has indicated nothing else, it has shown how many obstacles stand in the way of a simple solution to the population problem — or a complicated one, for that matter. By way of illustrative capitulation, let us see how the various proposals seem to fit the several criteria, in the large (Table 1).[146] That is only one observer's judgment of the present situation, but whatever appraisal is made of specific items it would appear that the overall picture is mixed. There is no easy way.

2. Family planning programs do not compare unfavorably with specific other proposals — especially when one considers that any *actual* operating program is disadvantaged when compared with any competitive *ideal* policy. (As any practical administrator knows, when an "ideal" policy gets translated into action it develops its own set of realistic problems and loses some of the shine it had as an idea.) Indeed, on this showing, if family planning programs did not exist, they would have to be invented: it would appear that they would be among the first proposals to be made and the first programs to be tried, given their generally acceptable characteristics.

In fact, when such proposals are made, it turns out that many of them call for *more* family planning not less, but only in a somewhat different form. In the present case, of the proposals listed above, at least a third put forward in effect simply another approach to family planning, often accepting the existing motivation as to family size. In any case, family planning programs are established, have some momentum, and, importantly, would be useful as the direct instrument through which other proposals would take effect. So that, as a major critic acknowledges, "there is no reason to abandon family-planning programs." [147]

What is needed is the energetic and full implementation of present experience; this is by no means being done now. Much more could be done on the informational side, on encouragement of commercial channels of contraception, on the use of para-medical personnel, on logistics and supply, on the training and supervision of field workers, on approaches to special targets ranging from post-partum women to young men under draft into the armed forces. If the field did well what it knows how to do, that in itself would in all likelihood make a measurable difference — and one competitive in magnitude with other specific proposals — not to mention the further impetus of an improved contraceptive technology.

TABLE 1. ILLUSTRATIVE APPRAISAL OF PROPOSALS BY CRITERIA

	Scientific readiness	Political viability	Administrative feasibility	Economic capability	Ethical acceptability	Presumed effectiveness
A. Extension of voluntary fertility control	High	High on maternal care, moderate to low on abortion	Uncertain in near future	Maternal care too costly for local budget, abortion feasible	High for maternal care, low for abortion	Moderately high
B. Establishment of involuntary fertility control	Low	Low	Low	High	Low	High
C. Intensified educational campaigns	High	Moderate to high	High	Probably high	Generally high	Moderate
D. Incentive programs	High	Moderately low	Low	Low to moderate	Low to high	Uncertain
E. Tax and welfare benefits and penalties	High	Moderately low	Low	Low to moderate	Low to moderate	Uncertain
F. Shifts in social and economic institutions	High	Generally high, but low on some specifics	Low	Generally low	Generally high, but uneven	High, over long run
G. Political channels and organizations	High	Low	Low	Moderate	Moderately low	Uncertain
H. Augmented research efforts	Moderate	High	Moderate to high	High	High	Uncertain
Family planning programs	Generally high, but could use improved technology	Moderate to high	Moderate to high	High	Generally high, but uneven on religious grounds	Moderately high

3. Most of the proposed ideas are not new; they have been around for some time. So if they are not in existence, it is not because they were not known but because they were not accepted — presumably, for reasons like those reflected in the above criteria. In India, for example, several of the social measures being proposed have been, it would seem, under almost constant review by one or another committee for the past 10–15 years — withdrawal of maternity benefits, imposition of a child tax, increase in age of marriage, liberalization of legal abortion, incorporation of population and family planning in the school curriculum.[148] In Mainland China, reportedly, later age of marriage is common among party members,[149] and in Singapore a 1968 law restricts maternity privileges beyond the third child for employed women and makes public housing available to childless couples.[150] As for general social development — compulsory education, industrialization, improved medical care, etc. — that is in process everywhere, though of course more can always be done (but not very quickly). So it is not correct to imply that it is only new ideas that are needed; many ideas are there, but their political, economic, or administrative feasibility is problematic.

4. The proposals themselves are not generally approved by this set of proposers, taken together. All of them are dissatisfied to some degree with present family planning efforts, but that does not mean that they agree with one another's schemes to do better. Thus, Ohlin believes that "the demographic significance of such measures (maternity benefits and tax deductions for children) would be limited. By and large those who now benefit from such arrangements in the developing countries are groups which are already involved in the process of social transformation" and that "changes in marital institutions and norms are fairly slow and could not in any circumstances reduce fertility sufficiently by itself when mortality falls to the levels already attained in the developing world." [151] Ketchel opposes several "possible alternatives to fertility control agents":

> Financial pressures against large families would probably be effective only in developed countries in which there are large numbers of middle-class people. In underdeveloped countries practically no financial inducements to have children now exist to be reversed, and the imposition of further taxes upon the many poor people would depress their living standards even further. . . . In order to be effective, economic pressures would probably have to be severe enough to be quite painful, and when they reached a level of painfulness at which they were effective, they would probably seriously affect the welfare of the children who were born in spite of the pressures. . . . The same objection applies to the use of financial rewards to induce people not to have children because such programs would make the families with children the poorer families. . . . The age at which people marry is largely determined by slowly changing cultural and economic factors, and could probably be changed quickly in a population only by rather drastic measures (in which) an inordinately severe punishment for violators would be required. . . . Statutory regulations of family size would be unenforceable unless the punishment for exceeding the limit was so harsh that it would cause harm to the lives of the existing children and their parents. Such possible procedures as vasectomizing the father or implanting long acting contraceptives in the mother would require a direct physical assault by a government agent on the body of an individual.[152]

Meier argues against the tax on children on both humanitarian and political grounds.[153] To the U.N. Advisory Mission to India, "it is realised that no major demographic effects can be expected from measures of this kind (maternity benefits), particularly as only a small proportion of families are covered . . . but they could contribute, together with the family planning programme, to a general change in the social climate relating to childbearing." [154] Earlier, in supporting a family planning effort in India, Davis noted that "the reaction to the Sarda Act (the Child Marriage Restraint Act of 1929) prohibiting female marriage (below 14) shows the difficulty of trying to regulate the age of marriage by direct legislation." [155] Myrdal warns against cash payments to parents in this connection, as a redistributional reform, and supports social awards to the children in kind.[156] Kirk believes that "it might prove to be the height of folly to undermine the existing family structure, which continues to be a crucial institution for stability and socialization in an increasingly mobile and revolutionary society." [157] Raulet believes that "Davis' main observation . . . that alternatives to the present stress on familism will ultimately be required . . . obviously makes no sense for most less developed countries today . . . Aside from the repressive tone of some of (the proposed) measures, the most striking thing about these proposals is the impracticality of implementing them. . . . The application of social security measures and negative economic sanctions . . . are so far beyond the present economic capacities of these countries, and would raise such difficult administrative and economic problems, that they are probably not worth serious mention." [158] Finally, Ehrlich is contemptuous of the professors whose "idea of 'action' is to form a committee or to urge 'more research.' Both courses are actually substitutes for action. Neither will do much good in the crisis we face now. We've got lots of committees, and decades ago enough research had been done at least to outline the problem and make clear many of the steps necessary to solve it. Unless those steps are taken, research initiated today will be terminated not by success but by the problem under investigation." [159]

5. In a rough way, there appears to be a progression in national efforts to deal with the problem of population control. The first step is the theoretical recognition that population growth may have something to do with the prospects for economic development. Then, typically, comes an expert mission from abroad to do a survey and make a report to the government, as has occurred in India, Pakistan, South Korea, Turkey, Iran, Tunisia, Morocco, and Kenya among others. The first action program is in family planning, and most of the efforts are still there. Beyond that, it apparently takes (1) some degree of discouragement over progress combined with (2) some heightened awareness of the seriousness of the problem to move the effort forward. To date those conditions have been most prominently present in India — and that is the country that has gone farthest in the use of incentives and in at least consideration of further steps along the lines mentioned above. It may be that in this respect the Indian experience is a harbinger of the international population scene. It is only natural that on matters of such sensitivity, governments try "softer" measures before "harder" ones; and only natural, too, that they move gradually from one position to the next to realize their goals. Indeed, some proposals require prior or simultaneous developments, often of a substantial nature: for example, a loan system tied to age of brides may require a good system of vital registration for purpose of verification, instruction in population in the schools requires some

degree of compulsory education, tying family planning to health programs requires a medical infrastructure.

Finally, it is also worth noting that more extreme or controversial proposals tend to legitimate more moderate advances, by shifting the boundaries of discourse.

6. Proposals need to be specified — proposals both for action schemes and for further research. It is perhaps too much to ask advocates to spell out all the administrative details of how their plan is to operate in the face of the kinds of obstacles and difficulties discussed above, or even get permission to operate: the situations, settings, opportunities, and personalities are too diverse for that. But it does seem proper to ask for the fullest possible specification of actual plans, under realistic conditions, in order to test out their feasibility and likely effectiveness. The advocates of further research similarly ought to spell out not only what would be studied and how, but also how the results might be applied in action programs to affect fertility. Social research is not always readily translated into action, especially into administrative action; and the thrust of research is toward refinement, subtlety, precision, and qualification whereas the administrator must act in the large. Short of such specification, the field remains confronted with potentially good ideas like "raise the age of marriage" or "use incentives" or "substitute pension systems for male children" without being able to move very far toward implementation.

7. Just as there is no easy way, there is no single way. Since population control will at best be difficult, it follows that every acceptable step be taken that promises some measure of impact. The most likely prospect is that population control, to the degree realized, will be the result of a combination of various efforts — economic, legal, social, medical — each of which has some effect but not an immediately overwhelming one.[160] Accordingly, it is incumbent upon the professional fields concerned to look hard at various approaches, including family planning itself, in order to screen out what is potentially useful for application. In doing so, on an anyway difficult problem, it may be the path of wisdom to move with the "natural" progression. Some important proposals seem reasonably likely of adoption — institutionalization of maternal care, population study in the schools, the TV satellite system for informational purposes, a better contraceptive technology, perhaps even liberalization of abortion in some settings — and we need to know not only how effective such efforts will be but, beyond them, how large a money incentive needs to be to effect a given amount of fertility control and how effective those indirect social measures are that are decently possible of realization. It may be that some of these measures would be both feasible and effective — many observers 15 years ago thought that family planning programs were neither — and a genuine effort needs to be made in the next years, wherever feasible, to do the needed experimentation and demonstration. The "heavy" measures — involuntary means and political pressures — may be put aside for the time being, if not forever.

8. In the last analysis, what will be scientifically available, politically acceptable, administratively feasible, economically justifiable, and morally tolerated depends upon people's perceptions of consequences. If "the population problem" is considered relatively unimportant or only moderately important, that judgment will not support much investment of effort. If it is considered urgent, much more can and will be done. The fact is that despite the large

forward strides taken in international recognition of the problem in the 1960's, there still does not exist the informed, firm, and constant conviction in high circles that this is a matter with truly great ramifications for human welfare.[161] Such convictions must be based on sound knowledge. Here it would appear that the demographers and economists have not sufficiently made their case to the world elite — or that, if made, the case has not sufficiently been brought to their attention or credited by them. Population pressures are not sharply visible on a day-to-day or even year-to-year basis nor, short of major famine, do they lend themselves to dramatic recognition by event. Moreover, the warnings of demographers are often dismissed, albeit unfairly and wrongly, on their record of past forecasts: [162] after all, it was only a generation ago that a declining population was being warned about in the West. It is asking government leaders to take very substantial steps indeed when population control is the issue — substantial for their people as well as for their own political careers — and hence the case must be not only substantial but virtually incontrovertible. Accordingly, the scientific base must be carefully prepared (and perhaps with some sense of humility about the ease of predicting great events, on which the record is not without blemishes). Excluding social repression and mindful of maximizing human freedom, greater measures to meet the problem must rely on heightened awareness of what is at stake, by leaders and masses alike.

What is beyond family planning? Even if most of the specific plans are not particularly new, that in itself does not mean that they are to be disregarded. The questions are: which can be effected, given such criteria? how can they be implemented? what will be the outcome?

This paper is an effort to promote the discourse across the professional fields concerned with this important issue. Given the recent stress on family planning programs as the "means of choice" in dealing with the problem, it is natural and desirable that counter positions should be put forward and reviewed. But that does not in itself settle the critical questions. What can we do now to advance the matter? Beyond family planning, what?

Notes

1 As one example, see "Declaration on Population: The World Leaders' Statement," signed by 30 heads of state, in *Studies in Family Planning*, no. 26, January 1968.

2 For example, see Kingsley Davis, "Population Policy: Will Current Programs Succeed?" *Science*, vol. 158, November 10, 1967, pp. 730–739; Robert G. Potter, Ronald Freedman, and L. P. Chow, "Taiwan's Family Planning Program," *Science*, vol. 160, May 24, 1968, pp. 848–853; and Frank W. Notestein, "Population Growth and Its Control," MS prepared for American Assembly meeting on World Hunger, Fall 1968.

3 See, for example, the section on "Goals" in Davis, *op. cit.*, pp. 731–733, and the 1968 presidential address to the Population Association of America, "Should the United States Start a Campaign for Fewer Births?" by Ansley J. Coale.

4 For current targets of some national family planning programs, see table 8, p. 39, and accompanying text in Bernard Berelson, "National Family Planning Programs: Where We Stand," prepared for University of Michigan Sesquicentennial Celebration, November 1967, which concludes: "By and large, developing countries are now aiming at the birth rates of Western Europe 75 years ago or the United States 50 years ago."

5 For a first effort to outline the matter, see point 12, pp. 46–51, in Berelson, *op. cit.*

6 Howard C. Taylor Jr. and Bernard Berelson, "Maternity Care and Family Planning

as a World Program," *American Journal of Obstetrics and Gynecology,* vol. 100, 1968, pp. 885–893.

7 Davis, *op. cit.,* pp. 732, 738.

8 Paul R. Ehrlich, *The Population Bomb,* Ballantine Books, 1968, p. 139.

9 S. Chandrasekhar, "Should We Legalize Abortion in India?" *Population Review,* 10, 1966, pp. 17–22.

10 Melvin M. Ketchel, "Fertility Control Agents as a Possible Solution to the World Population Problem," *Perspectives in Biology and Medicine,* vol. 11, 1968, pp. 687–703. See also his "Should Birth Control Be Mandatory" in *Medical World News, October* 18, 1968, pp. 66–71.

11 Ehrlich, *op. cit.,* pp. 135–36. The author appears to dismiss the scheme as unworkable on page 136 though two pages later he advocates "ample funds" to "promote intensive investigation of new techniques of birth control, possibly leading to the development of mass sterilizing agents such as were discussed above."

12 Kenneth E. Boulding, *The Meaning of the Twentieth Century: The Great Transition,* Harper & Row, pp. 135–36. For the record, I note a statement that appeared too late for consideration but does argue for "mutual coercion, mutually agreed upon by the majority of the people affected": Garrett Hardin, "The Tragedy of the Commons," *Science,* 162, December 13, 1968, p. 1247.

13 William B. Shockley, in lecture at McMaster University, Hamilton, Ontario, reported in *New York Post,* December 12, 1967.

14 Sripati Chandrasekhar, as reported in *The New York Times,* July 24, 1967. Just as this paper was being completed, the same author "proposed that every married couple in India deny themselves sexual intercourse for a year . . . Abstinence for a year would do enormous good to the individual and the country" (as reported in *The New York Times,* October 21, 1968). The reader may wish to consider this the 30th proposal and test it against the criteria that follow.

15 Davis, *op. cit.,* p. 738.

16 Davis, *op. cit.,* p. 738.

17 Sloan Wayland, "Family Planning and the School Curriculum," in Bernard Berelson et al., eds., *Family Planning and Population Programs,* University of Chicago Press, 1966, pp. 353–62; his "Population Education, Family Planning and the School Curriculum," MS prepared for collection of readings edited by John Ross and John Friesen, *Family Planning Programs: Administration, Education, Evaluation,* forthcoming 1969; and two manuals prepared under his direction: *Teaching Population Dynamics: An Instructional Unit for Secondary School Students and Critical Stages in Reproduction: Instruction Materials in General Science and Biology,* both Teachers College, Columbia University, 1965.

18 Pravin Visaria, "Population Assumptions and Policy," *Economic Weekly,* August 8, 1964, p. 1343.

19 Ehrlich, *op. cit.,* p. 162.

20 Richard L. Meier and Gitta Meier, "New Directions: A Population Policy for the Future," University of Michigan, revised MS, October 1967, p. 11.

21 UNESCO Expert Mission, *Preparatory Study of a Pilot Project in the Use of Satellite Communication for National Development Purposes in India,* February 5, 1968, especially the section on "The Population Problem," pp. 13–14, paras. 61–66.

22 Wilbur Schramm and Lyle Nelson, *Communication Satellites for Education and Development — The Case of India.* Stanford Research Institute, July 1968: "Family Planning," pp. 63–66.

23 Sripati Chandrasekhar, as reported in *The New York Times,* July 19, 1967. Here again I note for the record a very recent "Proposal for a Family Planning Bond," by Ronald J. Ridker, USAID — India, July 1968. This memorandum is a comprehensive and quite detailed review of the issues involved in providing 20-year bonds for couples sterilized after the second or third child. Along this same line, see another late suggestion of a bond linked both to age of marriage and to number of children, in *Approaches to the Human Fertility Problem,* prepared by The Carolina Population Center for the United Nations Advisory Committee on the Application of Science and Technology to Development, October 1968, p. 68.

24 Edward Pohlman, "Incentives for 'Non-Maternity' Cannot 'Compete' with Incentives for Vasectomy," Central Family Planning Institute, India, MS 1967?

25 T. J. Samuel, "The Strengthening of the Motivation for Family Limitation in India," *The Journal of Family Welfare,* vol. 13, 1966, pp. 11–12.

26 Davis, *op. cit.,* p. 738.

27 Julian Simon, "Money Incentives to Reduce Birth Rates in Low-Income Countries: A Proposal to Determine the Effect Experimentally"; "The Role of Bonuses and Persuasive Propaganda in the Reduction of Birth Rates"; and "Family Planning Prospects in Less-Developed Countries, and a Cost-Benefit Analysis of Various Alternatives," University of Illinois, MSS 1966–1968?

28 Stephen Enke, "Government Bonuses for Smaller Families," *Population Review,* vol. 4, 1960, pp. 47–54.

29 Samuel, *op. cit.,* p. 12.

30 Michael Young, in "The Behavioral Sciences and Family Planning Programs: Report on a Conference," *Studies in Family Planning,* no. 23, October 1967, p. 10.

31 Dipak Bhatia, "Government of India Small Family Norm Committee Questionnaire," *Indian Journal of Medical Education,* vol. 6, October 1967, p. 189. As the title indicates, this is not a proposal as such but a questionnaire soliciting opinions on various ideas put forward to promote "the small family norm."

32 Stephen Enke, "The Gains to India from Population Control," *The Review of Economics and Statistics,* May 1960, pp. 179–180.

33 Joseph J. Spengler, "Agricultural Development Is Not Enough," MS prepared for Conference on World Population Problems, Indiana University, May 1967, pp. 29–30.

34 J. William Leasure, "Some Economic Benefits of Birth Prevention," *Milbank Memorial Fund Quarterly,* 45, 1967, pp. 417–25.

35 Marshall C. Balfour, "A Scheme for Rewarding Successful Family Planners," Memorandum, The Population Council, June 1962.

36 W. Parker Mauldin, "Prevention of Illegitimate Births: A Bonus Scheme," Memorandum, The Population Council, August 1967.

37 Ehrlich, *op. cit.,* p. 138.

38 Bhatia, *op. cit.,* p. 188.

39 Samuel, *op. cit.,* p. 14.

40 Davis, *op. cit.,* p. 738.

41 Richard M. Titmuss and Brian Abel-Smith, *Social Policies and Population Growth in Mauritius,* Methuen, 1960, pp. 130–31.

42 Bhatia, *op. cit.,* p. 189.

43 Titmuss and Abel-Smith, *op. cit.,* pp. 131–36.

44 Davis, *op. cit.,* p. 739.

45 Bhatia, *op. cit.,* pp. 189–90.

46 Samuel, *op. cit.,* pp. 12–14.

47 Spengler, *op. cit.,* p. 30.

48 Bhatia, *op. cit.,* p. 190.

49 Davis, *op. cit.,* p. 738.

50 Bhatia, *op. cit.,* p. 190.

51 Titmuss and Abel-Smith, *op. cit.,* p. 137.

52 Samuel, *op. cit.,* pp. 12–14.

53 Davis, *op. cit.,* p. 738.

54 Ehrlich, *op. cit.,* pp. 136–37.

55 A. S. David, *National Development, Population and Family Planning in Nepal,* June–July 1968, pp. 53–54.

56 James Fawcett, personal communication, September 1968.

57 Samuel, *op. cit.,* p. 12.

58 Goran Ohlin, *Population Control and Economic Development,* Development Centre of the Organization for Economic Cooperation and Development, 1967, p. 104.

59 W. Phillips Davison, personal communication, October 4, 1968. Davison suggests a good pension (perhaps $400 a year) for men aged 60, married for at least 20 years, with no sons.

60 David, *op. cit.,* p. 53.

61 Davis, *op. cit.,* p. 738.

62 Young, *op. cit.,* p. 10.

63 Titmuss and Abel-Smith, *op. cit.,* p. 130.

64 Kingsley Davis, personal communication, October 7, 1968.

65 Ehrlich, *op. cit.*, p. 138.

66 Bernard Berelson, Amitai Etzioni, brief formulations, 1962, 1967.

67 Philip M. Hauser, in "The Behavioral Sciences and Family Planning Programs: Report on a Conference," *Studies in Family Planning*, no. 23, October 1967, p. 9.

68 Davis, *op. cit.*, p. 738.

69 David, *op. cit.*, p. 54.

70 Judith Blake, "Demographic Science and the Redirection of Population Policy," in Mindel C. Sheps and Jeanne Clare Ridley, eds., *Public Health and Population Change: Current Research Issues*, University of Pittsburgh Press, 1965, p. 62.

71 Davis, *op. cit.*, p. 737.

72 Meier and Meier, *op. cit.*, p. 9. For the initial formulation of the proposal, see Richard L. Meier, *Modern Science and the Human Fertility Problem*, Wiley, 1959, chapter 7, esp. pp. 171 ff.

73 Philip M. Hauser, " 'Family Planning and Population Programs': A Book Review Article," *Demography*, vol. 4, 1967, p. 412.

74 United Nations Economic and Social Council. Commission on the Status of Women. "Family Planning and the Status of Women: Interim Report of the Secretary-General," January 30, 1968, esp. pp. 17 ff.

75 Roger Revelle, as quoted in "Too Many Born? Too Many Die. So Says Roger Revelle," by Milton Viorst, *Horizon*, Summer 1968, p. 35.

76 David M. Heer and Dean O. Smith, "Mortality Level and Desired Family Size," paper prepared for presentation at Population Association of America meeting, April 1967. See also David A. May and David M. Heer, "Son Survivorship Motivation and Family Size in India: A Computer Simulation," *Population Studies*, 22, 1968, pp. 199–210.

77 Ehrlich, *op. cit.*, pp. 161–66, *passim*. The author makes the same point in his article, "Paying the Piper," *New Scientist*, 14 December 1967, p. 655: "Refuse all foreign aid to any country with an increasing population which we believe is not making a maximum effort to limit its population . . . The United States should use its power and prestige to bring extreme diplomatic and/or economic pressure on any country or organization [the Roman Catholic Church?] impeding a solution to the world's most pressing problem."

78 Ehrlich, *op. cit.*, p. 138. In the earlier article cited just above, he calls for a "Federal Population Commission with a large budget for propaganda," presumably limited to the United States (p. 655).

79 S. Chandrasekhar, "India's Population: Fact, Problem and Policy," in S. Chandrasekhar, ed., *Asia's Population Problems*, Allen & Unwin, 1967, p. 96, citing a Julian Huxley suggestion of 1961.

80 Meier and Meier, *op. cit.*, p. 5.

81 Davis, *op. cit.*, pp. 731–33.

82 Davis, *op. cit.*, pp. 738, 739.

83 Steven Polgar, in "The Behavioral Sciences and Family Planning Programs: Report on a Conference," *Studies in Family Planning*, no. 23, October 1967, p. 10. See also the recent suggestion of research on "the possibilities for artificially decreasing libido," in *Approaches to the Human Fertility Problem, op. cit.*, p. 73.

84 National Academy of Sciences, Committee on Science and Public Policy, *The Growth of World Population*, 1963, pp. 5, 28–36. This recommendation has of course been made on several occasions by several people: "we need a better contraceptive." For an imaginative account of the impact of biological developments, see Paul C. Berry, *Origins of Positive Population Control, 1970–2000*, Working Paper, Appendix to *The Next Thirty-Four Years: A Context for Speculation*, Hudson Institute, February 1966.

85 For example, see Sheldon J. Segal, "Biological Aspects of Fertility Regulation," MS prepared for University of Michigan Sesquicentennial Celebration, November 1967.

86 In passing it is worth noting that such expectations are not particularly reliable. For example, in 1952–1953 a Working Group on Fertility Control was organized by the Conservation Foundation to review the most promising "leads to physiologic control of fertility," based on a survey conducted by Dr. Paul S. Henshaw and Kingsley Davis. The Group did identify a lead that became the oral contraceptive (already then under investigation) but did not mention the intrauterine device. The Group was specifically searching for better ways to control fertility because of the population problem in the

developing world, and considered the contraceptive approach essential to that end: "It thus appears imperative that an attempt be made to bring down fertility in over-populated regions without waiting for a remote, hoped-for transformation of the entire society . . . It seems plausible that acceptable birth control techniques might be found, and that the application of science to developing such techniques for peasant regions might yield revolutionary results." (*The Physiological Approach to Fertility Control, Report of the Working Group on Fertility Control,* The Conservation Foundation, April 1953, p. 69.)

[87] Z. Dvorak, V. Trnka, and R. Vasicek, "Termination of Pregnancy by Vacuum Aspiration," *Lancet,* vol. 2, November 11, 1967, pp. 997–98; and D. Kerslake and D. Casey, "Abortion Induced by Means of the Uterine Aspirator," *Obstetrics and Gynecology,* vol. 30, July 1967, pp. 35–45.

[88] A. S. Parkes, "Can India Do It?" *New Scientist,* vol. 35, July 1967, p. 186.

[89] These are only illustrative magnitudes. Actually, the five million does not really represent 5/22nd of the birth rate since an aborted woman could again become pregnant within a period of months, whereas a newly pregnant woman would not normally become so for over a year. Thus it may be that abortion needs to be combined with contraceptive practice and used mainly for contraceptive failures or "accidents" in order to be fully effective as a means of fertility limitation in the developing countries.

[90] Report in *The New York Times,* November 17, 1967. The then-Minister had earlier suggested a substantial bonus (100 rupees) for vasectomy, the funds to be taken from U.S. counterpart, "but both Governments are extremely sensitive in this area. Yet in a problem this crucial perhaps we need more action and less sensitivity" (S. Chandrasekhar, in *Asia's Population Problem, op. cit.,* p. 96).

[91] United Nations Advisory Mission, *Report on the Family Planning Programme in India,* February 1966. See Chapter XI: "Social Policies to Promote Family Planning and Small Family Norms."

[92] Bhatia, *op. cit.*

[93] Central Family Planning Council, Resolution No. 8, January 1967, in *Implications of Raising the Female Age at Marriage in India,* Demographic Training Research Centre, 1968, p. 109; and *Centre Calling,* May 1968, p. 4.

[94] Samuel, *op. cit.,* p. 12.

[95] United Nations Advisory Mission, *op. cit.,* p. 87.

[96] *Planned Parenthood,* March 1968, p. 3.

[97] Report in *The New York Times,* September 12, 1968.

[98] *Planned Parenthood,* April 1968, p. 2.

[99] Davidson R. Gwatkin, "The Use of Incentives in Family Planning Programs," Memorandum, Ford Foundation, November 1967, pp. 6–7.

[100] Davis, *op. cit.,* p. 739.

[101] Ketchel, *op. cit.,* p. 701.

[102] For a review of this development see Richard Symonds and Michael Carder, *International Organisations and Population Control (1947–1967),* Institute of Development Studies, University of Sussex, April 1968.

[103] See footnote 17. At present population materials are being included in school programs in Pakistan, Iran, Taiwan, and elsewhere.

[104] As, for example, with Balfour, Mauldin, and Pohlman, *op. cit.;* and for the economic analysis, Enke and Simon, *op. cit.*

[105] Davis, *op. cit.* (footnote 64).

[106] In effect, Israel has a program of this general character, though not for population control purposes, but it is a highly skilled society especially from an administrative standpoint. I understand that the Ceylon Government has a program of "agricultural youth settlements," aimed jointly at youth unemployment and agricultural production but not population control. Of the 200,000 unemployed youth aged 19–25, the Government plans to settle 20–25,000 in the 1966–70 period.

[107] Taylor and Berelson, *op. cit.,* p. 892.

[108] Davison, *op. cit.* and revised figures.

[109] UNESCO Expert Mission, *op. cit.,* p. 23.

[110] Schramm and Nelson, *op. cit.,* pp. 164–68, *passim.*

[111] For the negative answer, see Enke and Simon, *op. cit.* Data from family planning budgets and national development budgets contained in five-year development plans.

112 Enke and Simon, *op. cit.;* see also Paul Demeny, "Investment Allocation and Population Growth," *Demography,* vol. 2, 1965, pp. 203–232; and his "The Economics of Government Payments to Limit Population: A Comment," *Economic Development and Cultural Change,* vol. 9, 1961, pp. 641–644.

113 Berelson, *op. cit.* (footnote 3), p. 20.

114 Warren Robinson, "Conceptual and Methodological Problems Connected with Cost-Effectiveness Studies of Family Planning Programs" and David F. Horlocher, "Measuring the Economic Benefits of Population Control: A Critical Review of the Literature," Working Papers nos. 1 & 2, Penn State–U.S. AID Population Control Project, May 1968.

115 Even in the United States, where a recent study concluded that "Altogether, the economic benefits (of family planning programs) alone would be at least 26 times greater than the program costs": Arthur A. Campbell, "The Role of Family Planning in the Reduction of Poverty," *Journal of Marriage and the Family,* vol. 30, 1968, p. 243.

116 Pohlman, *op. cit.*

117 Mr. Pohlman has under preparation a major MS on this subject, entitled *Incentives in Birth Planning.*

118 Simon, "Family Planning Prospects . . . ," *op. cit.* (footnote 27), p. 8.

119 Spengler, *op. cit.,* pp. 29–30. The Population Council is just now completing an analysis of the possible effects and costs of incentive programs with differing assumptions as to acceptance and continuation.

120 Enke, "The Gains . . . ," *op. cit.* (footnote 32), p. 179.

121 Balfour, *op. cit.*

122 Coale, *op. cit.,* p. 2. However, the author does point out, a few sentences later, that "it is clearly fallacious to accept as optimal a growth that continues until overcrowding makes additional births intolerably expensive."

123 Davis, *op. cit.,* p. 738.

124 For example, The World Leaders' Statement, *op. cit.;* and the Resolution of the International Conference on Human Rights on "Human Rights Aspects of Family Planning," adopted May 12, 1968, reported in *Population Newsletter* issued by the Population Division, United Nations, no. 2, July 1968, pp. 21 ff.

125 The issue was sufficiently alive in classical times to prompt the great philosophers to take account of the matter in their political proposals. In Plato's *Republic,* "the number of weddings is a matter which must be left to the discretion of the rulers, whose aim will be to preserve the average of population (and) to prevent the State from becoming either too large or too small"—to which end certain marriages have "strict orders to prevent any embryo which may come into being from seeing the light; and if any force a way to the birth, the parents must understand that the offspring of such a union cannot be maintained, and arrange accordingly" (Modern Library edition, pp. 412, 414). In Aristotle's *Politics,* "on the ground of an *excess* in the number of children, if the established customs of the state forbid this (for in our state population has a limit), no child is to be exposed, but when couples have children in excess, let abortion be procured before sense and life have begun . . ." (Modern Library edition, p. 316).

126 After noting that economic constraints have not been adopted in South Asia, though often proposed, Gunnar Myrdal continues: "The reason is not difficult to understand. Since having many children is a main cause of poverty, such measures would penalize the relatively poor and subsidize the relatively well off. Such a result would not only violate rules of equity but would be detrimental to the health of the poor families, and so of the growing generation." *Asian Drama: An Inquiry into the Poverty of Nations,* Pantheon, 1968, vol. 2, pp. 1502–3.

127 Frank W. Notestein, "Closing Remarks", in Berelson et al., editors, *op. cit.:* "There is a real danger that sanctions, for example through taxation, would affect adversely the welfare of the children. There is also danger that incentives through bonuses will put the whole matter of family planning in a grossly commercial light. It is quite possible that to poor and harassed people financial inducements will amount to coercion and not to an enlargement of their freedom of choice. Family planning must be, and must seem to be, an extension of personal and familial freedom of choice and thereby an enrichment of life, not coercion toward its restriction." (pp. 828–29).

128 Coale, *op. cit.,* p. 7.

129 Coale, *op. cit.*, p. 7.

130 Coale, *op. cit.*, p. 6.

131 Figures based on monthly reports from national programs. Since most of the Indian achievement is in sterilization, it may have a more pronounced effect. For a sophisticated analysis of the Taiwan effort that concludes, "What we are asserting with some confidence is that the several hundred thousand participants in the Taiwan program have, since entering the program, dramatically increased their birth control practice and decreased their fertility," see Robert G. Potter, Ronald Freedman, and L. P. Chow, "Taiwan's Family Planning Program," *Science*, vol. 160, May 24, 1968, p. 852.

132 Berelson, *op. cit.*, pp. 35–38.

133 In this connection, see the novel by Anthony Burgess, *The Wanting Seed*, Ballantine Books, 1963. At the same time, a longtime observer of social affairs remarks that "the South Asian countries . . . can, to begin with, have no other principle than that of voluntary parenthood . . . State direction by compulsion in these personal matters is not effective . . ." (Myrdal, *op. cit.*, p. 1501).

134 Gerald I. Zatuchni, "International Postpartum Family Planning Program: Report on the First Year," *Studies in Family Planning*, no. 22, August 1967, pp. 14 ff.

135 Howard C. Taylor, Jr., personal communication.

136 Edgar Snow, "The Chinese Equation," *The (London) Sunday Times*, January 23, 1966.

137 For example, the repeal of the free abortion law in Rumania resulted in an increase in the birth rate from 14 in the third quarter of 1966 to 38 in the third quarter of 1967. For an early report, see Roland Pressat, "La suppression de l'avortement légal en Roumanie: premiers effets," *Population*, vol. 22, 1967, pp. 1116–18.

138 See U.S. Department of Health, Education, and Welfare, Social Security Administration. "Social Security Programs Throughout the World, 1964."

139 Vincent H. Whitney, "Fertility Trends and Children's Allowance Programs," in Eveline M. Burns, editor, *Children's Allowances and the Economic Welfare of Children: The Report of a Conference*, Citizens' Committee for Children of New York, 1968, pp. 123, 124, 131, 133.

140 S. N. Agarwala, "Raising the Marriage Age for Women: A Means to Lower the Birth Rate," in *Implications of Raising the Female Age at Marriage in India*, Demographic Training and Research Centre, 1968, p. 21.

141 V. C. Chidambaram, "Raising the Female Age at Marriage in India: A Demographer's Dilemma," in *Implications, op. cit.*, p. 47.

142 Chandrasekhar, *op. cit.* (footnote 79), p. 96.

143 Kumudini Dandekar, "Population Policies," *Proceedings of the United Nations World Population Conference*, 1965, p. 4.

144 However, see David Chaplin, "Some Institutional Determinants of Fertility in Peru," manuscript, April 1968, for some evidence that welfare and labor regulations in Peru discourage the employment of women in low-fertility occupations (factory work) by making them more expensive to employ than men. Laws thus designed to promote maternity do so only by default since the higer fertility of the disemployed women will occur outside the protection of adequate medical and welfare institutions.

145 Actually, recent research is calling into question some of the received wisdom on the prior need of such broad institutional factors for fertility decline. If further study supports the new findings, that could have important implications for present strategy in the developing countries. See Ansley J. Coale, "Factors Associated with the Development of Low Fertility: An Historic Summary," *Proceedings of the United Nations World Population Conference*, 1965, vol. 2, pp. 205–209; and his paper, "The Decline of Fertility in Europe from the French Revolution to World War II," prepared for University of Michigan Sesquicentennial Celebration, November 1967.

146 As the roughest sort of summary of Table 1, if one assigns values from 5 for High to 1 for Low, the various proposals rank as follows:

Family planning programs	25
Intensified educational campaigns	25
Augmented research efforts	24

Extension of voluntary fertility control	20
Shifts in social and economic institutions	20
Incentive programs	14
Tax and welfare benefits and penalties	14
Political channels and organizations	14
Establishment of involuntary fertility control	14

[147] Davis, *op. cit.*, p. 739. The same critic was a strong advocate of family planning in India, and quite optimistic about its prospects even in the pre-IUD or pill era and with a health base. See Kingsley Davis, "Fertility Control and the Demographic Transition in India," in *The Interrelations of Demographic, Economic, and Social Problems in Selected Underdeveloped Areas*, Milbank Memorial Fund, 1954, concluding: "Although India is already well-launched in the rapid-growth phase of the demographic transition, there is no inherent reason why she should long continue in this phase. She need not necessarily wait patiently while the forces of urbanization, class mobility, and industrial development gradually build up to the point where parents are forced to limit their offspring on their own initiative and without help, perhaps even in the face of official opposition. . . . Realistically appraising her situation, India has a chance to be the first country to achieve a major revolution in human life — the planned diffusion of fertility control in a peasant population prior to, and for the benefit of, the urban-industrial transition" (pp. 87–88).

[148] See, for example, Visaria, *op. cit.*, p. 1343; Bhatia, *op. cit.*; Samuel, *op. cit.*, p. 12; U.N. Advisory Mission, *op. cit.*, Chapter XI; Chandrasekhar, in *Asia's Population Problem, op. cit.*; Myrdal, *op. cit.*, p. 1502; *Implications . . . , op. cit.*; and "Shah Committee Recommends Liberalization of Abortion Laws," *Family Planning News*, September 1967, p. 23.

[149] Snow, *op. cit.*

[150] K. Kanagaratnam, personal communication, August 8, 1968.

[151] Ohlin, *op. cit.*, pp. 104, 105.

[152] Ketchel, *op. cit.*, pp. 697–99.

[153] Meier, *op. cit.*, p. 167.

[154] United Nations Advisory Mission, *op. cit.*, p. 87.

[155] Davis, *op. cit.*, 1954, p. 86.

[156] Myrdal, *op. cit.*, p. 1503.

[157] Dudley Kirk, "Population Research in Relation to Population Policy and National Family Planning Programs," paper presented at meetings of the American Sociological Association, August 1968.

[158] Harry M. Raulet, *Family Planning and Population Control in Developing Countries*, Institute of International Agriculture, Michigan State University, November 1968, pp. 5–6, 49–50.

[159] Ehrlich, *op. cit.*, p. 191.

[160] It begins to appear that the prospects for fertility control may be improving over the decades. After reviewing several factors that "favor a much more rapid (demographic) transition than occurred in the West" — changed climate of opinion, religious doctrine, decline of infant mortality, modernization, fertility differentials, grass roots concern, and improved contraceptive technology — Dudley Kirk shows in a remarkable tabulation that the later a country began the reduction of its birth rate from 35 to 20, the shorter time it took to do so: from 73 years (average) in 1831–1860, for example, to 21 years after 1951, and on a consistently downward trend for over a century. (In his "Natality in the Developing Countries: Recent Trends and Prospects," prepared for University of Michigan Sesquicentennial Celebration, November 1967, pp. 11–13.)

[161] Nor, often, among the general public. For example, in mid-summer 1968 the Gallup Poll asked a national sample of adults: "What do you think is the most important problem facing this country today?" Less than 1 percent mentioned population. (Gallup release, August 3, 1968, and personal communication.)

[162] For an old but enlightening review, see Harold Dorn, "Pitfalls in Population Forecasts and Projections," *Journal of the American Statistical Association*, vol. 45, 1950, pp. 311–34.

II-2. Apprentice-Type Practice: Developing a Research Proposal and Conducting a Pretest to Check Its Feasibility

Two separate projects are involved for this exercise, one using a questionnaire and the other using laboratory-type observations. The first apprentice-type project you did, Exercise I-2, was a complete project, carried through to a write-up of the results. The projects for Exercise II-2 will not be completed. Instead, the task is to carry through to a research proposal and do a pretest, or pilot study, to see if your plan is workable or if and how it needs revising. Exercise I-2, on conformity, dealt with an aspect of internal functioning. As the first project for Exercise II-2, we will take as the broad problem the relation between a group and its social environment, or other persons and groups with which the group is in interaction. For the second project, we will consider possible factors related to differences in group effectiveness in problem solving.

First project
for Exercise II-2
Some background   Human groups do not exist in isolation but in some kind of environmental setting, both physical and social. While the task of developing some kind of accommodation to both its physical and social environment will not necessarily determine how the group will be specifically organized and function, still the pattern of accommodation will set some limits on the kinds of organization and operation possible. To take an obvious example, suppose the group of interest were a family and the head of the family decided to follow the occupation of movie actor. This decision limits the possible communities of residence for the family (e.g., Oshkosh, Wisconsin, would no doubt be excluded as a possible choice) and would also have some effect on the kinds of individuals and groups with which the family would be likely to interact.

Now you need to decide what part of the general topic you will select and try to develop a manageable problem to investigate. Suppose you decide to focus on families as the kind of group you will be interested in, and focus on the interaction of families with their social environments.

You might start to get ideas by selecting a familiar instance of the general kind of group and studying it fairly thoroughly — your own family. One way to proceed would be to do a retrospective participant observation study of your family, using an informal interview guide on yourself to aid your recall.

Pick at least two points in time and for each point describe the pattern of interaction with the major portions of the family's possible social environment: political, economic, religious, recreational, extended family (relatives not living in the same household with you at the times of observation), other friends. After describing the pattern at each of the two points in time, compare the descriptions to see how much change in pattern occurred.

Then try to develop some explanation, or hypothesis, to account for the change in pattern (or lack of it) for the family observed. Some likely candidates for factors accounting for change might include: (*a*) significant life-cycle changes, such as births, deaths, marriages, divorces, graduation from high school or college (*b*) extensive geographic mobility, requiring readjustment of relations with the social environment; (*c*) extreme social mobility, or change in socioeconomic status, either up or down.

Then try to develop a more general explanation that might account for more than just your own family. This more general explanation, or hypothesis, would be used to guide your selection of factors that might be observed about many families, to test your generalization.

Narrowing the
problem

What follows is a possible way of narrowing the problem to manageable form, then some suggestions for developing a research proposal and conducting a pretest. With your instructor's permission, you need not do what is suggested but may pick some other narrowed problem. Even so, you should read the rest of what follows, because the kinds of decisions you will need to make will be analogous ones. And, I would urge at least these restrictions on whatever problem you do choose: the independent variable should be "change in socioeconomic status of families" and the dependent variable some aspect of "change in interaction with social environment"; the data collecting technique should be a questionnaire. Dealing with change is not always an easy matter, and I think you need some experience in doing so; questionnaires are widely used in the social sciences and I think you should have some minimal practice in trying to develop one.

In particular, for this project the topic will be narrowed to the effect of change in the socioeconomic status of families as related to change in the pattern of interaction with extended family members. Extended family includes any relatives living outside the family of interest's dwelling unit. Family, in this study, will include all persons in the same dwelling unit who function largely as a single unit. For example, a roomer who does not eat meals with the rest and whose income is not included in the resources available to the rest would be excluded, while a foster child who participates as a member of the unit would be included, even though there is no blood tie.

Since the interest is in change, information will be needed about at least two points in time. You would like to pick those points to be reasonably sure that any potential respondent would have been with the same family during the period between. Therefore, I suggest you use life-cycle rather than calendar time and in particular take as one period the last year of high school for the respondent and the earlier period as five years prior to that. These choices will minimize the chances that one of the periods asked about would include military service for the respondent or that he or she would have married during the period and hence not be with the same family throughout. If you try to go much earlier than this for the initial period of observation, memory problems will likely be too great for you to get satisfactory data. And, if you take an interval much shorter than five years, for many families not much change might have occurred.

Developing a plan   Your task is to prepare an analysis plan, make it precise, develop a two-page-maximum questionnaire to obtain the information needed, conduct a pretest, and decide on the basis of the pretest whether your questionnaire will do the job you want it to or needs revising. Since your questionnaire is supposed to be designed for use with many people, you will need to prepare a code manual (discussed later) for the information to be obtained from the questionnaires, which would enable you to transfer the information to punch cards. If you were to obtain a thousand or so interviews, it would not be feasible for you to flip back and forth through the questionnaires and so the use of some device to allow mechanical processing of the data would be desirable. The pretest will consist of having two people, probably fellow class members, take the questionnaire on a self-administered basis. Please read through all the rest of the comments on this project before beginning to work on it further.

Your independent variable, change in family socioeconomic status, needs to be divided into categories. You will need three major categories: increase; no change; decrease. But you will probably want at least initially to subdivide the first and third. Thus you would want to divide the range possible for increase into categories ranging from a large amount of increase to a small amount of increase. Similarly, you would want to be able to examine categories from a small amount of decrease through a large amount of decrease in socioeconomic status.

Your set of dependent variables will be whatever aspects of extended family interaction you want to consider. For each aspect picked you will also need to set up three major categories covering increase, no change, and decrease, and again you will probably want to use subcategories for both increase and decrease.

If you place change in socioeconomic status in the heading, then, it would schematically look something like this:

Change in family socioeconomic status over 5-year period						
Increase				*No change*	*Decrease*	
High • • • *Low*					*Low* • • • *High*	

As you think about the kind of information needed to place a family in one or another of these categories, it should occur to you that you are going to have to decide what items you will use to determine socio-economic status level as of a given point in time, as well as what criteria you will use to determine amount of change through time. That is, will you use income, occupation, education, some indicator of "general style of life" or perhaps some combination of these? And, how much change in income, for instance, will you consider as a high or medium increase or decrease? Bear in mind the standard caution, for these items as well as those selected to serve as dependent variables: Is the information wanted likely to be possessed by the respondent, and if so can you set up the conditions so that he will be likely to give it to you? You will particularly have to come to grips with such questions as how much difference has to occur before you do not classify it as "essentially no change" but as something else. People are not going to remember in highly precise terms, although they can probably give you some kind of reasonable range. Since your basic data will not be highly precise, you will need some kind of range for "no change" as well as the other categories used. Incidentally, it would not be satisfactory for you just to ask the respondent to indicate whether there was a small increase or essentially no change, for instance. What is a "small" change to one respondent might not be to another. You are the one wanting to analyze any relationships found and you should not abdicate your responsibility for determining how those relationships will be viewed.

As far as the rest of your analysis plans, in the form of dummy tables, you need to decide what aspects of interaction with extended family members you will pick to examine. Whatever results you got from your retrospective participant observation of your own family may help you decide, but here are some suggestions. Interaction can vary quantitatively, qualitatively, or both. That is, it can change in frequency and in kind, both with respect to the means of interaction and its content.

The means of interaction may be more or less personal, ranging from face-to-face interaction to telephone calls to letters or other documents. The overall frequency of interaction, including all means, can vary as can the relative frequency or "mix" of different means of interaction. For example, at one time interaction may have been once a week face-to-face interaction and is now once a week telephone calls or exchange of letters. Or, it could have been daily telephone calls and once a week face-to-face and is now telephone calls twice a week and an exchange of letters once a week, and so on. And the content can vary, such as recreation, ritual functions (such as births, weddings, funerals, or other significant life-cycle events), aid of one kind or another, such as baby-sitting services or house-painting or financial assistance, and so on.

You need to settle on what aspects you will use for this study and how you will examine them. For instance, you might use as one kind of aspect a joint classification of the means and frequency of interaction, and as another aspect some classification of the content of the interaction. This is up to you.

A work, or auxiliary, table might be helpful to you. You could set up a small table showing the relationship between existing socioeconomic status and existing extended family interaction as of one of the points of time. This could help you to determine what items you will ask about on your questionnaire and what categories you will use. For instance, for various means of interaction you might ask about frequency of contact using as possible categories: at least once a week; less than once a week and up to a couple of times a month; about once a month; a few times a year; once a year or less.

Remember that you would need for each family inquired about the same information in the auxiliary table for each of two time periods. Then you could make some decisions about how this information could be used to get you to your basic analysis table classifications. For instance, is a change from once a week to a few times a month a comparable amount of change in your opinion as a change from a few times a month to about once a month and so you would classify both as, e.g., moderate decrease? Or what *will* you do?

Once you have figured out the items that will be in your analysis table and in any auxiliary tables you might use to aid you, and have figured out the procedures you will use to place the information from any given questionnaire into one or another category, you are ready to begin developing your questionnaire in earnest. Let me raise one last point for your consideration. Will you ask the respondent to tell you about his own pattern of interaction or give you some summary information for the family as a whole? I would urge you to consider the first choice for this exercise. Further, will you use the most frequent interaction shown with *any* member of the extended family or try to get some kind of summary or average for this? It is possible that only a few members of the extended family are interacted with at all, and if you take an average of some kind, how will you handle these hypothetical cases: Someone sees one cousin three or four times a week and no other members of the extended family at all, while someone else sees one cousin twice a month, an aunt a few times a year, and so on, but sees no member as often as once a week? For this exercise, I would advise you to consider asking your questions about kind, overall frequency, and means of interaction (or whatever you pick) only with respect to the most frequently interacted with member of the extended family.

In my comments I have tried to mention items I thought you would be most likely to overlook before trying to write your questionnaire and then find yourself in difficulty. Other items needing decision will no doubt come up as you work with your dummy tables and then start designing questions to obtain the information you will need to fill them. As far as the questionnaire itself, reread the general advice given in the text about sequencing of items for each topic and be aware that you will have to decide whether to ask about both time periods each time you ask about any items, or whether to group all the items for one time period and then repeat.

One way of checking on the phrasing of your questions, the categories selected as possible responses, and the length of time it will take to complete your questionnaire is to give it to yourself as though it were developed by a stranger. Was the statement used to gain entry satisfactory? Were there any questions you found a bit insulting or abruptly phrased? Were there any questions for which the categories allowed were not sufficient to enable you to place yourself in one of them, or were any ambiguous enough that more than one category would be applicable? Were there any places where you felt the need to amplify, and so some neutral probe questions would be desirable additions? Were the categories allowed as responses for some questions so similar that a small table could be prepared with the categories along the heading and the items inquired about along the side, so that you could quickly just check the appropriate categories for a series of items? Can you think of any other ways in which the questionnaire could be laid out physically to make it more feasible to remain within the bounds of a two-page questionnaire? Then, after answering this series of questions for yourself, put in any revisions you think are needed for the questionnaire to be filled in satisfactorily on a self-administered basis.

As a practical approach for getting ideas and then developing an analysis plan and questionnaire, I think you might benefit most from this exercise if you work in small groups to get ideas and develop rough plans. Then work individually on designing the questionnaire you want to use, the code manual for your questionnaire, and your evaluation of the results of the pretest. Before making a few remarks about code manuals and then summarizing what you are to do, let me make these suggestions aimed at trying to ensure that your group conversations will produce ideas rather than chit-chat. (1) Do not work in groups larger than five in number. (2) Be sure everybody contributes. "No fair" for someone to serve just as recording secretary. (3) Take notes from time to time and do not hesitate to summarize periodically, especially summaries of what the group has so far decided about objectives, variables, categories, and so on. (4) When you are not talking, *listen,* do not rehearse what you intend to say next.

If only because the human mind is finite, data are always summarized some way, and the means of doing this is a more or less formal code manual. I will comment on a relatively formal version. When you "code" you assign a symbol of some kind to a categorization of data. Typical symbols are numbers, since if you have many data you will want to use mechanical aids in manipulating them and most of the mechanical aids are designed to work with numerical or algebraic symbols.

A useful way to arrange a code manual is to prepare a heading like this:

Item	*Source*	*Location*

There will be some source from which the information is to be obtained, such as question number 22 in an interview, or observation trial number 8 in a series of trials. The entries under the item column will be a brief verbal description of the categories, and the location refers to the place you will store the information, such as column 18 in an 80-column punch card, and also lists across from each category the numerical symbol assigned to it which would appear in column 18.

You usually begin the manual with some identifying information to be punched into the card, such as the number of the interview to be coded. This portion of the code manual might look as follows:

Item	*Source*	*Column number and code*
Number of interview	Upper right-hand corner of face sheet (first page)	Cols. 1–4 (use number as it appears on face sheet)

If you had more than 9,999 interviews (*most* unlikely, in light of what we know about sampling) you would have to use five columns to identify the interview rather than four. Each interview would be given a number with enough digits to fill the four-column field in the example shown. Thus interview number 3 would be coded as 0003.

In general you use as many columns as you need to cover the number of categories used. If you wanted to code detailed occupation, which you could then recombine in various ways for analysis, and you wanted to use, say, 82 categories, you would need to use a two-column field. The maximum number of categories that can be coded using just one column is 12, although it is often wise to use just digits 1 through 9 for your code in any one column.

Let's take another example of coding an item, this time not identifying information. Suppose in a questionnaire you were interested in relative power of husband and wife in family decision-making, and in question 21 you asked about who usually makes the decisions in a number of areas. Part A of the question had to do with familial recreation, part B with economic purchases, and so on. You might code part B for question 21 as follows:

Relative decision-making:	Question 21,	(col. 32)
Economic	part B	
Husband only		1
Husband/wife equally		2
Wife only		3
All other possibilities		4
Answer to question		
not ascertained		9
(omitted, refusal,		
illegible, etc.)		

Looking at this illustration, you can probably see that while coding it is better to use the maximum detail you think you might want. It would be much wiser, probably, to divide the rather catch-all category of "all other possibilities" since if you *later* decide to lump them together that is a relatively easy matter, by simply requesting the machine (in its language) to count all the cards with a punch of either, say, 4 or 5 or 6 without distinguishing between them separately. But if you want to subdivide or break out some subcategories for an all-other-possibilities kind of category, that would be much harder. You would have to get out the interviews, recode them, repunch the cards, and so on.

Once you have your questionnaire developed, preparing a code manual for it is a fairly simple process, just as developing a questionnaire is relatively easy once your analysis plans are clear. In essence, you follow the advice given to Alice in Wonderland when she was not sure how to proceed: begin at the beginning, continue to the end, and then stop. Begin with your identifying information, using as many columns as you need. Then continue with question 1 of the interview, using as many of the next available columns as you need to cover responses to it, and continue through the questionnaire. However, finding a place to put answers to each question asked may not be the end of your code manual.

For instance, you might decide you want to code some summary measures, based on the combination of responses to a series of questions. In this project, to take one possible example, you might instruct the coder to look at the responses to questions 12, 13, 20, and 21, with the first two dealing with some item five years before high school graduation and the last two dealing with the last year of high school. Depending on the pattern of responses, you might set up an additional column in your code manual with the categories covering degree of change on the item during the period.

It is true that this kind of inspection and summarizing can be done mechanically, with appropriate instructions to the machine. I mention the possibility just to stress that in coding you are by no means limited to a rigid pattern of one column for each question. Remember that the purpose of coding decisions, as with so many other decisions in the planning stages, is to enable you to handle your information in such a way that it is easier for you to see whatever patterns are present for the variables and relationships you chose to examine.

Steps you are to do

1. Develop your analysis plan, using whatever dummy tables you might need.
2. Develop a questionnaire to obtain the information needed for your analysis plan. The questionnaire is limited to two pages maximum and should be prepared in duplicate, for pretesting purposes.
3. Develop a code manual for your questionnaire.
4. Carry out a pretest of your questionnaire, by having two people (preferably your classmates) answer the questionnaire on a self-administered basis.
5. Although this would not normally happen in a pretest, I think you should try to help each other with your pretests by noting in the margin next to a question any difficulties you see with it — for instance, categories not mutually exclusive.
6. Use your code manual to code the two completed questionnaires returned to you. For this exercise, on the questionnaire (in the margin) you may enter in parentheses beside the question the column number to be used and the code assigned.
7. Analyze the results of the pretest by deciding which of your questions needs rewording or whether other changes in your questionnaire need to be made and by deciding which of the codes in your code manual are unworkable and need to be revised, if any. Write up your evaluation of your pretest.
8. Turn in the two completed questionnaires, as coded by you; your code manual; your evaluation of your pretest; your analysis plans, including any dummy tables developed to aid you.

SECOND PROJECT FOR EXERCISE II-2

So far, you have used observations collected in the field (for the project in Exercise I-2) and used questioning for the first project in this exercise. The second project for Exercise II-2 will use laboratory-type observations. Further, the earlier projects mentioned involved studying naturally occurring situations, which you made no attempt to manipulate or interfere with, but this time you will deliberately form the situations and observe differences between them.

Suppose you became interested in why some groups seem more effective than others in accomplishing some task. Perhaps you just returned home from a committee meeting and were either pleased or dismayed at the functioning of the group. You might suspect differences in effectiveness are common to other groups besides committees, such as families, or cities, or industrial organizations, and decide to try to investigate why this should be so.

The general topic to be investigated for this part of Exercise II-2, then, is effectiveness of group problem-solving. Preferably, we would like the groups to be real rather than artificial (such as role-playing groups) and would like the tasks set for the groups to be of comparable difficulty. We would like to be able to manipulate the situations somewhat, to try to decide what might be related to differences in effectiveness.

Since you will both be designing the project as well as serving as members of the groups manipulated for the pretest of your research proposal, this imposes limits on what is feasible for you to do. Because you will be aware of the bases for forming the groups and of what is to be observed about them, there may be some troublesome measurement effect in the results shown by the pretest.

As you think about the general boundary conditions imposed for this exercise, you might be led to consider using game-playing groups. Then you would have *bona fide* groups and you could also control on task difficulty by having all at least play the same kind of game.

I suggest the following game, often played by children to pass the time on auto trips. Whoever is "it" tells the others, "I have something in my hand and it is usually found at the ————." The blank is filled in with zoo, or seashore, or farm, or whatever appeals to the chooser. But it should be something found only at the location specified. For instance, if zoo fills in the blank then anteater would be acceptable as a choice but ants would be "no fair." As in the Twenty Questions game referred to in the text, the rest of the players are limited to questions that can be answered with just yes or no.

You could measure degree of success by the length of time or the number of questions, or both, it takes the players to identify the item chosen. Any question asked by any player would count, except for those receiving a "don't know" reply.

Now you need to decide what might be related to the effectiveness of the group in solving its task. You could turn to folk wisdom and you might come up with: two heads are better than one; too many cooks spoil the broth. Now what? As an aside, this is one of the main difficulties with commonsense explanations. It is not that no explanation can be found but that too often too many, and often rather contradictory, explanations are available.

If you took commonsense explanations and decided to proceed systematically and logically to find out which, if either, is correct and under what conditions, then you would be proceeding in a "scientific" fashion rather than a commonsense one. In a very real sense, examination of scientifically acceptable procedures can be construed as an examination of how to improve our commonsense modes of finding out. Undoubtedly, by this point in the book it has occurred to you that much of what is being discussed could be called systematized common sense. And so — at least, I hope — it is. By systematizing procedures and turning useful ones into habit you free your energy and creative talent for application to those matters which can not be anticipated and seem inevitably to arise.

You might decide that for the small-sized groups with which you will be dealing the folk wisdom about the virtues of two heads compared to one might be pertinent and so you want a moderate size, and the same size, say, four or five players doing the guessing. As you think about this you would probably decide that five would be a better choice than four, since if disputes arise about which questions to ask, a tie-breaker would be present.

To get ideas for the rest of your plan you might try to recall your experience in various groups in which you have participated, such as committees, or several couples selecting the evening's activity for a Saturday date for all to spend together, or even family decision-making on what to do for a summer vacation. In which instances was the task accomplished smoothly, in which not, and why? This kind of systematic exploratory examination of a familiar instance of the general kind of group you are interested in is often helpful, when feasible for you to do.

You might decide that the pattern of division of labor (or coordination of the various roles occupied in the group) within committees on which you served was important to success, as probably was an efficient search strategy, or systematic exploration of possibilities. But while you can form groups according to a specific size and give them comparable tasks to do, it is not likely to be feasible for you to *impose* particular divisions of labor (since even if you did so on a manifest basis, a different pattern might emerge informally) or particular search strategies (for the same reason), in order to examine directly the effect of differences in these on group success.

So, you can try something that is often helpful when you are temporarily stymied: Try to think of a related problem, that is, one that is more generalized, or more specialized, or analogous, or more accessible. Suppose you try to think of possible conditions related to the emergence of more efficient coordination patterns, or of more efficient search strategies, or both.

Returning to conventional folk wisdom, this time you might come up with "necessity is the mother of invention." Let us say you feel the more the group is restricted in the resources available to it, the more it is likely at least to attempt to organize itself more efficiently, both with respect to the pattern of coordination developed and how quickly this is done, as well as with respect to its strategy. Suppose you decide you will form situations in which the groups are increasingly restricted as far as solving their tasks, and see what differences in success occur.

For this game-playing problem, you can restrict the groups either on the time available to them or the number of questions they can use, or both, before the group would be classed as failing in its task of identifying the object sought. Since any question asked by any player counts, some pattern of organization and some search strategy will likely be essential if there is to be any hope of success.

Here are some suggestions for you to consider, and use or not, as you choose. Classify degree of success according to four headings: high; medium; low; failure. Select three groups to play the game. You would be wise to use some random selection of members or some other way to avoid having friends play, since they will already have worked out some pattern of accommodation in their interactions.

Group A plays the game with no restrictions on time or number of questions. Playing this first game, in view of all, also provides the same *minimum* amount of practice for the other two groups by observing. Here, incidentally, is where measurement effect is likely to be especially troublesome. Having read this far, even the unrestricted group is aware of what is being done and looked for and may, more or less unconsciously, try to finish in the shortest length of time and using as few questions as it can.

To try to minimize this problem somewhat, all groups in the pretest should try to play as though only the particular restrictions in force for a given trial are known to them. Also, as a practical matter, the object to be guessed should probably be told the observers before each trial starts, to avoid whispered guessing on the part of the observers. Further, gasps and groans from the observers as the game proceeds are taboo.

Groups B and C should probably *not* observe each other's efforts. Have Group B play one game restricted only on number of questions. Twenty-one would be a good limit, since it can easily be divided into thirds for use in deciding high, medium, or low success. Then Group C plays, restricted only on time. Twelve minutes (or perhaps one-third the time it took the unrestricted group?) would be a good choice since it can be divided into thirds. Then Group B plays again, this time restricted on both time and questions, and Group C plays again, with both restrictions. You can flip coins to decide whether B or C goes first in the singly restricted case and for which goes first in the doubly restricted case.

Each situation, varying by kind and number of restrictions, can serve as experimental situation, with the other four as comparisons. Note that dividing success into thirds is a little more complicated for the doubly restricted situations. For instance, high could mean "less than or equal to 4 minutes *and* less than or equal to 7 questions." Medium could then mean "both more than 4 minutes or more than 7 questions *and* less than or equal to 8 minutes and less than or equal to 14 questions."

The stub for your analysis plan dummy table would be something like this:

*Situations, by number
and type of restrictions*

No restrictions
One only
   Questions
   Time
Both questions and time
   Group first restricted on questions
   Group first restricted on time

You need to decide what categories you will use for degree of success, for your heading, and decide what procedures will be used to determine the category in which a particular group should be placed.

Steps you are to do

1. Decide how you will select items to be guessed, how you will pick groups and observe them, and so on. That is, in general you need to decide whether you will follow the above suggestions or try something else, making similar *kinds* of decisions along the way.
2. Conduct pretest to see if your plan is workable.
3. Write up your judgment of the workability of your plan, based on the pretest results.
4. Turn in your analysis plans and any dummy tables developed; your write-up of the pretest results.

II-3. ON YOUR OWN: COMPLETE RESEARCH PROPOSAL

By now you should be through with your "review of the literature," even for those times you had to go back and check something because you had another bright idea while developing your plans. Also, your analysis and data collection plans should be roughly complete. Finish preparing your research proposal, following the outline for a detailed protocol document given at the end of Part II of the text.

Be sure to act as consultant for yourself on your protocol. Your instructor may ask each of you to serve as consultant for one other student in the class, but if not, try to set up such an exchange on an informal basis. I have found that these peer-level consultations can be very helpful for the students involved. No matter how hard your instructor tries to place himself back in the position of being a novice researcher, some things troubling you may go right by him because you are simply not on the same level. But sometimes a fellow novice can easily spot them and either make some useful suggestions or at least help you more clearly formulate what is bothering you, so that your instructor may be able to aid you. More than half the difficulty in solving any problem seems to disappear when you have a well-formulated question to try to answer.

Take the consultant task seriously, and do not be too concerned with giving the image of being either a nice guy or a nasty guy. Remember that at this point whether or not the consultant agrees that where the researcher wants to get is worth getting to is largely irrelevant. The consultant's job is not to dispense praise or blame, but to *help*.

Possibly the hardest part of occupying the role of consultee is to develop enough impartiality about your work that you can tolerate criticisms and suggestions without coming apart at the seams. I realize this is easier said than done, for any of us, but it *is* essential if you are to minimize your chances of fooling yourself as you go along.

Your instructor may want you to turn in your revised (if any revisions were necessary) protocol now, for any final critique he may have to offer, or he may decide to have you carry out your plans as soon as possible and turn in everything in one package at the end. If you are to turn in your protocol, you might be wise to make a copy of it first, and, because of time pressures, begin work on any parts for which you think major changes are extremely unlikely to be suggested.

PART III

Second Portion of the Research Process

from collecting observations through writing report

In questions of science the authority of a thousand is not worth the humble reasoning of a single individual.

GALILEO GALILEI

1. Introduction

The imagery used in Part I that the game of science is representable by a never-ending cycle is just one way of noting the successive impingement of one step in the basic game on the others. Making decisions in earlier stages is guided by an anticipation of the needs of later stages, and the options available to you at later stages hinge on prior decisions made.

Consequently, many of the points that could be made in a discussion of that portion of the research process devoted to collection of information, its analysis and interpretation, and the preparation of a report covering the entire process for a particular project have already been touched, at least briefly. Some points mentioned in the text have been further elaborated in the Exercise Sets accompanying Parts I and II of the text.

The kind of thinking and procedures needed for data collection have been mentioned in a discussion of the task of developing a plan for collecting the information desired for a specific problem. Similarly, the analysis stage to come later had to be anticipated while discussing setting up an initial plan for analysis of data to be collected. The later intent to develop as accurate ds descriptions as possible guided decisions on general strategy and controls, just as deciding on the sampling procedure to employ was guided by the intent to produce as accurate du descriptions as you can later. Interpreting the results from your particular project requires you to provide perspective by assessing where we are on a given topic now that your results are available and where we might go from here. Similar procedures were employed to place your problem in initial perspective, using both the results obtained by others and your own creative imagination. And, at least by implication, a discussion of guides for evaluating reports prepared by others is in part a discussion of guides for best preparing your own report.

Therefore, Part III will be rather briefer than the others in this book. This relative brevity should not be interpreted as meaning that lesser importance is attached to the second portion of the research process. On the contrary, the decisions and procedures described in the first, or planning, portion are aimed at enabling you to carry out the second portion as satisfactorily as you can.

During the first portion of the process, you essentially moved down the right side of the cycle of science, from an initial idea to the point where you were ready to collect observations related to that idea. The second portion of the process essentially takes you up the left side, to a completion of a turn of the cycle and to setting the stage for beginning the next turn.

Your first task is actually to collect observations, guided by the plans you have developed. Then you must make sense of them, again guided by your plans. In order to make sense of them, you need to describe them; you need to identify whatever patterns are present. This amounts to moving along the cycle from *obs* to *ds*.

But your description of the patterns in your sample of observations (*ds*) is a means to an end. Information comes to us in bits and pieces, or samples. Yet it is the larger chunk, or parent class, from which the pieces come that we want to see described and explained. Your next task, then, is to generalize. This means you need to move from *ds* to *du* along the cycle: Decide the extent to which you feel the pattern in the sample is applicable to its universe, or parent class.

After this, you face the task of trying to provide answers to the question, So what? That is, you must assess what you have done. To do this, you look both backward and forward. You look back to the objectives with which you began, your initial idea, and assess the relevance of your results to the objectives with which you began. This assessment roughly amounts to completing a turn of the cycle. But you also need to look forward, or assess the implications both of what you have learned and the way you chose to learn it (or content *and* method) for guiding future work on the general topic. This assessment

roughly amounts to setting the stage for the next turn of the cycle.

Finally, you need to prepare a report on your project. You need to decide what you should report and how you should report it. No matter how well done a study might be, the results need to be made known to others if the game of science is to yield cumulative and self-correcting knowledge. Because science is by its very nature a cooperative enterprise, results that remain unknown to others represent private, not public, knowledge, and are therefore useless in raising the probability that future instances of the basic game will be well played.

Throughout both portions of the research process, there are various guides for procedures to be followed. Their purpose is to minimize the chances of fooling yourself whenever you draw conclusions based on what has been done. A good researcher will proceed more carefully than a poor one, but there is no magic in the guides. Following guides that have proved helpful to others while playing the game should make it less likely that you will mislead yourself, but they can hardly guarantee this. Let us now turn to the second portion of the process in more detail.

2. Collect Data

The principal caution to observe throughout the data collection stage of the research process is that you not become careless in carrying out the plan you have developed. This does not mean you must be absolutely rigid and never deviate from the details of your plan. In practice, this is not likely to be possible anyway. Few things are more certain than that something unexpected will happen. You want to be able to make those alterations that

will best enable you to deal with the unexpected when it does occur. The very act of trying to devise a plan should have sharpened your thinking about where you want to go and why. With a fairly clear idea about where you want to get, then when alterations are necessary you will be better able to vary your course to come as close as you can manage.

Data collection involves three main tasks. First you must secure access to the data decided on, both initial and continued access until data collection is complete for the project. Second, you need to build in quality control checks. Third, you need to be concerned with the mechanics of collecting and processing information.

2.1 ACCESS. Every study has some access problems. You must solve problems related to both initial access — being allowed to obtain information at all — and to continued access — being allowed to complete the collection of information.

Sometimes access problems are easily solved, requiring only an inexpensive purchase of records already in the public domain or else the location of appropriate materials in some library, hoping not too many other people want to use the same source materials during the period you have to complete collecting your information. But securing access can range through all levels of difficulty, possibly proving unsolvable with existing techniques. In addition, what was at one time a fairly simple access problem may change to a more difficult one, and vice versa.

For instance, not many years ago a researcher wanting to use a questionnaire had minimal difficulty in persuading people to talk to interviewers. Surveys were somewhat novel. Most people were both flattered that their comments were wanted and impressed by the rationale given as to why the sampling procedures meant it would *not* be just as good to take some other house down the block. The access problem for studies using this technique is no longer as easy to solve.

Various commercial companies have used the device of having salesmen misrepresent themselves in person and over the telephone as disinterested survey takers in order to gain entry. This causes one kind of difficulty for the serious researcher.

A good rationale for doing the study and proper identification devices can help overcome the suspicion that the interviewer is really just a salesman and his questionnaire will turn out to be a gimmick to disguise a sales pitch. Sending advance letters to the occupants of the households selected and having some advance publicity given the study in the local news media can also aid in stamping your study as legitimate, but even these are not always enough.

In addition, there has been an unfortunate increase recently in fear of all strangers because of possible random and senseless violence. This fear is particularly pronounced among residents of certain parts of our large urban areas. And on the other side of the coin, it is less rare now for prospective interviewers to show great reluctance, and perhaps even refuse, to conduct interviews in certain districts within our large cities. Whether the fear is justified or not on either side is beside the point, as long as it exists.

This makes it much more difficult to obtain the probability sample of respondents that was planned. Again, the devices already mentioned to legitimate your study can be tried, in order to overcome this second kind of difficulty in obtaining access. But as long as large numbers of people are too mistrustful of all strangers even to come to the door or otherwise allow the interviewer to get close enough to present his credentials or give his rationale, this aspect of the access problem for interview studies will remain a difficult one to overcome.

And, of course, no matter how well designed the sample or the rest of the parts to the study, if the plan cannot be carried out in practice — for whatever reason — the "results" are just that much more suspect. In general, then, it is wise to do some kind of pretest or preliminary feasibility study, no matter what the kind of observations wanted, to check if you *will* be able to get what you want in the way you planned and within the time period allocated for data collection.

You should routinely check what is in a published report about how the access problem was solved and be sure to include some information on this in your own reports. For instance, if a researcher states he did an interview survey with a random sample of the population, note what he says about the proportion of refusals. Then stop to judge whether or not you think the proportion is high enough to cast doubt on any generalizations made about the sample *actually* obtained. Reminding yourself to ask whether the details of the method used are clearly described, as well as whether any critical omissions resulted because of those details, should help you spot any difficulties here.

On a more positive note, access problems for both laboratory and field versions of experiments involving human beings seem to be a little easier to solve nowadays than they once were. It is not certain why this is so. Perhaps the general public is more sophisticated now and has a better grasp of the logic underlying experimentation and its usefulness in yielding understanding of what is going on and why. Or perhaps as massive amounts of money become committed to health, education, welfare, space programs, transportation, and the like, those in charge of these matters feel the need to obtain more satisfactory answers than those so far obtained by other methods.

At any rate, there does seem to be a more prevalent attitude now than in the past that if we really want to know (especially before huge expenditures are made) such matters as whether one type of educational approach is better than another, or the effects of prolonged isolation in very small groups for the purposes of lengthy space flights or undersea explorations, or the likely effects of one or another costly mass transit system, we had better do some systematic experimentation to find out. To be sure, for some problems simulated experiments are carried out with the aid of a computer, but at least the acceptance of the underlying logic is there — even for cases where application may involve human beings rather than other physical objects — and to some extent acceptance of that logic seems to be carrying over to acceptance of nonsimulated experiments as well.

Typically, solving initial and continued access problems depends on what might be called legitimation and diplomacy. Especially if a social science project is complex, it is wise to secure substantial legitimation of the project. In general, you should try to get the backing of the most influential units in whatever group you want to study, so that you may enter at the highest possible level. Working your way down seems to be much easier than the reverse.

For instance, if you wanted to study families, you would initially try to secure acceptance of the project by the adults, not the children. Similarly, if you wanted to study high school classroom situations or unions or industrial organizations, you would contact first the principal or the leaders of the union or industrial organizations. Just this is not always enough, and you will often find it helpful to have an advisory committee made up of representatives of all the important segments of the community or other social organization to be studied. Depending on whether or not the legitimation you achieve is deemed satisfactory by those from whom you want information, gaining access may be correspondingly easy or hard.

Once initial access is achieved, you need

to have continued access to information until your data collection is complete. Accomplishing this often rests on how diplomatic you or your representatives are. More bluntly, a better term for what is necessary to have continued access might not be diplomacy but common courtesy. Remember that it is you who are seeking to impose on others, not the reverse, and so it is your obligation and not theirs to provide justification as to why information should be given you.

The better and more understandable your rationale is for doing your project — any project, at any level — the better your chances will be of both gaining and keeping access. Perhaps the easiest way to proceed is to mentally put yourself in the place of those from whom you want information. Then, with the roles mentally reversed, ask yourself what you would want to know about the project in order to convince yourself to cooperate. At a minimum you would want to know who, what, and why, or under whose auspices (persons or groups) the study is being conducted, and what kind of information is needed and for what purpose. Since the researcher is likely to have little to offer you in exchange for his interruption of your activities except the promise that you are contributing to a worthwhile addition to knowledge, you would certainly want to be convinced that the project will indeed be that.

Try to put yourself in the place of your advisory committee as well as those individuals or groups who will serve as sources of information, either as sources for direct observation or because they can provide answers to questionnaires or because they control the use of whatever records you may be interested in. And your answers to the questions they would be likely to ask you should be considered ones. If the suspicion arises that you do not really

know what you are doing, access to information may end abruptly. Unfortunately, it may not just end for you. Whether you do a creditable job or a poor one may make it just that much easier or harder for the next researcher who might want to use the same sources of information, and you should keep this in mind.

These various matters of legitimation and diplomacy may well involve facing some ethical issues. The data collection phase of the research process is one of the two where you are most likely to encounter questions of ethics. Report preparation and publication is the other.

These two phases of the overall process are the ones in which what you do is most likely to impinge on your fellow human beings. In the remaining phases you primarily use your own reasoning ability and nonliving aids such as available literature or mechanical devices for processing information. If anyone "gets hurt" it will only be you. This is not necessarily correct for the data collection and report phases.

I suppose the shortest and most obvious advice to be given is to follow some version of the Golden Rule: do nothing to hurt your neighbor deliberately. Neighbor, in this version, includes both those who serve as sources of information and any present and future colleagues in the general scientific enterprise who might want to conduct investigations using the same or similar data sources.

Side effects from what you do when you collect data and what you say in any report you write are always possible. It is your obligation, as an ethical individual, let alone as an ethical scientist, to try to ensure that possible side effects are neutral, or at least not damaging.

More specifically, in the data collection and report publication stages you may need to wrestle with questions of preserving the anonymity of persons or groups and of the use of subterfuge. Under the latter I include such matters as the use of hidden tape recorders or cameras, and deliberate misrepresentation of the purposes of the project or what will actually be done in the course of the research, in order to obtain the information you would like to have.

Opinion is divided, especially on the issue of the use of subterfuge. There is much less disagreement that the anonymity of data sources should be preserved unless the information is already in the public domain or unless permission is explicitly obtained to identify individuals or groups. But as far as the use of subterfuge is concerned, I have heard well-intentioned (although not necessarily convincing, at least to me) arguments on both sides.

I suppose the easy thing to say here is that this is a matter for the conscience of the individual researcher, and perhaps this is the best thing to say. But we all have our more or less biased opinions, scientists included, and here is mine for your consideration: I am against the use of subterfuge, for both ethical and practical reasons. This does not mean I would object to telling (for example) subjects in a proposed experiment that the purposes of the research require that the subject not be made fully aware in advance of the procedures to be used and why, then leaving it up to the individual subject to decide whether or not he is still willing to participate. It does mean that as a citizen I would strongly object to being told something was to be done and only later realize that I had been intentionally deceived.

I suspect that my citizen feeling is widespread and it seems to me that the scientist *qua* scientist has an obligation to respect these feelings. I think it is not only more ethical for him to do so, but I believe it may be far more practical. If a trust is violated, the result is likely to be closure of that source of information to any future research, for the particular investigator involved as well as any who might follow.

For instance, a rather plaintive letter to the editor appeared on this point in one of the 1970 issues of *The American Sociologist*. It seems that the writer of the letter wanted to do some research with college students at his academic institution and found that it was impossible to convince the subjects that he was telling the truth about the purposes of his experiment. Having them believe him was evidently critical for his research project and so he was expressing his unhappiness at the difficulties caused later researchers when prior ones practice deception. Since student turnover is quite rapid, it is unlikely that the particular students approached had already been deceived in a research project. Instead, the student grapevine had no doubt done its usual efficient job of alerting later students to what had happened to earlier ones.

In these days of rapid communication generally, it seems possible that when the use of subterfuge is later discovered, the result might well be the closure of an entire *area* of investigation, such as the internal workings of labor unions, or jury deliberations, or medical school training practices, or the conditions in a country that foster or hinder popular uprisings. Scientific knowledge is gained by a cumulative process in which it is rare indeed that a *single* study's results can be considered definitive. In my judgment, I doubt that the gain in knowledge from a single study using some sort of subterfuge can outweigh the possible practical risk, quite apart from any ethical issues.

2.2 QUALITY CONTROL. Assuming any access problems are well enough solved, you need to concern yourself with quality control. A small pretest, or pilot study, can be useful in helping you spot points where you need to institute quality control checks you might otherwise overlook, as well as helping you see how to improve your handling of access or even mechanical tasks.

As discussed earlier, you can allow yourself to be quite flexible and imaginative in selecting premises to be used in a theoretical argument if, once selected, the entire argument is carefully checked for strength and soundness. Similarly, you can be flexible and imaginative in ways of finding out *if* these ways are then carefully checked to see that the quality of what is obtained through their use is satisfactory.

Quality control procedures typically involve a kind of "inspection sampling," in that small samples of the items and procedures are checked. For instance, suppose you did a fairly complicated study involving a probability survey of households in a large metropolitan area. To check on the block-listing of households you can pick a subsample from the blocks picked for the original sample and check that block-listing for the subsample was reasonably correct. The better the subsample, the more firmly grounded are conclusions about what it shows. Thus, you would not pick just any blocks to check, but you would pick a probability sample of the blocks originally selected.

In addition to checking on the quality of the original block-listing, the subsample can be used to check on interviewer quality. For the subsample, have the interviewing supervisor or someone you consider to be an exceptionally good interviewer visit the dwelling units again and reinterview.

Once the reinterview is completed the original interview is taken out and the two compared, with the respondent asked to help reconcile any discrepancies that might be present, such as items originally forgotten and now recalled or vice versa. This

procedure, more formally known as taking a PES, or post-enumeration-survey, is used to check both on whether the interviewers are going to the right units and on the general quality of the interviewing done, in order to estimate the amount of response error (and there will always be some) that exists.

You might think that respondents would object to being asked to answer the same questionnaire twice. In my experience and in that of other survey research workers with whom I have talked, this is not so *as long as* the respondent is given a clear and understandable explanation for the imposition on him. I have found that respondents selected for a PES are usually pleased to see that the researchers are concerned enough about the quality of the information obtained to want to do some checking.

After, or preferably during, the time the questionnaires are coming in from the field, pick a sample of items in the questionnaire that can serve as consistency checks and routinely check these on all questionnaires before they are processed. For example, those stating they are married should be above some minimum age.

During the coding, pick a sample of completed questionnaires and have them recoded by the coding supervisor or someone you think is a good coder. This gives you a check on the quality of the coding job being done.

All tabulations can be checked as they are returned from machine processing to see that the overall total is correct and the marginals add to the proper total. In addition, a sample of the cells in the tables can be recomputed.

These various kinds of checks based on inspection sampling are typically referred to as internal consistency checks. How many of them you need to make depends on which items are critical for the purposes of your study and how much of your resources you can afford to allocate for quality control purposes. If your initial quality control checks reveal that the quality is high, you can breathe a well-earned sigh of relief. If they do not, and it is not feasible for you to correct most of the errors, then you have an obligation to use your checks to estimate the amount of error and to adjust your later generalizations accordingly.

After all, it is no disgrace in science to have to work with data that are not as adequate as you might like. Disgrace, if any, comes because you have not made your basic observations, whatever form they come in, as accurate as was practical, or — much worse — if you pretend in your report that your data are more accurate than you know them to be. In the first instance you run the risk of unnecessarily misleading yourself and so not playing your specific game of science as well as you might have. In the second instance you are deliberately fooling others, and so retarding progress in the general game.

In addition to internal consistency checks, you can make some external consistency checks as well. If outside estimates of some items inquired about are available, check your results with these to see how reasonable your findings seem. For instance, whatever the main purpose of some interview study you might do, you probably asked questions on age and marital status, guessed at sex and race, and so on. You can make comparisons of the distributions on such items with census distributions for the area from which the sample was picked (allowing for probable changes between the last decennial census and the time your survey was taken, or using any intercensal official estimates that might exist). Then, if your sample results for those items you *can* check seem consistent with independent estimates, you would have somewhat more confidence that your study might be adequately representative for the items you cannot check.

As well as checking with outside estimates when possible, make any other logical checks for reasonableness you can. A researcher familiar with the details of the procedures followed for his particular study and with his general subject can often spot something about his data that just does not look right, even though it may take him a while to pinpoint just exactly what it is his developed intuition tells him is wrong. These various kinds of checks for reasonableness are sometimes referred to as checks by convergence of evidence, as well as called external consistency checks.

Similar checks can be made for studies involving data in other forms than answers to questions and using other procedures. If you are making direct observations, you should build in checks on intraobserver and interobserver reliability. If you are using some physical measuring instrument, be sure to check periodically that it is measuring and recording properly. These checks are analogous to the checks described for the use of questionnaires and interviewers as data collecting and recording instruments. Adaptations of the other kinds of internal consistency checks cited for a questionnaire survey can be used in other kinds of studies. No matter what the type of study, though, some external and internal consistency checks should routinely be made.

Building in systematic ways of checking what is done is as important (although the details may vary) for small and seemingly simple studies as it is for large and complex ones. This is sometimes hard for the beginner to take seriously, especially if he only reads about what should be done and does not gain some practice in trying to do it.

Unhappily, I suspect there is another reason besides lack of exposure to the practical problems that occur in doing research work. This reason lies in the habits and attitudes so often fostered by the student's exposure to our usual processes of education. A premium is placed on learning material rapidly and on being right on certain selected occasions only.

If it turns out that a student makes mistakes he is not given much encouragement or incentive to find and correct them, especially if those mistakes occur on the written tests so often solely used to judge his competency in a subject. Rather, he typically resigns himself to taking his lumps in the form of a poor grade and goes on to something else. Seldom is he given any incentive to go back and try to learn the material again and this time correctly.

Some of the newer instructional approaches, however, such as the use of programed learning materials, do involve what seem to me to be more realistic procedures both for attaining and judging mastery. Under this approach a certain level of competency, rather than speed, is stressed. If the student does not achieve at the 80 percent level of competency, say, when he is tested (and the tests do not always consist solely of written examinations) he reviews the material and tries again until he does, with the speed of his review and the number of times he must go over the material largely irrelevant to the process of judging him. Of course, the better job he does of learning the material correctly the first time and of locating his errors quickly, the sooner he can move on to new material. But what counts is that he is finally right, not that he is rapid.

Under this approach it is assumed that the student is human, that he possesses the humility to realize that since he is learning new material he will undoubtedly make some mistakes, that he has the maturity to recognize that the appropriate reaction to mistakes is neither to skip over them nor to feel personally threatened or humiliated by them but to correct them, and that he has the self-confidence to believe that if he does try again he will be able to find his mistakes and he will be able to correct them. It seems to me this is a far healthier and realistic approach to take, not only to the processes of education, but certainly to the conduct of research and perhaps the conduct of other areas of life as well.

After all, few of us commit suicide or go into a deep depression over an unhappy love affair. We pick ourselves up and try again — perhaps a bit more cautiously the next time, but nonetheless we do try, we don't just give up. Similarly, experienced scientific researchers almost automatically follow a rule of thumb that leads to a certain amount of both useful humility and self-confidence: Nobody's perfect, errors are bound to occur, and therefore systematic ways of catching and correcting as many of them as possible should be built into the overall design and conduct of *any* study.

2.3 MECHANICS. The beginner sometimes seems to feel he need not concern himself with the mechanics related to collecting and processing his information. This is not so. The research process, like the chain it resembles, is only as strong as its weakest link. Naturally, you need not record every observation or do every computation yourself, but you do need to oversee and control what goes on.

A number of handbooks and other detailed descriptions covering mechanics are available. For instance, there are a variety of physical aids for processing and manipulating data. If you become involved in a complex project, you may need to resort to some of the more sophisticated of these aids, such as computers. Gaining a basic understanding of the abilities and limitations of any mechanical aids you might consider using gets easier all the time. Operator manuals are available, of course, and they are increasingly being phrased in readable English. Further, for some of the more sophisticated aids such as computers, self-teaching or programed instruction materials are widely available now and cover from simple to advanced levels of understanding and application.

While you do not need to understand the internal workings of such devices as computers, you do need to have a grasp of the principles involved in their operation and should be aware of what such devices can and cannot do. Similar comments apply to the use of desk calculators, tape recorders, and the like. You should clearly keep in mind, though, that any mechanical aids you might use are just that: aids. One way of saying this is that every such device is potentially a **GIGO** device: garbage in, garbage out. It is up to you to try to ensure that this potential is not realized.

Other matters covered in detail in handbook-like materials include the specifics of setting up the processing of interviews, conducting training of interviewers and coders, keeping field notes, the relative efficiency of different experimental designs, and the like. One item that sometimes does not receive the attention it might is setting up a system of careful record-keeping.

It is remarkably easy to forget details, even when engaged in a project, but especially after you have begun work on another project and another researcher comes along and wants to use portions of your information. At the time, you may feel that you could never forget the decision you made on how to handle a troublesome matter or exactly what tabulation number 28 contains, but you very likely will forget and so you need to set up an efficient record-keeping system.

Since there are good handbooks available and since this book is pitched at an introductory level, let me here merely stress again that you should be sure to oversee the steps in the collection, storage, and processing of your information. This is so for ethical as well as practical reasons.

As researcher, you are responsible for what happens to your collected basic data. Especially if you have "sensitive" information, as well as to preserve the anonymity of any subjects or respondents used, ultimately it is *your* responsibility to ensure that none of your data become "lost, strayed, or stolen." Apart from these ethical considerations, there is the practical dividend that a researcher thoroughly familiar with what was done throughout his project usually develops his intuition thereby. This developed intuition can be invaluable when it comes to interpreting any patterns identified and in spotting clues that can be helpful in deciding where to go next as far as research on a topic.

3. ANALYZE AND INTERPRET

Your first task is to identify accurately any patterns existing in the particular sample of observations collected. This is tantamount to developing *ds* descriptions,

in terms of the cycle of science diagramed earlier. Once your *ds* descriptions are developed, and in practice along with developing them, your second task is to decide how generalizable these patterns are. In other words, you need to develop *du* descriptions. Third, you need to interpret, or assess, what you have learned and so complete the cycle by again placing your project in perspective.

Before you can adequately identify patterns in your data, or decide the likelihood that these patterns are applicable to the parent class for your sample, or assess the implications of your results for general knowledge about the topic, you need to be clear on what was done. Thus whether your analysis turns out to be relatively easy or quite difficult, as far as forming strong and sound arguments for any conclusions made, depends largely on how systematically and clearly procedures were set up and followed.

If the kinds of decisions that should have been faced in the planning stages were not, then the same kinds of decisions have to be faced now if anything beyond anecdotal material is to be salvaged from the study, and reconstructing is typically more difficult than starting fresh. Reconstructing, after the fact, just what kind of sample was actually selected and what the implications of this selection are for its probable representativeness, as well as just what kinds of controls were in fact applied and whether they were in essence applied uniformly or haphazardly, can be far from easy. The analysis stage is the one in which, in homely but apt terms, the chickens are likely to come home to roost.

3.1 IDENTIFICATION. Your first analysis task is to identify any patterns present in the sample of observations actually obtained. Several approaches can be employed to aid you in trying to discover whatever patterns exist. There are some standard logical procedures to use, there are various mathe-matical and statistical tools available, and there are some common ways to vary your examination of the data.

Foremost among the aids available to you at this stage is the thinking you undertook in advance of collecting your information. If this was carefully done, you already will have thought about how to manipulate your data to make it manageable and about how you will put it into more or less explicit tables showing the cross-classifications and joint-classifications of interest.

While doing this you will have decided on the number of categories you will use for your variables, guided by an understanding of the mechanics involved in processing information. Thus you will have kept the maximum detail you thought you might want for later analysis, since it is relatively easy to decide to collapse categories or to combine them in alternative ways for analysis purposes but mechanically difficult to get *more* detail to analyze. The basic documents, whatever they might be, would have to go through several handling stages again (recoding, repunching, retabulating, and so on) and each time they are handled an additional possibility for error exists. You also will have decided *how* you will examine relationships, such as the use of absolute numbers or relative ones like percentages or ratios. And you will have speculated on possible patterns you might find and their meaning, so you will have some "standard" patterns in mind to compare with your results.

Whenever you decide, as you must in any study, which variables are of interest to you, which ones you want to relate, which will be used separately and which simultaneously or jointly, and how you will try to see the relationships between the variables, a "table" is present. It may be explicitly and physically prepared or only roughly designed in your head. None-theless it is there. The kinds of procedures likely to be useful for deciphering the table's meaning are similar whether or not it is explicitly prepared, and so I will describe what might be done with formally prepared tables.

Of course, first be sure internal consistency checks have already been made, and have the title of the table clearly in mind so that you feel sure you know just what is being related to what. Then begin taking the table apart, beginning broadly and then working more narrowly. Characterize your entire sample of units according to the variables contained in the stub and heading. You can begin with either, although you may find it preferable to characterize by any independent variables first. To describe the entire sample you must look at the cells for the row marginal and the column marginal. Recall that the row marginal is that column whose cells tell you what the entire sample is like as far as the categories used for the variables in the stub (or rows), and the column marginal is that row whose cells tell you what the entire sample is like as far as the categories used for the variables in the heading (or columns).

Once you know what your sample as a whole is like with respect to the variables of interest, you have some kind of base with which to compare the results in the rest of the table. Now begin looking at the body of the table, noting the pattern for major categories first.

If you have any joint classifications, look at the categories for each variable separately, describing the general outline and intensity of the pattern you see when each variable's effect is singly examined. Then look at the joint, or simultaneous, effects present.

To aid in later write-up of your report, as well as simply to keep things clear in your own mind, it is helpful to note what you see as you go along. After you look at each marginal, write a sentence or two on the kind of clustering you see in the total sample. As you examine the effects of each single variable in a joint classification, put down both your judgment on what you see and any comments on how the pattern for each is related, if at all, to the pattern shown for the overall sample when you looked at just the marginals. Do the same kind of describing and looking back at the prior broader patterns as you study joint effects.

While the practiced researcher may not have to do so, as a practical matter the beginner will find it wise to put in all the totals he thinks he might like to examine, even though this may involve some duplication of information scattered in the table. Suppose you jointly classified two variables in your stub, one with four categories and one with five. To be specific, suppose you classified all United States cities according to the four Census regions and then within each region you classified cities by size into quintiles, or fifths, with the top quintile containing the largest fifth of the cities and the bottom quintile containing the smallest. The stub of your table would look like this:

All U.S. cities, by
region and population size

Northeast
   Top quintile
   Second quintile
   Third quintile
   Fourth quintile
   Bottom quintile

North Central
   Top quintile
   Second quintile
   Third quintile
   Fourth quintile
   Bottom quintile

South
    Top quintile
    Second quintile
    Third quintile
    Fourth quintile
    Bottom quintile

West
    Top quintile
    Second quintile
    Third quintile
    Fourth quintile
    Bottom quintile

You might find that you can mentally compare the pattern in the rows for the categories under the first (region) variable of the joint classification, in order to see its effect when taken alone. But you will probably find it difficult to mentally add up all the rows labeled top quintile, then all the rows for the second quintile, and so on, and then compare these mentally-added-up rows to see the effect of the second (size) variable by itself. If you put some extra rows at the bottom of the table, analyzing the information will be easier. This is worth doing even though it involves some extra labor, since you will not bother putting all the extra rows in the table when you place it in the appendix of your report. At least these rows would appear at the bottom of the table when you try to analyze it:

All cities
    Top quintile
    Second quintile
    Third quintile
    Fourth quintile
    Bottom quintile

In fact, you probably could make your analysis job easier for yourself if you also repeated the rows for the four regions in a single place at the bottom of the table. The same comments, for the same reason, apply to adding extra columns if you have joint classifications in the heading. Remember that the appendix to your report needs to contain data in a form that the reader can examine for himself if he wishes, but this does not mean that you cannot expect him to do some rearranging and make some effort in combining material. Auxiliary or work tables, extra columns and rows, and the like do not have to appear in any published form unless you choose for them to and can afford the added publication cost. Your task is to analyze the basic information as well as you can, and you should feel free to do whatever you can to make that job as easy for yourself as possible while you systematically attempt to see any patterns present.

Whether you physically or only mentally make the combinations needed, the procedure followed should be similar: first look at the marginals, then the major breaks (as the categories for the first variable used in a joint classification are usually called), then the minor breaks (categories for the second variable), and then at the joint effect of the variables. In each case you are looking for the shape and intensity of any patterns shown, and in each case you would be wise to note your conclusions before going on.

The pattern for the marginals is contrasted with the rest of the table in order to see whether association or independence is shown in the body of the table. If association is present, then you go on to describe it in some detail.

In the city illustration above, suppose the variable contained in the heading were median family income, grouped according to different levels. (Median family income for a city is the income that divides the families in the city into two equal halves, with half the families having an income above the median and half an income below it.) Looking at the column marginal tells you what the total set of cities is like as far as the proportion of them with certain median income levels. Thus you could do some kind of job of predicting median income level if you knew only that the units involved were cities. What you would like to know is whether you can do a better job of predicting if you know *more* than that. In particular, you would like to know whether you can do a better job by knowing the region of location for a city, or the size group it belongs in, or both region and size group simultaneously. If independence is present the answer is no, while if association is present the answer is yes, and how *much* better job you can do if you have additional information depends on the pattern of the association present and how pronounced the pattern is.

This does not mean that showing independence is necessarily disappointing. This may have been what you were hoping to find, in order to support some inference by eliminating other possible inferences. If you think back to the original analysis plan developed and discussed in Exercise I-2, partial support for the inference that conformity occurred because of norm internalization would have been provided if conformity could be shown to be *independent* of the strength of the sanctions present in differing situations of the same type.

In addition to following the general procedure for trying to see *any* pattern of association (first characterizing the total sample and then looking at the effect of singly and simultaneously classified variables), you compare what is found with the patterns you spent some time thinking about when you were planning your study. In order to develop even rough criteria for theoretical significance, you did some speculating on possible clear-cut patterns and how you might interpret them. You should already have decided which of these "standard" patterns indicate support for some explanation and which indicate revisions

are needed. How much support or how much revision your study actually indicates depends on how close the pattern that *did* occur is to one or another of the patterns speculated on earlier. And of course, before drawing firm conclusions about the extent to which one of the earlier-speculated-on patterns has empirically occurred, you should first check whether anything in the details of your method could have led to illusory results.

Typically, the clear-cut patterns speculated on in the planning stages will have rested on the use of one or both of the two basic principles of elimination, one for eliminating conditions as not being necessary and the other for eliminating conditions as not being sufficient. Even so, it never hurts to look over your data to see whether any unanticipated applications can now be made of either principle. For instance, can you take whatever was used as independent variable and now turn the problem around and use it as dependent variable?

Suppose you were interested in studying the relation between the amount of formal education of the heads of families and the occupational level occupied, perhaps ranked by some measure of occupational prestige or by median income received annually by holders of similar jobs. And suppose you decided to look at the relationship by using percentage distributions.

Schematically, this might be shown as in the sample table below. For each row, corresponding to an occupational level, you would look across the columns to see what the percentage distribution of educational levels is like, and then compare the rows. Doing this amounts to using occupational levels is like, and then compare the rows. cational level as the dependent one.

Let us say you found that as the occupational level increased, so also did the per-

Occupational level (by median income received)	Educational level (by years of school completed)					Total
	High	•	•	•	• Low	
High						100%
•						100
•						100
•						100
•						100
Low						100
Total						100

centage of family heads with at least some college training. From this you might suspect, knowing that formal education is typically completed before entering full-time employment, that perhaps a certain level of education is a necessary condition to get a job that pays more than a particular level of income.

But will completing some level of education guarantee some occupational level or above? To shed some light on this, you would now let educational level be the independent variable and occupational level be the dependent one, and recompute the percentages so that each *column* would now add to 100 percent. Now, within each educational level category you look at the distribution of occupations, and then compare the columns.

Suppose you found that the clustering of occupations with the same income level is not strongly pronounced within the differing levels of education. Then you might conclude that although it is possible that a particular level of education might be necessary to secure a particular occupational level, evidently it is not sufficient — it will not guarantee attaining that occupational level. In other words, getting a certain amount of formal education might be essential if a person wants to be able to compete for jobs at or above some level, but this alone will not guarantee he

will be successful in the competition. In order to make this kind of inference, you had to analyze the same basic data on your sample of family heads, but in two different ways.

The procedures suggested are general or *logical* ways to proceed to get the main pieces of information you would like to know when summarizing and identifying a pattern. They are: (*a*) locating patterns by beginning broadly and working more narrowly, looking for association or independence and the extent of either as you proceed; (*b*) speculating on possible clear-cut patterns and their interpretation in order to compare them with actual patterns found; and (*c*) any use of either principle of elimination that was not anticipated earlier but now seems justified, or any other ways of varying your approach that occur to you. You want to know the general outline or shape of the pattern, its intensity or the extent of clustering within the pattern, and the spread or variation shown around any particular shape and intensity of pattern present. There are a number of statistical aids available to help yield this kind of information.

Statistical techniques generally divide into two major types. One type involves descriptive statistics, or ways of summarizing the pattern in a set of data. This type is the one most likely to be useful to you in trying to develop your *ds* descriptions. The other type involves inferential statistics, or ways of helping judge the likelihood that what is going on in the sample can justifiably be said to be going on in its parent class as well. This latter type is more likely to be useful to you in trying to develop your *du* descriptions.

Descriptive statistics are used for three principal tasks: to measure central tendency, variance, and correlation. Or, in the terms used earlier, measures of correlation aid in describing the general outline of the pattern of relationships, measures of central tendency aid in describing clustering, and measures of variance aid in describing spread. Depending on the particular kind of statistical measure used to describe or summarize any of the three, the answers you get are slightly different.

For instance, assume the yearly income for each of a set of families was given by this set of values:

$$ 2,000
$$ 2,400
$$ 6,000
$$ 2,000
$$ 25,000
$$ 8,000

Which measure should you use as the best estimate of clustering, or typical income for the set of families?

Answering this depends on what the options are, but even more importantly on what you want the term "typical" to mean. In the example, the most frequently occurring value is $2,000. If you want to think of typicality as the most frequently occurring value in a distribution of values, then you use the "mode" to summarize clustering, because that is the definition of the mode.

If you want to think of typicality as the middle value in the distribution, with half

the items above and half the items below that value, then you use the "median" because that is the definition of the median. In the example, there is an even number of items, so no one is in the middle. Here you would take the two middle values, add them up and divide by two, which in this case gives six plus eight divided by two or $7,000 as the median. (Of course, any value between $6,001 and $7,999, if you are rounding to the nearest dollar, would serve to divide the distribution so that an equal number of items are above and below the median, but the customary way of computing the median for an even number of items is as I have just described it.) There are still other ways of describing clustering statistically, chief among these being the arithmetic mean.

It is the arithmetic mean you are using when you say your average score for a series of quizzes is, say, 85 points. To obtain this figure you add up all the points you received for all the quizzes and divide by the number of quizzes. (Did you notice by now that the way to find the median when there is an even number of items is by taking the arithmetic mean of the two middle values?) In the income example given, the mean is $45,400 divided by 6, or $7,567 to the nearest dollar.

The arithmetic mean gives you a kind of balancing point. If you visualize the mean as a sharp knife blade, and each of the dollars for the families or each of the quiz points earned as having a constant weight, then if you spread these weights out appropriately on a thin strip of something, at some point along the strip the knife could be placed underneath and the strip would be stably balanced. The balance point is the mean value. More formally, this is stated by saying that the arithmetic mean for a distribution is that value for which the deviations around the mean (or differences between the actual scores or incomes and the mean score or mean income, with some of these differences being positive and some being negative) add up to zero. That is, the sum of the positive deviations exactly equals the sum of the negative deviations, or they balance.

Another way of thinking about the mean is as a "socialistic" kind of measure. If all the dollars available to the six families were added up and then the total were divided into equal shares for each family, the mean would tell you the number of dollars in each of these equal shares.

In the income example given, which was deliberately skewed rather than symmetrical, you have three different figures to mull over, $2,000, $7,000, and $7,567, coming from describing central tendency according to the mode, the median, and the mean respectively. Each gives a different kind of information.

I have described the computation and some interpretation of these three measures because they are extensively enough used that you ought to be a little familiar with each even if you never formally study any statistics or read research reports in professional journals, and you cannot really understand a measure unless you know how it is computed as well as why. Even articles in the semipopular press, such as the better news magazines or such newspapers as the *New York Times* or *Wall Street Journal* refer to these measures without further elaboration, assuming that the reader knows how to interpret them. You are particularly likely to see the median and the mean referred to. (If the term mean is not qualified as to kind or if just the term "average" is used, the customary understanding is that the arithmetic mean is the measure involved.) I will make just brief remarks on measures for the other two descriptive problems, summarizing spread and covariation.

A common way of looking at spread is the range, or difference between the two extreme values in a distribution. Further, the range can be divided into equal pieces and these are given different names, depending on how many pieces are used. Commonly used divisions are halves, thirds, quarters, fifths, tenths, and hundredths. Dividing a distribution into four pieces is called using quartiles, into five pieces using quintiles, into ten using deciles, and into a hundred is the familiar use of percentiles (*percent,* or according to one hundred). I see little point here in describing some of the other measures of spread, such as the standard deviation, which is a particular kind of measure of spread around a mean value. If you go on to become a producer of scientific knowledge, you will soon enough learn how to compute the measures of most utility for your discipline. Instead, I hope that from this discussion you will keep in mind the three basic tasks for which descriptive statistics are used. Then if you do study statistics you will be better able to keep your eye on the proverbial forest rather than losing sight of it among the trees devoted to specific ways of accomplishing these tasks, each giving slightly different but related information.

The third major task is to describe covariation or correlation. Measures of correlation are designed to get at the extent to which variables travel some systematic path together. The measure you are most likely to come across in research reports and even occasionally in the semipopular press, is the Pearsonian correlation coefficient, which in reports is often given simply as r and is understood to be this particular measure. If you ask the extent to which the variables can be described as traveling a linear (or straight line) path, then r is what you compute to help answer the question.

If the variables travel this path in the same direction, so that the more of one variable the more of the other, then the correlation is called direct and the correlation coefficient will be positive. If they travel in opposite directions, so that the more of one variable the less of the other, then the correlation is called inverse and the correlation coefficient will be negative. The sign (plus or minus) tells you whether the correlation is direct or inverse, while the magnitude (size) of the correlation coefficient tells you the extent to which the path is likely to be a straight line. If the coefficient is near zero, a straight line does not describe the path well, while if it is near one (either plus one or minus one) then a straight line gives an excellent fit and few points (or units) are off the line.

Theoretically, you could always plot your cross-classified data on graph paper, using the standard X and Y coordinates, although it is not always practical to do so. Suppose you plotted some hypothetical data, with the following "scatter diagram," as it is called, being the result.

Variable Y

Variable X

The scatter diagram shows a "path" highly visible to an eye inspection, yet a single straight line would be a poor choice as a summary of that path. But often it is not feasible to prepare a scatter diagram, and I trust you can see that even for the diagram shown *some* straight line could be drawn through the points. The question becomes,

which straight line would be the best one to draw, in the sense that the deviations of the points from the line are minimized overall? The way you compute the correlation coefficient, using standard computing formulas available, guarantees that *if* you tried to draw a straight line through the distribution then the formula gives you the best one in the sense of minimizing the deviations.

There are other formulas to use if you suspect a straight line is not a good summarizing choice but a curved one might be, and this gets into curvilinear correlation. And, if you want to try to describe the path taken by three or more variables simultaneously, then you can use multiple correlation techniques. And so on.

I mention just the names and the general purpose of the measures here, because to understand them you not only need to learn what the formulas are for the differing measures, but far more important, you need to learn the assumptions that must be met for the legitimate use of each, and to do this you need to study some mathematics. Otherwise, if you just blindly pick a measure, or leaf through a statistics book and find some formula that appeals to you and plug in some numbers whether or not you are justified in doing so for this particular formula, then you are engaging in a form of number magic rather than adding to knowledge.

Even if there were no other good reasons (and there are) for studying mathematics in general and not just that branch known as probability theory and its applied branch called statistics, one good reason would be to guard against being fooled by number magic practiced by others. Probably this is not done with a deliberate intention to deceive, but whether consciously intended or not, the illusory aspect is still there and still just as damaging as far as being sure that what we "know" is likely to be "true." An equally good reason is to guard against your own unconscious use of number magic, even though your intentions may be honorable. Good intentions are of course desirable, but we all know what road they may pave, and unfortunately good intentions are no substitute for understanding what you are doing.

I will stress that one of the most unhappy deceptions of all is to deceive yourself or allow others to deceive you into thinking you can learn to use sophisticated measurement techniques without learning the mathematical reasoning that underlies them. Trying to learn statistics or any other branch of mathematics without making the effort to learn the reasoning involved and without working a good many mathematics problems to ensure that you have grasped the principles is, to use one of the more popular ways of saying this, like trying to learn to cook without using heat.

The result may well be a sorry mess, but while a cooking mess is easily detected as such by anyone, this is not always true with a mathematics mess unless the reader knows some mathematics himself. If you do not think you have the time to learn some, you will do yourself and your readers most service if you stick to a careful eye inspection of the outline and intensity of the patterns in your data, using measures you do understand, even though they may not be the mathematically optimal ones you might have used.

A well-chosen and carefully thought out and described percentage distribution should not be underestimated. That much mathematics can take you a long way toward understanding what is going on and why. When that is not far enough, sit down and learn the mathematics needed

to take you further. Fortunately, even if it is not feasible for you to take formal classes, aids such as programed instruction books on different topics in mathematics, some even going back to reviews of elementary school arithmetic, are becoming more widely available. If you do the problems in them faithfully, you can teach yourself quite a bit in a relatively short time.

3.2 GENERALIZATION. Concluding that your results for your sample are more generally applicable rests on two bases: accurately describing the pattern present in your sample; justifiably eliminating the interpretation that your sample pattern is solely a chance result and so cannot be generalized beyond the specific sample. How well you can provide the first base depends on the quality of the observations available and the ds descriptions used to summarize them. Providing the second depends on the outcome of a three-step process, related to three interpretations of the term "probability," or "likelihood." The first interpretation has to do with the calculation of *a priori* possibilities, the second with long-run empirically established frequencies, and the third with the weight to be attached to evidence.

The first interpretation is the one used when you state that the likelihood of a given face turning up when a die is tossed is one-sixth. There are six faces to the die, and *a priori* each possibility is equally likely.

This interpretation of probability underpins the mathematics used in statistics of inference, the other main branch of statistics. Statistics of inference are used to aid in doing two related tasks. The customary terms given are (1) estimation of parameters and (2) hypothesis testing.

You are engaged in the first kind of

task when you compute the likelihood that an interval around an estimate made from a random sample will contain the universe value somewhere within the interval. The universe value is a fixed one (a parameter). Values computed from samples will vary, but they form an orderly distribution if the samples are random (each set of units drawn in the same manner from the same universe with a chance of selection that is independent of and equal to the chance for any other set). This distribution is called the sampling distribution for the estimate.

Based on a mathematical consideration of the *a priori* possibilities that could appear in the sampling distribution it is true that (*a*) the distribution of the estimates made from *random* samples is such that the estimates tend to cluster around the universe value and (*b*) the larger the random sample the more likely it is that an estimate made is closer to the universe value than would be an estimate from a smaller sample. Of course, it is in the nature of probability interpreted in an *a priori* possibilities sense that rare things do have some chance of happening and so you always have the risk that you happened to get one of the samples for which an estimate made from it is rather far away from the universe value. (Recall from the discussion of random sampling in Part II that what you compute is the likelihood that your *procedures* for sample selection will yield a sample for which the confidence interval around an estimate from it will cover the universe value.)

Doing an adequate job of making *du* descriptions, or descriptions of the parent classes for your observations, hinges not only on accurately describing what is going on in the sample but also in part on using the logic, and perhaps even the specialized techniques, involved in statistics of inference. In essence, these techniques are designed to try to get answers to the question: Could the pattern I have observed and described for the sample reasonably have been expected on the basis of chance alone? This implies comparing what actually occurred with what might have been expected, solely on the basis of chance.

The comparing is done to decide whether chance is a reasonable "alternative interpretation" to the one you would like to make, namely, that the association observed exists in the parent class as well. Once you compute (which we are not going to get into the details of at all here — learning inferential statistics usually follows learning descriptive statistics since you need to know what kinds of summarizing measures might be made) that in the long run only in 5 or 12 or whatever times out of 100 samples of the same kind from the same universe could the results be expected to occur by chance (that is, the confidence interval around the estimate would not cover the universe value), whether you consider your result to be due to chance or not is up to you to justify. It is conventional to set 5 in 100 or 5 percent as the upper proportion before the decision that chance produced the results is chosen as a more likely interpretation than the one you would prefer to make instead. But the figure 5 percent is *chosen,* not given. There may be times when you decide that, even though the result could have occurred by chance more than 5 percent of the time, you still feel (based primarily on your use of the other two interpretations of the term "probability" to be discussed later) that your *ds* description can justifiably be used as a *du* description as well.

Whether you formally make the computations needed or only informally estimate the answers if they were or could be computed, the same kind of question is asked: Could what is observed have oc-

curred by chance alone? And the same kind of reasoning is used: preparing as strong and sound an argument as you can that chance can be eliminated as a legitimate alternative interpretation.

Returning to the two main tasks for statistics of inference, suppose you took a sample of people from a large city and found that the proportion of Protestants was about 60 percent. One question you might ask yourself is whether this estimate is a pretty good approximation to the proportion of Protestants in the entire city. This would be a problem in the estimation of parameters.

But suppose you ask what the likelihood is that you would get a sample with 60 percent Protestant if in fact the proportion in the city is quite different from 60 percent, perhaps 30 percent, 50 percent, 75 percent, or whatever you decide to guess for the proportion of Protestants in the entire city. This would be a problem in hypothesis testing.

You somehow decide on a guess to use for the universe value and then you ask about the likelihood that *if* the universe value is as guessed then you would obtain an estimate as far away from that value as your sample estimate turned out to be. Determining what guess to make is outside the province of statistics proper. It may come from a hunch, an examination of equally likely possibilities, a statistical frequency empirically established by a series of studies, and so on.

In the example, you might say you have no reason to believe there is any difference between the proportion Protestant and the proportion non-Protestant and so you guess the universe value as 50 percent and compute the likelihood that you would have a proportion as large as 60 percent if the "true" proportion were 50 percent. Or, if 10 years ago 90 percent of the city was

known to be Protestant, you might ask what the likelihood is that you would get a sample with 60 percent *if* there had been no change in the religious make-up of the city?

The answer rests on two things: the computed chances that your sample estimate would be as far away as it is if your guess about the universe value is correct; and the particular guess made for that universe value. You face the risk of making two kinds of errors, Type I and Type II, or the risk of rejecting a correct guess and the risk of accepting a false one.

Computing how frequently a particular sample result could be expected to occur if your guess were correct about the proportion Protestant in the city (and the computations will yield somewhat different answers if your universe guess is 90 percent than if it is 75 or 30 or some other percent) can aid you in deciding what to infer from your project. For instance, you might have set up this decision rule: if the expected occurrence of the sample estimate, under the hypothesis that the universe value is 90 percent, would be at least as rare as 5 in 100 similar samples, *reject* the hypothesis that the universe value is 90 percent; if the expected occurrence is greater than 5 in 100, *accept* the hypothesis. Then, depending on how frequently it turns out that your sample estimate could occur if your universe guess were correct, you decide either that there has been a change in the religious make-up of the city (i.e., your universe guess was wrong), or that your sample result is consistent with the guess that the proportion Protestant remains close to 90 percent. Using this decision rule means you are willing to set at no greater than 5 in 100 the risk of rejecting your universe guess when it is correct. (This would be a Type I error, and the level at which you set its risk is

your "level of significance.") But there is another kind of error you would like to avoid as well, the risk of accepting your universe guess when it is actually incorrect. (This would be a Type II error, accepting a false hypothesis.)

Deciding what to pick as your best guess for the universe value when you are engaged in hypothesis testing is outside the province of statistics. Similarly, deciding what weight to give to the risk of a Type I versus a Type II error is outside too. Once you decide on the "best guess" to be used in computations, and once you decide how important each type of error is to you and so which type you want to minimize, there are statistical techniques to aid you in going on from there. But these are decisions for you, the researcher, not a statistical consultant (in human or textbook form) to make. Making these decisions partly turns on the other two interpretations of probability or likelihood.

The second interpretation is that of a long-run statistical frequency. In this sense likelihood refers to what empirically occurs, judged by the results of a series of repeated investigations, not by what the *a priori* possibilities might be.

It is the second interpretation of probability that is used when you state that the likelihood that any particular human birth will be a male child is slightly more than half. On *a priori* considerations you could argue that since there are two sexes, each is equally likely to appear for a given birth and so the chance of a male birth is one-half. You could argue this way, but you would be empirically wrong. True, there are two sexes, but based on a series of repeated observations (long-run birth records) the statistical frequency of a male birth is not one-half, but slightly more than half. Similarly, the chance of your

dying when you reach a given age is not one-half. *Empirically,* the possibility that you will die is not equally likely to the possibility that you will not die, but varies throughout the life cycle.

(As an aside, how do we in practice decide whether a particular coin is a fair one or not? By an appeal to experience— it is empirically true that in the long run coins tend to conform to the mathematical model of a situation in which there are only two possible outcomes, each is independent of the other, and each is equally likely to occur. Because of our *experience,* any coin that does not so conform is suspect, *not* because the model says anything about such empirical events as tossing coins. It doesn't. Models in mathematics, unlike the "as if" models science tries to provide, are perfectly general. It is in this respect that so much of the power provided by mathematics resides. The mathematician's models must be internally consistent and all conclusions about the implications of the model deductively valid. Whether a set of empirical events can be shown to meet the assumptions in the model is a matter to be determined, and by the scientist and not the mathematician. Mathematics provides a set of explored implications of various assumptions. These can be a set of ready-made solutions to many problems if scientists can find ways to formulate their problems so that these solutions then become applicable. Much scientific activity in general is devoted to just that task. The fact that so many mathematical models *have* been shown to have empirical correspondences and so powerful mathematical tools become available for use is testimony to the historically mutual influence of science and mathematics on one another.)

Statistics of inference, based on mathe-

matical models about *a priori* possibilities, represent one step to aid making the judgment that a given *ds* description is or is not generalizable to become a *du* description as well. Consistency and convergence with what is already known, i.e., statistical frequencies established empirically by replications of studies, represent another. Still a third step is given by the third interpretation of probability.

A third interpretation of probability relates to an evaluation of the weight of evidence. It is this interpretation you are using when you state the likelihood that team A will win the game, that it will rain before noon tomorrow, or that currently underdeveloped countries will or will not be able to skip successfully some of the less desirable stages in modernization that occurred in the history of now modernized countries. These kinds of statements amount to judgments of the weight to be given various pieces of related evidence.

These judgments build on the application of the other two interpretations of likelihood, on the general knowledge a scientist possesses, and on less obvious factors involved in the way he makes judgments. In deciding whether a particular study's results are generalizable and to what extent, a scientist uses whatever information he can get from the use of statistical inference techniques; he uses whatever information he has about available empirically established frequencies; and he also uses, for instance, his personal assessment of the risks of one type of error over another. A chance of 5 in 100 may be regarded by one scientist as an acceptable risk but as too high by another scientist, especially for certain types of problems, such as the effectiveness of a medical treatment that may produce undesirable side effects. Or, one scientist may feel that a

series of mutually supporting results, none of which is very strong by itself, may merit generalization, while another scientist might decide otherwise.

While various procedures are undertaken to try to ensure minimal disagreement on what the evidence *is*, there can still be honest disagreement on the weight that should be given the existing evidence when it comes to generalization and then assessment stages. Ultimately, the decision any scientist comes to about whether and to what extent his objectives have been realized — that he can or cannot justifiably make the kinds of generalizations he wanted to be able to make — will depend on his judgment of the weight of the total evidence available to him.

3.3 ASSESSMENT. Once the *du* descriptions have been arrived at, assessment is needed. The results need to be assessed in light of where we are now as far as our understanding of some topic. Providing this kind of perspective completes a turn of the cycle. Assessing what now seem profitable next steps to take to further our understanding of the topic sets the stage for the next turn of the cycle.

Providing perspective on where we are now that your results can be added to the store of knowledge on the topic requires going back to the objectives with which the project was begun. If the study was a reconnoitering or a reconnaissance level one, what pieces to the puzzle were located, or what is the precision with which the outlines of a piece are now known? What explanations might be developed, even if vague and tentative, to account for the pieces? If the study was a testing level one, what can now be said about earlier existing explanations? Have some possible explanations been eliminated, and do some of the remaining ones now seem more confirmed or else in need of revision? If so, what are the details of the filling in, or the more sharply delineating, or the confirming or denying?

As well as providing perspective about where we are now that your results are available, perspective should be provided about where we should go from here. That is, what is your assessment of what now seem to be the most profitable next steps?

As far as procedures for doing this assessment, the discussion on using what is known (Part II, section 3.1) is entirely applicable here. In the earlier stage you had to try to make sense out of other people's findings and decide where to go next. The difference in this stage is that your results are available now and they were not then. But the same procedures and advice apply at this later stage as well, and rather than repeat them let me simply urge you to re-read that section.

4. WRITE REPORT

The purpose of writing material is to affect the reader precisely as the author intended. It is quite possible, then, that "the report" turns out to be several reports aimed at slightly different audiences. Even so, you want to interest, inform, and convince the reader. One aim may be stressed more than others, depending on the audience. Some of the details that would leave your colleagues unhappy if they were omitted may bore your advisory committee, for instance. And if your project is complex, you may be issuing interim reports from time to time. But in general, I think if you follow the topical outline suggested in Part II, to the extent that you somewhere cover the subtopics for the major headings, this will give you a good start toward at least informing your readers.

Go over the outline of topics to be covered. Adapt the major headings if you need to. Then go over *each* topic, with an eye to deciding on the main items to be used in the paragraphs. It is often helpful to list a series of "topic sentences" or phrases stating the main ideas to be covered under each topic. Beside each of these topic sentences jot down phrases for the detailed points you want to make. Each separate topic sentence or main idea will become a paragraph, while the details elaborating the main idea will be contained in the various sentences within the paragraph.

After you have finished your initial draft, look it over at least three times. First check that the outline used does cover the subtopics adequately. Then go over each subtopic and check the organization of the set of paragraphs for it. Finally, check individual sentences in the paragraphs to see if you can state something more simply or in a more interesting fashion.

How carefully you prepare your detailed outline and then actually follow it when writing your report will be the main determinant of how well you inform your reader. Remember that he has not gone through all the thinking you have while inspecting various options in order to choose the particular ones you did. Nor should he be expected to engage in a detailed analysis and interpretation of the evidence, comparable to what you should have done. His interests lie in learning and evaluating your major justifications for the choices you made, and your considered distillation of what you feel has been learned and why you feel so. Treat those interests with respect, by providing him in as coherent a fashion as you can the major items he needs to grasp and judge what you have done.

And treat him with the courtesy due anyone willing to make the effort to read your report. Because he does not have the background you have, at least on this project, he is in the position of being an intelligent layman. Since he is a layman, you need to be as clear as you can, but since he is intelligent you should not belabor points that might be better shown in some other fashion, such as one or another graphic device.

Few things are more deadly dull in a report than a long rehearsal in the text of figures for which the main point could be summarized by a small text table or a chart of some kind. Of course, you cannot just put a pie chart or bar chart in your report and then ignore it. You need to tell the reader how to interpret the chart and you need at least a few comments in the written text about your assessment of the significance of what is graphically shown. After all, any text table or other graphic device represents a *selection* from the basic and more complex data available. Presumably that selection rested on your judgment of what a thorough analysis revealed was important enough to stress. Why not say so? State what you think is important and why. From the source note to the text table or chart (referring to the number of the appendix table from which the data were selected for graphic treatment and in which more detailed and possibly qualifying information can be found), your reader can turn to the table and further check your judgment for himself if he wishes.

Many kinds of graphic devices can be prepared, but they typically serve one of three purposes. If you want to show trend, then you can use a line graph. Form the familiar X and Y coordinates and indicate the scale you are using along each axis, such as percentage along the Y axis. For instance, you might plot the trend in the proportion voting Democratic in national elections over the past twenty or so years for the rural and urban portions of your state of residence. You would use separate lines for urban and rural, perhaps a solid line for urban and a dashed line for rural. To plot the points on each line you locate the time of the national election in order to place the point along the X axis and then move it up the Y axis until you have the percentage of, say, urban dwellers in the state that voted Democratic at that election.

If you want to make comparisons between components, then a pie chart might be used. Pie charts often appear in local newspapers around taxing time, showing you what portion of your tax dollar goes for which purposes. Depending on the politics of the local paper, a pie showing the split of the national tax dollar may appear alongside the one for the local tax dollar.

Pie charts are easily made, although special paper containing the diagrams can be purchased. Use a compass or else take a half-dollar and trace around it. Lightly pencil two lines through the circle, intersecting at the center and at right angles to one another. Each of the four pieces that result is worth 25 percent. After you decide how big a wedge of the pie will be used for each category, draw in the size of the wedges with darker lines. The first cut is usually made by beginning in the middle of the top half of the pie. When you complete dividing the circle, erase the pencilled intersecting lines used initially to quarter it.

The main caution to follow with the use of pie charts, as with any other graphic device, is that you not make them so detailed that the point of using a graphic device is lost. If the reader has to study a complicated "key" telling him what each of some ten or twelve pieces represents, or each of seven or eight lines on a line graph, you have hindered rather than helped him.

Bar charts are used to make comparisons when different bases are used, instead of components of the same base as in pie charts. For instance, you might want to compare the freshman class at four colleges on a particular item, perhaps percentage married at the time of entry into college. Make the usual X and Y coordinates, putting percentage along the Y axis. Then you would prepare four bars resting on the X axis, one for each of the colleges, and showing the percentage married in the freshman class.

Rather than describing anything other than these three frequently used graphic devices, I urge you to spend fifteen minutes or so browsing through the introductory section of the *United States Summary* (Volume 1) of the latest Census of Population. This will be available in any library.

The introductory section summarizes the main findings, for the United States as a whole, that a staff of experts feel are present in a set of data far more complex than you are ever likely to obtain, and the findings are illustrated by a variety of well-chosen graphic devices. Spending just fifteen minutes or so looking at these should give you ample ideas for devices you might adapt for your own report.

You should not only help your reader to interpret any graphic devices you use, but also generally help him to read what you have written: tell him what he has just finished reading; tell him what he

should remember as important; tell him what he is going to read next. Remember that one of the aims of your report is to *inform* him. The easier you make it for your reader to acquire information, the more successful you are likely to be in meeting this aim.

The outline you use and the revisions you make in your initial draft to state your points more clearly, as well as graphic devices and other helps to the reader's understanding, are essentially aimed at informing your reader as best you can. But this is a scientific report, and you also want to convince him that your conclusions are justified.

Remember to ask about your own report the same "suggested questions" that you would use to evaluate a report written by a stranger. Check your logic. The entire document can be thought of as a single argument, with subarguments throughout as well. Try to make these as strong and sound as you can. Then let the report sit for a few days. Reread it as though it were written by someone else, and make a final evaluation for completeness and other aspects of quality. Then make any revisions you need to. If you do this systematically, you should greatly increase your chances of convincing your reader as well as informing him.

There remains the job of interesting him. It is true that to some extent a report aimed at your professional colleagues is aimed at a captive audience. If they have reason to believe that your report will provide them with information relevant to their own work they will, no matter how reluctantly, wade through reams of the murkiest prose. But surely you should feel a twinge of conscience if you force them to do so to learn about your project. After all, your advisory committee, if you have one, will not tolerate such treatment. A murky report will be quickly returned to you, perhaps with a none too polite order to return your report when it is written in English. Don't other potential readers deserve the same consideration?

Graphic devices can add interest as well as clarity to your report. Going through the sentences in the initial draft of your report to try to find simpler and more interesting ways to say the same thing clearly can help. And, if you write as though your report were to be read aloud, you can often spot a livelier way to say what you want to say.

One final caution about what should be put in a report remains to be mentioned. Just as you cannot observe everything, you cannot report everything. But beware of "data cooking." It is often tempting to omit data that deviate from an otherwise fairly clear-cut pattern. It may be tempting, but it is not ethical. You have an obligation to state clearly when information has been omitted from consideration, and why, and to try to present the complete data you obtained in the appendix of your report. And at least in a report aimed at your professional colleagues, be extra careful to be clear about what was done.

Hopefully, your colleagues will consider that what you have done can be used by them. This means that some of them will try to repeat, as well as build on, your results. They are likely to become frustrated and irritated if it is not clear what you did to obtain your results. You can understand their feelings if you think about what your own reactions would be if you tried to follow the instructions that were not uncommon for recipes in grandmother's day. "Take a pinch of this and a good-sized lump of that, bake in a moderate oven, and after twenty minutes test to see if it is done" can be maddening instructions to try to follow, especially if you are not already an accomplished cook.

5. CONCLUDING REMARKS

The research process divides into two main portions, with two principal parts to the first portion and three to the second portion. The first portion entails both deciding on a problem to investigate and developing a plan to do so. During the second portion of the process data are collected, then analyzed and interpreted, and a report is prepared covering the entire project.

The principal fault to watch out for in the problem selection part is proceeding to the other stages without as thorough a grasp as you can manage of just what the specific problem is that you want to investigate. With respect to developing a plan, common failings to guard against are either plunging ahead without a plan that is ade-quate and appropriate for the problem, or else sitting and hoping ideas will come without making much of an effort to assist them in coming. Others must have wrestled with similar or analogous problems, in your own or more or less closely related disciplines. Find out what they have done and try to adapt it. And don't be afraid to use your own creative imagination as well, as long as you then go on to check that what you come up with is in fact a satisfactory procedure.

There are three cautions for the second portion of the process. Don't become careless in carrying out your plan, but instead build in quality control checks along the way. Be sure you look back when you complete your project and give substantial attention to evaluating both what was learned and the way chosen to try to learn it, in order to guide future efforts. Finally, give sufficient time and care to preparing and revising the final report on your project. No matter how well done a study might be, if the report is not read the findings have little chance of being used and so scientific knowledge is just that much less cumulative. This cumulative aspect is of great importance in aiding progress along the cycle of science and so raising the probability that future instances of the basic game will be well played.

The preceding remarks have been directed mainly to those of you who will eventually become producers of scientific knowledge. But even if you never engage in the production of scientific information in the future, being aware of the kinds of decisions that need to be made throughout the cycle of science should aid you in judging results produced by others. Whenever you come across some stated finding on a subject that you would like to know more about, especially when the statement appears in the more mass-oriented communications media, my hope is that after reading this book and completing its exercises you will almost automatically use what you have learned to "work backward" from the finding. If the finding were to be a fully justified one, what would the researcher have had to do? What kinds of evidence would be needed, and in particular, what kinds of controls and sampling would be required? How reasonable does it seem to you that such evidence is obtainable at all? Is enough information given for you to be able to judge the likelihood that the needed evidence was in fact obtained?

Rapidly going through a series of questions related to the basic one, "How *could* and *does* he know?" may save you some

troublesome unlearning later. As the old saying warns, "The things you don't know won't hurt you nearly so much as the things you know that ain't so."

I also hope you will have gained an understanding of what science can and cannot do, based on the aims of the game and how it is played. Once a decision is made as to what societal goals are desirable, for instance, science *may* be able to describe some way ("the conditions under which") a goal could be achieved. Sometimes there may be more than one way to reach a goal, and then science might be able to state which ways are more efficient than others — given some clear criteria for "efficiency." But there is no guarantee that science will be able to find even *one* way, no matter how much we all might want to achieve a particular goal, and there is certainly no guarantee that a way will be quickly found.

Massive amounts of money and personnel, or "crash programs," may work — but they may not. As one joke common among research workers puts it, "Sometimes a crash program seems to be like trying to get nine women pregnant simultaneously in hopes that at least one will give birth in a month."

Some things just cannot be hurried, no matter how much we might wish otherwise. But on the other hand, if no support is given to reasoning and research activity engaged in trying to find ways to achieve desirable goals, it seems almost certain that no way will be found. That is, one method of ensuring that *none* of the women will give birth — even if no sooner than nine months — is simply no longer to try to get any of them pregnant, but instead to turn to such unhelpful activities as pleading with them to produce beautiful and healthy children and beating them when they do not do so immediately, or to such displacement-type activities as pounding the table or burning down the hospital.

On occasion, one of the most useful things science may be able to tell us is that we are trying to do the impossible. For instance, by exploring the implications of various goals for the behavior needed to achieve them, it may be that science can tell us that reaching goal A requires certain kinds of behavior that are incompatible with the behavior required to reach goal B, at least under existing conditions, and so some attention needs to be given either to deciding on priorities or altering the existing conditions or both.

But setting goals and ordering priorities among them has traditionally been reserved for the citizen role, and has not been part of the activities of the scientist *qua* scientist. Keeping the two kinds of roles distinct (making decisions about what goals are desirable to achieve; and exploring the conditions under which that achievement is or is not likely to occur, and the implications of those conditions for other goals we might have) seems to me to be a division of labor worth preserving. I believe it is well to keep the division clear even when those roles are occupied by the same individual. It is sometimes tempting to blur the roles and so turn over to just certain of us some of the hard decisions that should (and in fact do) beset us all. This temptation should be resisted, I think. Expertise in deciphering the conditions under which events occur and change does *not* automatically carry with it any special qualifications for deciding which of those events we should try to prevent, which we should try to guarantee, and which we should not try to manipulate at all but instead should adapt ourselves to.

Exercise Set III

III-1. Some Desirable Skills: Analysis and Use of Graphic Devices; Writing

This exercise is in three parts. For Part A you will be given a simple set of raw, or unclassified, data. Then you are asked to prepare a table that might be used to analyze the data, fill in the table, carry through a series of possible steps in analysis of the data, prepare some simple graphic devices to illustrate certain findings, and suggest ways a similar project might be carried out in the future to avoid some difficulty noted in eliminating a particular alternative interpretation. For Part B you will be given a specific puzzle to solve, using certain pieces of information provided you, and asked to justify your conclusions as you go along. For Part C, you are asked to turn some typically obscure prose into clear and readable English.

PART A

Background

The data were obtained from the ten sections of an introductory course in social research given at California State College at Hayward in fall quarter 1968. Each of the sections played four Twenty Questions games. In each of the sections the size of the group of players (minus the leader) varied in the same manner. The first group to play was of size three, followed by size four, then by size five, and last by size six. A different set of individuals (except for the leader) was used for each game. All games were played in view of the entire section. Success in playing the game was measured according to the number of questions needed by the group to guess the object selected by the leader. Any question asked by any member of the group was counted and the group members were permitted to discuss among themselves, if they wished, which questions to ask.

Data

A. Number of questions required by groups of size three: 17, 20, 19, 16, 22, 24, 28, 21, 24, 30
B. Number of questions required by groups of size four: 13, 13, 11, 13, 12, 15, 14, 22, 26, 22

232

C. Number of questions required by groups of size five: 7, 5, 10, 15, 13, 16, 16, 18, 26, 32

D. Number of questions required by groups of size six: 13, 11, 11, 13, 20, 18, 19, 16, 24, 26

Some comments

You have four size categories for the groups. The categories can be thought of as representing one variable, size, and you could use them to examine the proposition that at least in small groups the larger the group the more likely it is to be successful (perhaps reasoning that "two heads are better than one" and therefore the more sources of ideas the better).

The categories can also be thought of as representing another variable, balance. Thought of in this way, the odd-numbered groups can be lumped into a single category, unbalanced, and the even-numbered groups lumped into the category "balanced." You could then use this variable to examine the proposition that a group is more likely to be successful if it is unbalanced since then a tie-breaker person is present. (Recall that any question asked by any player counts and so if the group is not to waste questions it will have to organize itself to come to some agreement about which questions to ask; in groups as small as these decisions are typically decided by vote and hence a tie-breaker may be important as a way of avoiding impasses. As a matter of fact, the games originally were played in order to make comparisons of the observed patterns of division of labor and operating norms that evolved, especially in the more successful compared to the less successful groups, but of course we can reanalyze the available data as we choose.)

And, you can think of the categories as representing a joint classification of balance and size, enabling you to see both the separate and simultaneous effects of the two variables on degree of success in game-playing. The questions that you are asked to answer below are designed to take you through a process of first separately and then simultaneously looking at the effects of the two variables, so please prepare your table in a way that will make it easy for you to do this.

Table preparation and completion

Prepare a dummy table and then fill it in with the data given earlier. Jointly classify balance and size, preferably in the stub. Use these categories for degree of success:

High: one to ten questions
Medium: eleven to fifteen questions
Low: sixteen to twenty questions
Failure: more than twenty questions

Once you have your table prepared and filled in, continue with the rest of this exercise by answering the following questions on a separate sheet of paper.

Selected questions to answer from an analysis of your table

1. What conclusion can you draw about the degree of success achieved by the set of groups as a whole, regardless of size or balance? (*Hint:* look at the column marginal cells. Also, you would be wise to at least mentally convert the numbers into percents.)

2. First look at the effect of "balance" by itself.

   a. What proportion of the unbalanced (odd-numbered) groups would you *expect* to achieve "high" success if balance were independent of (i.e., "unrelated to") success?
   b. What proportion of the unbalanced groups actually *did* achieve high success?
   c. What proportion of the balanced groups would you expect to achieve high success if balance were independent of degree of success?
   d. What proportion of the balanced groups did achieve high success?
      (*Hint:* To answer parts *a* and *c*, look at your answer to question 1.)

3. Does it seem that balance is a variable worth using to aid you in predicting degree of success, and why do you say so?
   (*Hint:* Compare your answers to the parts of question 2.)

4. Using the data in your table, show in *pie-chart* form the balanced and unbalanced groups, according to the four categories for "degree of success." (Trace around a fifty-cent piece twice, once to give you a circle for the balanced groups and once to give you a circle for the unbalanced groups. Lightly sketch in two pencilled lines for each circle, with the lines at right angles to each other and intersecting at the center of the circle. Each of the four quarters of the circle is now worth 25 percent, and you can estimate which part of the total "pie" should be allotted to each success category. Draw in these segments with darker lines and erase your pencilled lines. Note that to complete the pie you will have to convert numbers to percentages.) Use a separate sheet of paper, and place the two "pies" beside each other, using the one on the left for balanced groups and the one on the right for unbalanced groups. Use the following "key" for success categories:

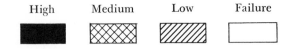

| High | Medium | Low | Failure |

5. Having looked briefly at the effect of balance by itself, now look at the effect of size by itself.

   a. What proportion of the *smaller* groups (sizes 3 and 4 combined) would you expect to achieve *at least moderate* success (high and medium combined) if size and success are unrelated?

b. What proportion of the smaller groups *did* achieve at least moderate success?

c. What proportion of the *larger* groups (sizes 5 and 6 combined) would you expect to achieve at least moderate success?

d. What proportion of the larger groups *did* achieve at least moderate success?

6. Does it seem that size is a variable worth using to aid in predicting degree of success, and why do you say so?

7. Using the data in the table, show in *bar chart* form the proportion of groups that *failed* to guess the object, within *each* size class. (You will have to convert some numbers into percentages in order to prepare the chart. Use a vertical bar above each size class indicated.) An example, to be copied and completed, is below.

PROPORTION OF GROUPS THAT FAILED, BY SIZE OF GROUP

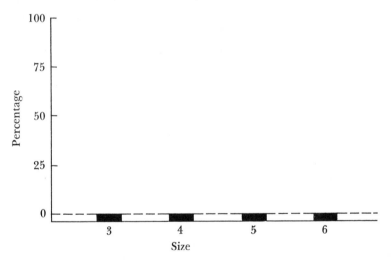

8. Now look at the effect of "balance" and "size" together. After doing so, read the lettered statements below. Then answer the question below.

a. *Within odd-numbered groups,* it is clear that the larger the group the more successful it is, since the larger group has a higher proportion with at least moderate success achieved and it also has a smaller proportion of failure.

b. *Within even-numbered groups* the pattern by size is unclear, since the smaller group not only had a higher proportion with moderate success but also of failure. However, there is some slight tendency for the smaller group to do better.

Which of the two statements above seems justified, based on the information given in the table? (neither; *a* only; *b* only; *a* and *b*)

9. What has been done so far by no means exhausts the analysis you might do of the information in the table. I have tried to select possibilities you might overlook, instead. For instance, you would no doubt examine each row and each column carefully, and so I have asked questions that require you to do some *combining* of rows and columns. But perhaps answering the questions so far has given you some flavor of what might be done. Now I want to turn to some other considerations. Specifically, let us consider whether the details of the method used might affect the results.

   a. The table does not mention *practice,* in the sense of at least observing prior groups in the same section trying to play the same kind of game. It is possible that this variable, "amount of practice," could affect success as well, since those in the larger groups had the opportunity of observing the smaller groups' attempts to succeed. Perhaps the players in the larger groups picked up some tips on strategy or coordination. Let us see if there is any information in the table prepared that could shed light on the effect of this "practice" variable. First, based on what you know about the details of the method used (see Background section at the beginning of this exercise), arrange the groups in order on a scale (see example below), according to the amount of practice (in the observational sense defined above) each size group received.

   ---

   least   most
   practice   practice

   b. Suppose you felt there should be a *direct* correlation between amount of practice and degree of game-playing success. Based on the information in the table, which column(s) could lend support to your feeling, and why do you say so?

   c. Which column(s) tend to *deny* (or at least give "mixed" results to) this feeling, and why do you say so?

10. As noted in the discussion of the second project for Exercise II-2, in manipulated situations where the same people both design and participate in the situations to be observed, it is difficult to control in advance some possibly relevant factors. However, it should be possible to control a variable such as "amount of practice," at least when this variable is defined as the amount of observation of prior groups with a similar task to perform. Briefly describe how you might *redesign* playing the forty games, four in each of ten sections

of the course — this time so that you could later discount the effect of amount of practice. In order that you not merely take the "easy" solution of having all groups out in the hall until their turn comes (in which case, unless you can very well control the amount of conversation going on in the hall, each group may work out a pattern of interaction and strategy or even attempt some practice, and so you again are faced with some "muddying" factors) assume that all members of the section are present during the playing of all games, but each *section* plays its Twenty Questions independently of the other nine sections. Describe your design.

Once you have completed all parts to this exercise compare your answers and sketches with the ones given below.

SUGGESTED
ANSWERS FOR
EXERCISE III-1,
PART A
Table

NUMBER OF GROUPS PLAYING TWENTY QUESTIONS GAME, WITH BALANCE AND SIZE OF GROUP RELATED TO DEGREE OF SUCCESS

Balance[a] *and size*[b]	*Degree of success*[c]				*Total number*
	High	*Medium*	*Low*	*Failure*	
All groups	3	13	11	13	40
Unbalanced	3	2	7	8	20
Three	0	0	4	6	10
Five	3	2	3	2	10
Balanced	0	11	4	5	20
Four	0	7	0	3	10
Six	0	4	4	2	10

Source: sections of introductory social research class, California State College at Hayward, fall quarter 1968.

[a] Balance defined as follows: unbalanced contain an odd number of persons; balanced contain an even number.

[b] Size defined as the number of members in the group: 3, 4, 5, and 6.

[c] Degree of success grouped into categories according to the number of questions required for group to guess object selected: high = one to ten questions; medium = eleven to fifteen questions; low = sixteen to twenty questions; failure = more than twenty questions.

Questions

1. Few groups — less than 10 percent of the total — had high success. The remainder of the groups were fairly evenly split among the remaining categories of success, with roughly a third moderately successful, a third achieving low success, and a third failing.

2. *a.* About 8 percent, or the same proportion as was true for the groups as a whole (i.e., 3 divided by 40).

   b. Fifteen percent (or almost twice as high a proportion as expected). (Comparison of 3 divided by 20 with 3 divided by 40)

   c. Same answer as for *a*, or about 8 percent.

   d. None, or 0 percent.

3. Yes. Prediction of success based on knowledge of the group's balance or unbalance is much better than simply predicting on the

basis of knowing it is "a group." The latter prediction would tend to underestimate the degree of success of unbalanced groups and overestimate the degree of success of balanced ones. Of course, this conclusion rests on the assumption that the groups observed represent a "fair sample."

4. Pie charts for balanced and unbalanced groups, according to degree of success:

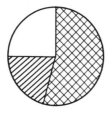 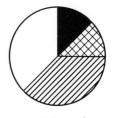

balanced   unbalanced

5.   *a.* Forty percent (16 divided by 40).
     b. Thirty-five percent (7 divided by 20).
     c. Forty percent, same as answer for *a.*
     d. Forty-five percent (9 divided by 20).

6. Not when size is divided merely into "smaller" and "larger" as defined in the question. Prediction based on knowing whether group is smaller or larger is not much better than one based just on knowing it is "a group." The latter prediction would slightly overestimate success for smaller groups and slightly underestimate success for larger groups.

7. Bar chart of proportion of groups that failed, within each size class:

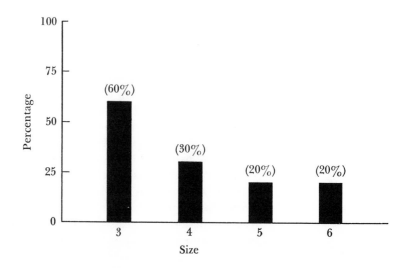

8. Both *a* and *b* justified by table.
9. *a.*

3	4	5	6
least practice			most practice

   b. Failure column seems mildly supportive. There is no *exception* to the pattern that the proportion failing decreases with practice, although there is a leveling off of the proportion for the larger groups.

   c. Any of the degree of success columns except Failure. In each there are exceptions to the pattern that increased practice seems to lead to increased success.

(*Note:* To see the answers suggested for parts *b* and *c* most easily you would *not* compute a percentage distribution for each column, with its total number serving as 100 percent. Rather, you would proceed as you did to answer question 7 earlier, and compute percentage distributions for the rows, with each row's total number serving as 100 percent. Then, for this question, you would compare the percentages that result in the cells contained in the columns.)

10. Assuming all members of each section are to be present for its four games played, one way would be to rotate the order of starting: give each size group an equal chance to be first, second, third, or last. If you had just eight sections, this would be simple. In two of the sections, size 3 begins, followed by sizes 4, 5, and 6; in two sections size 4 begins, followed by sizes 5, 6, and 3; in two sections size 5 begins, followed by sizes 6, 3, and 4; in two sections size 6 begins, followed by sizes 3, 4, and 5.

   However, you do not have eight sections to design for, but ten. What to do? I suppose one way would be to have two of the sections do something else and just use the data from the eight sections for which you rotate starting order. But, assuming you are committed to using all ten sections, you might proceed as follows. For the ninth section, have the smaller groups go first and flip a coin to see which begins. Then have the two larger groups play, again flipping a coin to see which starts. For the tenth section, reverse the process: larger groups first and flip a coin, followed by smaller groups and flip a coin. By this process (deliberate control through rotation for eight of the sections and a combination of deliberate control and randomization for the two remaining sections) you would hope that the effect of practice by observing others would "wash out" and so could be ignored.

PART B

For this part of Exercise III-1, I have slightly adapted a problem that appeared in a book on scientific method by an industrial chemist, David Killeffer, called *How Did You Think of That?* (Doubleday and Co., 1969).[1] The final solution to the problem is given in the book, but not how to reach that solution. To solve the puzzle you will have to work back and forth between the data given, speculate on what might be possible answers, and make trial fits of the pieces. As you reach each of your conclusions, write down the reasoning process — the evidence used — to reach the conclusion. Sometimes a conclusion will be reached by eliminating all other possible answers; sometimes it will be more directly reached. Here is the puzzle to solve.

Five men are playing poker. Each had a different number of cigarettes at the time the game started, and each is smoking a different brand. *How many cigarettes did each man have when the game started, and what brand is each man smoking?*

Here are the pieces of information you will need to solve the puzzle.

1. The names of the men are Brown, Perkins, Reilly, Turner, and Jones. The five brands of cigarettes are Luckies, Raleighs, Camels, Old Golds, and Chesterfields. The numbers of cigarettes at the start of the game are 20, 15, 8, 6, and 3. In no case is the order given in the preceding three sentences significant.
2. There are only 4 aces in the deck of cards used.
3. When someone "draws to an inside straight" in poker, this means he asks for only one card.
4. At the time of the game, only Raleigh cigarettes were cork-tipped.

At a given time:

5. Perkins asks for three cards.
6. Reilly has smoked half of his original supply, or one less than Turner.
7. The smoker of Chesterfields originally had this number of cigarettes: twice as many as he has now, plus half as many as he has now, plus 2½ more cigarettes.
8. The man who draws to an inside straight absentmindedly lights the tipped end of his fifth cigarette.
9. The man who smokes Luckies has smoked two more than anyone else, including Perkins.
10. Brown drew as many aces as he had cigarettes.
11. The Camel smoker asks Jones to pass Brown's matches.
12. No one has smoked all his cigarettes.

I think you might find it helpful to prepare the following diagram and put an X in each cell that can be eliminated as a possibility. Here is the solution of the puzzle in diagram form, with a blank cell telling you the item of information you want about a particular man.

Man's name	Number of cigarettes originally had					Brand smoked[a]				
	20	15	8	6	3	L	R	Ca	OG	Ch
Brown	X	X	X	X		X	X	X		X
Jones		X	X	X	X		X	X	X	X
Perkins	X		X	X	X	X	X	X	X	
Reilly	X	X		X	X	X	X		X	X
Turner	X	X	X		X	X		X	X	X

[a] L: Luckies; R: Raleighs; Ca: Camels; OG: Old Golds; Ch: Chesterfields.

What you are to do Reach the solution to the puzzle, and as you reach each conclusion along the way justify it, by citing the pieces of evidence used. Turn in your justified solution.

Here is an illustration of how one conclusion might be justified. From pieces of information 10 and 2, along with your knowledge of the numbers of cigarettes at the beginning of the game (item 1), you can conclude that Brown must have had three cigarettes to start with. (Therefore you can X all other cells for numbers of cigarettes for Brown and also place an X in the cells for three cigarettes for all other players.) You might briefly write this as "A. Brown: 3 cigarettes (items 1, 2 and 10)." Then if you need to use this conclusion as partial justification for others, you can refer to it by letter.

Solving the entire puzzle, justifying each conclusion as you go along, should take you between one and three hours of concentrated thinking.

PART C   For this part of Exercise III-1 you are to take some typically obscure prose and turn it into clear, readable English sentences. I have selected the requirements for graduation with a Bachelor's degree from your academic institution. If you are in junior college, get a catalog from the library for some academic institution that does grant a Bachelor's degree. (You can also do this if you are working with this book on your own and are not in any academic institution. Another possibility would be to take some section of the annual instructions that come with your income tax form, perhaps selecting the instructions on what can be deducted as business expenses.)

You do not have to cite the requirements for graduation with a particular major field of study unless you wish; I do want you to cover the general requirements for graduation with a Bachelor's degree. In your statement, also cover such ancillary items as whether or not an individual can receive credit for upper-division (junior and senior) level classes as long as he meets the prerequisites for the course or whether he must himself have at least junior standing; whether or not he can receive credit for graduate level courses taken while still an undergraduate; what proportion of his classes can be taken on a pass-fail basis and whether there are any restrictions on the kinds of classes taken on a pass-fail basis, such as only classes outside his major field of study. In other words, state both what he must do to graduate with a Bachelor's degree and the major options available to him in doing this. If this exercise accomplishes nothing else, you will find future contacts with any academic adviser you may have much more pleasant and profitable. Turn in your statement to your instructor.

III-2. APPRENTICE-TYPE PRACTICE: COLLECTING INFORMATION TO WRITING A REPORT

This exercise is intended to give you some guided practice on the second portion of the research process. You will start with a briefly described problem, then collect information, analyze it, and prepare a report on the project.

Previous apprentice-type exercises have involved observations taken in field and laboratory settings and observations in the form of answers to questions. This exercise will use observations in the form of already available records.

Since this exercise is only one of several you are asked to complete I have tried to keep it simple, especially since the data collection stage for any project tends to be time-consuming. For this exercise you are limited to the use of data available in one or another kind of record. I have selected a data source I thought would be readily accessible to you: the listing of the faculty contained at the back of the college catalog for your academic institution. Virtually all public, and many private, academic institutions have such a listing in the back of the catalog of courses offered by that institution. If yours does not, pick some other academic institution that interests you for one or another reason and locate its catalog in your local library.

I have selected a very simplified problem, basically having to do with a question of educational quality (a problem related to the adequacy of the formal "socialization" process), namely, the extent of homogeneity or "inbreeding" of the faculty. If we are willing to grant certain assumptions for the sake of the argument, then this exercise might have some intrinsic interest, as well as serve to illustrate certain phases of the research process.

These assumptions are as follows: (1) A student is better off in "getting an education" and so (hopefully) learning to think and judge for himself, if he is exposed to greater rather than lesser heterogeneity of viewpoint.

(2) A given professor's intellectual outlook on his discipline and his emphasis on certain topics within that discipline will be most colored by where he obtained his most advanced degree, since that is the stage of greatest professional commitment in his own training process. (3) Geographic areas within and outside the United States do have certain cultural similarities setting them apart from other areas — New England does somewhat differ in culture and general outlook from the deep South, for instance. (4) Academic institutions located in certain geographic areas of the country tend to share certain basic similarities of outlook (this is based on assumption 3).

"Inbreeding" might be defined in a number of different ways, of course. For instance, you could look at the inbreeding of the faculty by comparing the proportion with advanced degrees from the "Big Ten" universities with all others. Or, you could lump together all professors with degrees from academic institutions located in a major metropolitan area (say, with at least 500,000 total population) and contrast them with all other professors teaching at your institution. Partly to keep things simple, I have used the assumptions in the preceding paragraph to define the extent of inbreeding as the extent to which faculty members received their highest degrees in the same Census division of the United States or "outside the United States." A preliminary check of the catalog available to me revealed so few faculty members who received their highest degrees from some institution located outside the United States that it did not seem worthwhile to divide this category further; this may not be the case for your institution. And, for general interest purposes, you may find it useful to examine the proportion of the faculty whose highest degree was granted by an institution in your current state of residence, as well as the proportion from the Census division in which that state is located.

For convenience in this exercise, "faculty" is defined as including anyone contained in the faculty listing at the back of the college catalog, whether or not actively engaged in teaching. If this were not a practice exercise, you might decide to eliminate such persons as librarians and college deans from the listing before proceeding further.

Two factors were selected as possibly related to inbreeding and so aiding in making better predictions: the level of the highest degree attained; and the extent of commitment to the college. The suspected relationships are that the higher the level of the highest degree attained, the lower the level of inbreeding as defined above; the greater the extent of commitment to the particular institution at which the faculty member is currently teaching, the lower the level of inbreeding. Level of highest degree attained was divided into three categories, in descending order: any kind of doctorate; any kind of master's degree; and all other cases. Extent of commitment was divided into two categories in descending order: employed full-time and employed part-time. These two factors are to be *jointly* classified so that both their separate and simultaneous effects may be examined.

The faculty listing should contain (among other items) whether or not the faculty member is employed full-time and the name of the institution granting the faculty member's highest degree and what that degree is. You will need to use some additional sources to determine the rest of the information needed. The back of your dictionary, a recent almanac, or some reference volume available in your local library can be used to tell you in which state the institution granting the faculty member's highest degree is located. Census definitions, found in the front of the summary volume of the census data for the United States as a whole (as well as several other places, such as the *Statistical Abstract*), can be used to tell you in which division the state should be placed.

For your dummy appendix table (or analysis plan), I suggest that you place in the heading the location of the institution granting the faculty member's highest degree, using eleven categories: one for each of the nine divisions; one for outside the United States; one for the state in which the institution you are examining is located. In your stub, I suggest you place a joint classification of level of highest degree attained and extent of commitment, as follows:

Extent of commitment and
level of highest degree
attained
———————————————————

Full-time
   Doctorate
   Master's
   All other

Part-time
   Doctorate
   Master's
   All other

Total

Your heading might look as follows:

		Inside United States Census division[a]										(fill in state where institution is located)
Total	Outside United States	All	1	2	3	4	5	6	7	8	9	

[a] (The footnote would name the divisions and list the states included in each.)

For convenience in this exercise, we will *assume* that the listing of faculty members is complete as of the beginning of the current academic year. Some institutions list teaching assistants in a separate section at the end of the listing of regularly appointed faculty. If this is the case for your institution, omit this section of the list containing teaching assistants.

Before collecting the information, you should do some speculating on possible patterns that might be found and how you would interpret them. For instance, would you consider 20 percent in a single division a large amount of inbreeding or not? How about 30 percent? As you probably learned while completing Part B of Exercise II-1, the nine Census divisions can also be combined into four Census regions. What would you conclude about the extent of inbreeding if 30 percent were contained in a single Census region? How about 40 percent? What pattern would have to be shown for you to conclude that either level of highest degree attained or extent of commitment, or both, is *independent* of the amount of inbreeding? And so on.

SAMPLE
SELECTION

We will aim at a sample size of at least 100 faculty members for each of you to examine. There are several ways this sample could be selected.

If we knew, or were willing to count, the total number contained in the faculty listing we could select a sample of 100 people by using "simple random sampling without replacement." You would need to select 100 random numbers between 1 and the total number on the list, probably using a table of random numbers. A portion of such a table appears below:

```
9 1 4 9 9 1 4 5 2 3 6 8 4 7 9 2 7 6 8 6 4 6 1 6 2 8 3 5 5 4
8 0 3 3 6 9 4 5 9 8 2 6 9 4 0 3 6 8 5 8 7 0 2 9 7 3 4 1 3 5
4 4 1 0 4 8 1 9 4 9 8 5 1 5 7 4 7 9 5 4 3 2 9 7 9 2 6 5 7 5
1 2 5 5 0 7 3 7 4 2 1 1 1 0 0 0 2 0 4 0 1 2 8 6 0 7 4 6 9 7
6 3 6 0 6 4 9 3 2 9 1 6 5 0 5 3 4 4 8 4 4 0 2 1 9 5 2 5 6 3

6 1 1 9 6 9 0 4 4 6 2 6 4 5 7 4 7 7 7 4 5 1 9 2 4 3 3 7 2 9
1 5 4 7 4 4 5 2 6 6 9 5 2 7 0 7 9 9 5 3 5 9 3 6 7 8 3 8 4 8
0 4 4 9 3 5 2 4 9 4 7 5 2 4 6 3 3 8 2 4 4 5 8 6 2 5 1 0 2 5
4 2 4 8 1 1 6 2 1 3 9 7 3 4 4 0 8 7 2 1 1 6 8 6 8 4 8 7 6 7
2 3 5 2 3 7 8 3 1 7 7 3 2 0 8 8 9 8 3 7 6 8 9 3 5 9 1 4 1 6
```

Suppose the total number of faculty on the list were 450. You would select 100 random numbers by placing your finger blindly on a page of the table of random numbers and selecting all three digit numbers between 001 and 450 until you had 100 such numbers, with no duplicates (since we would not want to count a faculty member twice). If your finger happened to land on the fourth column and the third row above, then by moving your finger down the page three columns at a time your first three numbers picked would be: 048, 064, and 237. You could then return to the top of the page and go down columns 5, 6, and 7 to continue selecting numbers, and so on until you had 100.

Just to give you some practice with this method of sample selection, suppose that the number is 450 total on the list. Place your finger blindly on the random numbers above and select the first 20 random numbers between 001 and 450. Since you would want 100 such numbers, it would be mechanically easier to collect information on faculty members by rearranging the random numbers in numerical sequence (this also makes it easier to note duplicate numbers), numbering the faculty on the list and then selecting those faculty who should be in the sample. Rearrange the 20 numbers you have selected into numerical order. Perhaps even with this minimal practice you can see that this method of sample selection is hardly intellectually taxing, although it may be tedious.

If you feel reasonably certain that there is no relevant periodicity in the list, such as every fourth name being employed part-time, then there is a still easier way to select a probability sample. If you do suspect periodicity, the more tedious procedure described above should be used.

Let us assume, which seems reasonable from an eye inspection of the catalog available to me, that there is no relevant periodicity. Then we can use systematic sampling. After a random start, we will pick every kth individual on the list, where k is the interval between picks. What size should k be? We could set k arbitrarily, by deciding to take a 5 percent sample, say, and then k would be equal to 20. But since we want to be sure of having at least 100 faculty members in our sample, k should equal the total number on the list divided by 100.

We can make an estimate of the total number on the list by picking about three pages of the list, counting the number on those three pages and dividing that by three in order to get an average number for a page, then multiplying that average by the total number of pages on the list. Now divide your estimate of the total number on the list by 100 and if your division does not result in a whole number, drop the decimal portion. The answer is your sampling interval, k. Now use the portion of a table of random numbers that appeared earlier to get a random start. Place your finger blindly on the random numbers and take the first number between 1 and k that appears. For example, suppose k is 15 and your random start is 03. Select the 3rd faculty member on the list, then the 18th (3 plus 15), then the 33rd, and so on until you have gone through the list.

COLLECTING AND MANIPULATING DATA

Now you are ready to collect your information. Since you will have only around 100 faculty members to study and very little information to obtain about each, you can use the simplest possible data collection and manipulating aid: three-by-five-inch index cards. Use one card for each faculty member, placing the member's name and sample number in the center of the card, in case you have to go back and recheck the other information to be entered.

Even though this project is a simple one, I think you would be wise to prepare a short code manual, listing the variables you will be using, the categories for those variables, the source of the information, the codes assigned, and the location of the information on the card.

To illustrate what will be the longest portion of your brief code manual, and to save you the trouble of locating the appropriate definitions, here is what the portion of your code manual for the location of the academic institution granting the highest degree attained might look like.

Item	Source	Location and code
Location of institution granting highest degree attained:	Name of institution from faculty listing for ——— institution, 19——; state in which located from whatever listing of colleges and universities you used; grouping of states in divisions from U.S. Census of Population definitions	Front, upper right-hand corner of 3″ × 5″ card
Outside U.S.		0
Census division: New England	Includes: Maine, New Hampshire, Vermont, Massachusetts, Rhode Island, Connecticut	1
Middle Atlantic	New York, New Jersey, Pennsylvania	2
East North Central	Ohio, Indiana, Illinois, Michigan, Wisconsin	3
West North Central	Minnesota, Iowa, Missouri, N. Dakota, S. Dakota, Nebraska, Kansas	4
South Atlantic	Delaware, Maryland, District of Columbia, Virginia, West Virginia, N. Carolina, S. Carolina, Georgia, Florida	5
East South Central	Kentucky, Tennessee, Alabama, Mississippi	6
West South Central	Arkansas, Louisiana, Oklahoma, Texas	7
Mountain	Montana, Idaho, Wyoming, Colorado, New Mexico, Arizona, Utah, Nevada	8
Pacific	Washington, Oregon, California, Alaska, Hawaii	9

Notice that you might want to indicate when an institution is located in the state in which the institution studied is located. This might be done by assigning the code number 10 to that state. Then in the upper right-hand corner some cards will have two codes. You could keep them separate by entering the number of the division and then a diagonal under it and the number 10. For instance, suppose you are examining a California institution and a faculty member was awarded his degree from a California institution. The upper right-hand code for his card could be: 9/10.

Using your set of completed three-by-five-inch cards, sort them so that you may fill in the dummy analysis table you prepared. You will find it more efficient if you first sort on the major breaks in the stub, enter the information for the corresponding rows and then sort on the minor breaks and enter the information for the corresponding rows.

For example, suppose you placed extent of commitment in the upper left-hand corner of the card, using code 1 for full-time and code 2 for part-time. First sort (separate into piles) according to the codes for the upper left-hand corner. You will have two piles. Then using just the "full-time" pile, sort on the upper right-hand corner (location of institution granting highest degree). You will have ten subpiles, one for outside the United States and one each for the nine divisions. Count the number of cards in each subpile and enter the number in the appropriate cell for the "full-time" row. Then take the pile for the division in which the institution you are studying is located and count just those that also have a 10 in the upper right-hand corner. Enter this number in the cell for the state in which the institution studied is located, for the "full-time" row.

Now merge the cards for the "full-time" row. Using just this pile of cards, sort them on whatever corner in which you placed the codes for the level of the highest degree attained, say the lower right-hand corner. You will now have three subpiles. Sort each of these separately. Sort according to the upper right-hand corner codes, as you did for the entire set of "full-time" cards, and enter the numbers in the appropriate cells.

Repeat the procedure in the preceding two paragraphs for the "part-time" cards. Fill in the cells for the corresponding rows. Finally, merge all the cards together and sort on the upper right-hand corner to get the numbers that should go in the cells for the "Total" row at the bottom of the stub.

You should sort on *each* row rather than just sort to get level of degree attained, filling in the cells for those rows, and adding to get the cells for the rest of the rows, because you *just might make mistakes*. This can happen even with the best of intentions, and you would like to catch any errors and correct them before trying to analyze the table. If you sort on each row separately, you can make some internal consistency checks for the table, which should be an early step before going to the trouble of analyzing the results. Check that those items that should add up actually do. For instance, the numbers in the cells for the columns "Outside U.S." and "All" under the divisions should add to the numbers in the cells for the "Total" column. Some other checks for internal consistency can be made, and you should make them.

Your instructor probably divided you into sample-picking groups, giving each of you a separate random start. Before proceeding further you should verify that all of you in the same sample-picking group have the same numbers in the filled-in table.

COMPLETION OF THE PROJECT

Now you are ready to analyze your table, interpret the results, and prepare a report on the project. Convert each row of numbers into a percentage distribution. Then follow the guides for table reading that you learned in Exercise I-1.

Examine the marginal cells first, so that you know the extent of inbreeding for the sample as a whole. Then examine according to the major breaks and minor breaks separately, to see the effect of each of these on the kind of prediction of inbreeding you could make if you had this additional information. Note that you will have to do some combining of the numbers in some of the rows and compute additional percentage distributions to see the separate effect of the minor breaks. Then turn to the body of the table you prepared and examine the simultaneous effect of the two variables in the stub on your possible predictions. Characterize the patterns found according to the general shape or outline of the patterns and according to how pronounced, or intensely shown, it is.

While doing this, you may want to look at certain groupings of the divisions. As mentioned earlier, the divisions are grouped into regions as well by the Census Bureau. The four regions and the divisions they include are as follows: Northeast region includes New England and Middle Atlantic divisions; North Central region includes the East North Central and the West North Central divisions; South region includes the South Atlantic, East South Central, and West South Central divisions; West region includes the Mountain and Pacific divisions.

Compare the patterns that occurred with those you speculated on before collecting your data. What conclusions can you draw? Before making those conclusions too firmly, look back and evaluate the method used to obtain the results. Census groupings of states were used because they were already available and seemed a sensible way of grouping states. (A great deal of information is routinely collected for the various census groupings, and as a general rule you should try to collect your results so that they will be cumulative with what else is known unless you have a *very* good reason for deviating in such a way that your results will not be cumulative.) Do these groupings still seem reasonable to you or can you suggest a better grouping for the dependent variable used, defined as it was according to geographic-related inbreeding? Or do you now feel a different way of looking at inbreeding would be preferable in future studies, and if so, how and why? How about the independent variables used? Perhaps rather than looking at the relationship with level of highest degree attained, future studies might be better off if they looked at something else, perhaps the general field of specialization, such as social sciences, physical sciences, engineering, education, and the like.

Once you have your rough draft written, let it sit for at least a day. Then read it as though it were on a report you knew nothing about and evaluate it according to the guides in Part II of the text. Try to follow the topic headings suggested, and for this exercise use at least *two* graphic devices (small text table, pie chart, bar chart, and so on) in your Major Findings section, and be sure to include your completed table in an Appendix section. Make any final revisions in your rough draft that you think are needed. Try to have your final report no longer than the equivalent of eight double-spaced typewritten pages of *text,* or verbal material. Turn in your complete report.

III-3. On Your Own: Complete Your Project

By now you should have collected your data, analyzed and interpreted it, and prepared a rough draft of your report, according to the headings given in the Topical Outline in Part II of the text. Assume the role of a scientific reviewer toward your rough draft. Read as though the report had been prepared on a project you knew nothing about, checking to see that items that should be covered are, and providing answers to the suggested questions to ask given in the general guide for evaluating reports. Make any revisions you think are necessary and then turn in your final report.

Suggestions for Beginning Further Reading

There are two books to which I have turned many times in the past and fully expect to continue to do so in the future. Their influence pervades the book you have just finished reading. The first is *An Introduction to Logic and Scientific Method,* by Morris R. Cohen and Ernest Nagel (Harcourt, Brace and Company, 1934). This book is divided into two parts, with the first called "Formal Logic" and the second called "Applied Logic and Scientific Method." Each is well worth reading, but if your time is limited you might read the second part thoroughly and just sample from the first. The other book to which I am particularly indebted is available in paperback, *How to Solve It: A New Aspect of Mathematical Method,* by Georgy Polya (Doubleday Anchor, 1957). Professor Polya is a mathematician and so his illustrations are mainly from mathematics. But don't let that stop you from reading this excellent book. His approach is a general one toward problem solving, and if you skip every one of the mathematical illustrations (which would be too bad because they are really quite elementary and if you concentrate you should have no difficulty with them) and read just the rest of his discussion you will benefit immensely. Professor Polya is writing for beginners and he has a delightful style.

If you read just Cohen and Nagel, you should have a good grasp of what we try to do in science and why; if you read Polya too, you will possess a set of more specific approaches on how to accomplish this. If you would like to be able to do a good job of telling others (especially in written form) what you have done and learned, I urge you to read and then use the guides in Rudolf Flesch's *How to Write, Speak, and Think More Effectively* (Harper and Brothers, 1960). Whatever readability the book you have just finished may have can be credited to my attempts to follow Flesch's advice. As is not rare with advice, it is easier to recognize that it is sound than to apply it to oneself.

Whether you anticipate becoming a producer of scientific knowledge or not, I think you will find the above three books worth your time. But especially if you expect to remain a consumer only, you should read at least one more book. This one should be on the history of science.

There are many good ones, but my favorite is Morris Kline's *Mathematics: A Cultural Approach* (Addison-Wesley, 1962). In my opinion this book should be read by everyone interested in science in general and in the social sciences in particular. Professor Kline writes well, and he is addressing himself to nonmathematicians. He does an outstanding job of weaving the various historical threads together, and his unfolding of the way in which one after another image of the world becomes dominant for a time (there are "fashions" in science as well as out) is fascinating reading, as is his account of the interplay between the world of science and the practical interests of the everyday world.

If you read just the four books recommended above, you should have the background to become a well above average consumer of scientific knowledge and to have a good foundation to build on if you decide to become a producer too. Let me now give you a brief and biased selection of one or two items on various topics you might care to investigate. If you become a serious researcher you will have to get into the journal literature eventually, but for this list aimed at beginners I have selected only books, preferably paperbacks, and some programed or self-teaching books, and in my selection I have favored those authors who write with particular clarity.

History and philosophy of science.

> Dampier, W. C. *A History of Science* (Cambridge University Press and Macmillan, 1944).
>
> Frank, Philipp. *Philosophy of Science* (Prentice-Hall, 1957). This hefty paperback is a bit stiffer going than most other items on this list, but worth the effort.

General mathematics and logic.

> Dickoff, J., and P. James. *Symbolic Logic and Language: A Programmed Text* (McGraw-Hill, 1965). A thorough introduction to the useful tool of symbolic logic.
>
> Flexer, Roberta J., and Abraham S. *Programmed Reviews of Mathematics* (Harper and Row, 1967). This set of six small booklets gives an intensive review of certain topics, such as linear and quadratic equations.
>
> Hancock, John D.; Miriam S. Olken; and Dale G. Seymour. *Introduction to Modern Mathematics*, Series 1 and 2 (Behavioral Research Laboratories programed text, 1966 and later). This multivolume set of programed books makes learning mathematics almost painless, even for the most nervous beginner.

Selected techniques.

> Backstrom, C. H., and G. D. Hursh. *Survey Research* (Northwestern University Press, 1963). Paperback, but of a handbook nature, as is Mildred Parten's lengthier treatment, below.

Bruning, James L., and B. L. Kintz. *Computational Handbook of Statistics* (Scott, Foresman, 1968). Handbook in nature, and, as is typical with handbooks, best used after you have mastered the underlying logic (for example, as presented in Dixon and Massey, below). Assumptions needed for the use of various measures are briefly stated, followed by detailed computational illustrations.

Dixon, W. J., and F. J. Massey, Jr. *Introduction to Statistical Analysis* (McGraw-Hill, 1951). There are many good statistics books, and they appear in a steady stream. I like this one particularly. If you feel your mathematics is a little rusty, before reading Dixon and Massey you might like to browse through this short programed review: Clark, V. A., and M. E. Tarter. *Preparation for Basic Statistics: A Program for Self-Instruction* (McGraw-Hill, 1968).

Fisher, Ronald A. *The Design of Experiments* (London: Oliver and Boyd, first published 1935, 8th edition 1966). A classic for research workers.

Parten, Mildred. *Surveys, Polls, and Samples: Practical Procedures* (Harper and Brothers, 1950).

Plutchik, Robert. *Foundations of Experimental Research* (Harper and Row, 1968). One of the better among several recently published paperbacks on experimental design.

Smith, R. E. *The Bases of Fortran* (Control Data Corporation, 1967). One of the best programed introductions to Fortran (a widely used computer language) that I have come across. Entertainingly written.

Some general books on research methods in the social sciences. There are many methods books. I think the three cited below are among the better ones available.)

Kerlinger, F. N. *Foundations of Behavioral Research* (Holt, Rinehart and Winston, 1964).

Phillips, Bernard S. *Social Research* (Macmillan, 1966).

Selltiz, C., et al. *Research Methods in Social Relations* (Holt, Rinehart and Winston, 1959).

Finally, three paperbacks that soundly cover several topics and are written with an ease of style that is marvelous to read (but difficult to write!).

Agnew, N. Mck., and S. W. Pyke. *The Science Game: An Introduction to Research in the Behavioral Sciences* (Prentice-Hall, 1969). I came across this delightful book when I had virtually completed my own — and it's a good thing I discovered it so late, or I might never have finished. The map that serves as frontispiece, "The Island of Research," is alone worth the price of the book. Particularly good on different levels of language, but the entire book is well done.

Cameron, W. B. *Informal Sociology* (Random House, 1964). A series of essays on a number of topics. The first two, "The Elements of Statistical Confusion" and "Knowledge Without Numbers," are especially relevant, although the essay, "We and Us," is interesting for the kind of behind-the-scenes thinking that goes on in theory development. And I think all students, instructors, and administrators should read "Physical Setting and Intellectual Climate" (coauthored with Raymond Wheeler) and ponder its message.

Huff, Darrell. *How to Lie with Statistics* (W. W. Norton, 1954). Chapters 5 and 6, covering abuses of graphic devices, are particularly good, and I have already cited the last chapter, "How to Talk Back to a Statistic." Read it all; you'll enjoy it.

Index

LITTLE, BROWN AND COMPANY · BOSTON

083704